ISBN 978-1-5283-3276-7
PIBN 10921644

1 MONTH OF
FREE
READING

at
www.ForgottenBooks.com

By purchasing this book you are eligible for one month membership to ForgottenBooks.com, giving you unlimited access to our entire collection of over 1,000,000 titles via our web site and mobile apps.

To claim your free month visit:
www.forgottenbooks.com/free921644

English
Français
Deutsche
Italiano
Español
Português

www.forgottenbooks.com

Mythology Photography **Fiction**
Fishing Christianity **Art** Cooking
Essays Buddhism Freemasonry
Medicine **Biology** Music **Ancient
Egypt** Evolution Carpentry Physics
Dance Geology **Mathematics** Fitness
Shakespeare **Folklore** Yoga Marketing
Confidence Immortality Biographies
Poetry **Psychology** Witchcraft
Electronics Chemistry History **Law**
Accounting **Philosophy** Anthropology
Alchemy Drama Quantum Mechanics
Atheism Sexual Health **Ancient History**
Entrepreneurship Languages Sport
Paleontology Needlework Islam
Metaphysics Investment Archaeology
Parenting Statistics Criminology
Motivational

vania. Laws, statutes, etc. Banking ...

DIGEST

OF THE

BANKING, TRUST COMPANY

AND

BUILDING AND LOAN ASSOCIATION LAWS

OF THE

COMMONWEALTH OF PENNSYLVANIA.

COMPILED UNDER THE PROVISIONS OF AN ACT OF ASSEMBLY
OF THE COMMONWEALTH OF PENNSYLVANIA BY DIREC-
TION OF THE COMMISSIONER OF BANKING.

COMPILED BY

WILLIAM BROWN, JR. AND CHARLES L. BROWN,
Of the Philadelphia Bar.

CONTENTS.

CHAPTER 1.

Constitutional provisions relating to corporations.

CHAPTER 2.

Legislation relating to banks prior to banking act of 1850.

CHAPTER 3.

Banking act of 1850.

CHAPTER 4.

Legislation relating to banks from banking law of 1850 to the banking act of 1876.

CHAPTER 5.

Banking act of 1876.

CHAPTER 6.

Legislation relating to banks since the act of 1876.

CHAPTER 7.

Co-operative Banking Associations.

CHAPTER 8.

Trust Companies.

CHAPTER 9.

Building and Loan Associations.

CHAPTER 10.

Savings Institutions and Savings Banks.

CHAPTER 11.

Miscellaneous acts relating to Banks, Trust Companies, Building and Loan Associations, Savings Institutions, etc.

CHAPTER 1.

CONSTITUTIONAL PROVISIONS RELATING TO CORPORATIONS.

Creation of Corporations by Special Laws Forbidden.

Sec. 1. The General Assembly shall not pass any local or special law * * * * creating corporations, or amending, renewing, or extending the charters thereof; granting to any corporation, association or individual any special or exclusive privilege or immunity. * * * * *.—Article 3, Sec. 7.

Casting Votes of Stockholders for Directors or Managers.

Sec. 2. In all elections for directors or managers of a corporation, each members or shareholder may cast the whole number of his votes for one candidate or distribute them upon two or more candidates, as he may prefer.—Article 16, Sec. 4.

Foreign Corporations to Have Place of Business and Agent in State to be Served With Process.

Sec. 3. No foreign corporation shall do any business in this State, without having one or more known places of business, and an authorized agent or agents in the same, upon whom process may be served.—Article 16, Sec. 5.

Corporations Confined to Business of Charter and Only to Hold Real Estate for Business.

Sec. 4. No corporation shall engage in any business other than that expressly authorized in its charter; nor shall it take or hold any real estate, except such as may be necessary and proper for its legitimate business.—Article 16, Sec. 6.

Stocks and Bonds Only to be Issued for Money, Labor or Property Received.—Fictitious Increase of Stock or Indebtedness Forbidden.—Stock and Indebtedness Only to be Increased by General Law.—The Larger Amount in Value of Stock Must Consent to Increase.—Sixty Days' Notice of Meeting for Increase Must be Given.

Sec. 5. No corporation shall issue stocks or bonds, except for money, labor done, or money or property actually received; and all fictitious increase of stock or indebtedness shall be void. The stock and indebtedness of corporations shall not be increased except in pursuance of general law, nor without the consent of the persons holding the larger amount in value of the stock, first obtained, at a meeting to be held after sixty days' notice, given in pursuance of law.—Article 16, Sec. 7.

Banking Laws to Provide for Registry of Notes and Bills for Circulation.

Sec. 6. Every banking law shall provide for the registry and countersigning, by an officer of the State, of all notes or bills designed for circulation; and that ample security to the full amount thereof, shall be deposited with the Auditor General, for the redemption of such notes or bills.—Article 16, Sec. 9.

Legislature May Alter, Revoke or Annul Any Charter They May Think Injurious to the Citizens.—Only Charter of one Corporation to be Created, Renewed or Extended.

Sec. 7. The General Assembly shall have the power to alter, revoke or annul any charter of incorporation now existing, and revocable at the adoption of this Constitution, or any that may hereafter be created whenever, in their opinion, it may be injurious to the citizens of this Commonwealth in such manner, however, that no injustice shall be done to the corporators. No law hereafter enacted shall create, renew or extend the charter of more than one corporation.—Article 16, Sec. 10.

Three Months' Public Notice to be Given of Creation of Banks.—Bank Charters Limited to Twenty Years.

Sec. 8. No corporate body to possess banking and discounting privileges, shall be created or organized, in pursuance of any law, without three months' previous public notice, at the place of the intended location, of the intention to apply for such privileges, in such manner as shall be prescribed by law; nor shall a charter for such privilege be granted for a longer period than twenty years.—Article 16, Sec. 11.

Term "Corporation" in Article to Include Stock Companies Having Powers of Corporations Possessed by Individuals or Partnerships.

Sec. 9. The term "Corporations," as used in this Article, shall be construed to include all joint stock companies or associations having any of the powers or privileges of corporations not possessed by individuals or partnerships.—Article 16, Sec. 13.

CHAPTER 2.

LEGISLATION RELATING TO BANKS PRIOR TO THE BANKING LAW OF 1850.

Establishing a Banking House in this State by Companies Incorporated in Other States Prohibited.—Penalty.

Sec. 10. No company incorporated by the laws of any other of the United States shall be permitted to establish within this Commonwealth any banking house or office of discount and deposit, and all and every person or persons who shall in violation of this act be concerned in any such establishment, on conviction thereof in any court of justice within this State, shall for every such offence, forfeit and pay for the use of the same, the sum of two thousand dollars, and the private estates of such person or persons offending as aforesaid shall be liable for the payment of such forfeiture.—Act of 28th of March, 1808, Sec. 1, 4 Sm. L. 537.

Demand for Payment to be Made Before Bringing Suit on Bank Notes.

Sec. 11. No suit shall be sustained on any bank note or notes payable to bearer or order, on demand, unless demand shall have been first made for payment thereof at their banking house, office or treasury, and in case of non-payment, interest shall be recoverable on the same from the time of making such demand.—Act of 22nd of March, 1817, Sec. 1, 6 Sm. L. 441.

Incorporated Banks Only to Issue Notes. Penalties.

Sec. 12. No incorporated body, public officer, association or partnership or private individual, other than such as have been expressly incorporated or established for the purpose of banking, shall make, issue, re-issue or circulate any promissory note, ticket or engagement of credit in the nature of a bank note, of any denomination or amount whatsoever, other than such as have been issued by banks lawfully and expressly established; and no such incorporated body, public officer, association or partnership, shall receive any such note, ticket or engagement of credit, other than those above excepted, or those made and issued by it or himself, or under its or his immediate authority, and that for the mere purpose of cancelling or destroying the same, under the penalty, in the case of a public officer, of ten dollars, and in the case of a corporation, association or partnership, fifty dollars for each and every note so made, issued, re-issued, circulated, paid, or received, to be recovered by any person or persons suing for the same, before any alderman or justice of the peace within this Commonwealth, as debts under one hundred dollars are by law recoverable.—Act of 22nd of March, 1817, Sec. 2, 6 Sm. L. 441.

Mode of Proceeding to Enforce This Act.

Sec. 13. The mode of proceeding against any bank or other corporation under this act, shall be by summons served on the president, cashier or other chief officer, director or manager of such bank or corporation, and that where judgment shall be entered thereon, such judgment shall be as well against such bank or corporation as against such president, cashier, chief officer, manager or director, or so many of them severally, whereon such service shall have been made, and execution may thereupon forthwith issue, as well against such bank or corporation, to be levied upon any debts due to them as upon the shares of their capital stock or other property, real, personal or mixed, and against each such president, cashier, chief officer, director or manager, to be levied on his personal or real property, or if a sufficiency thereof cannot be found, or plaintiff shall so require, against their and each of their persons, to be proceeded on as is usual in the case of a capias ad satisfaciendum.—Act of 22nd of March, 1817, Sec. 3, 6 Sm. L. 441.

Penalties for Second and Subsequent Violations. Who May be Witnesses.

Sec. 14. For a second and each subsequent act of making, issuing, re-issuing, circulating, passing or receiving, otherwise than is hereinbefore excepted, any of the notes, tickets or engagements of credit aforesaid, the penalty or sum to be recovered shall be increased in an amount equal to the original penalty or sum mentioned in the first section of this act, but shall in no case exceed fifty dollars on an individual not a president, cashier, chief officer, director or manager of any bank or corporation, association or partnership, or five hundred dollars in the case of such bank or corporation, association or partnership; any such penalty or debt to be recovered where it exceeds one hundred dollars, before the court of common pleas of the proper county, in the manner and by means of process, judgment and execution, as is described in the second section of this act; and all sums recovered under this act shall be one-half thereof paid to the person or persons suing for the same, to his or their own use, and the other half into the hands of the treasurer or county commissioners of the county wherein the recovery shall be had, for the use thereof: Provided always, That no public officer or private individual shall be excluded from the performance of his duties, or from being a competent witness in any suit under this act, by reason of his being subject to the payment of county rates and levies therein, or by reason of one moiety of the sums to be recovered, being payable to the county treasurer or commissioners as is hereinbefore directed. Act of 22nd of March, 1817, Sec. 4, 6 Sm. L. 441.

Quo Warranto Against Banks May Issue After Two Convictions Where Judgments Unpaid.—Charter May be Declared Void.

Sec. 15. Whenever judgment shall have been had against any such bank or corporation, in any two suits in the court of common pleas, or before two different justices of the peace, and certified copies or transcripts of such judgments filed with the prothonotary of the court of common pleas of the proper county, and the same should have remained unpaid for three months, it shall be the duty of the Attorney General, or his deputy, in such county, to file in said court an information in the nature of a quo warranto, the process awarded on which shall be served by the sheriff or his deputy, on the president, cashier, or other chief officer, or any director or manager of such bank or corporation, and on a return of service in manner aforesaid, to the satisfaction of such court, they shall proceed therein as nearly as may be in the manner directed and practiced under writs of quo warranto; and in case of a verdict for the Commonwealth, the court, instead of the usual judgment in such cases, shall have power to inflict a penalty not exceeding five thousand dollars, and to adjudge the charter and corporate power of such bank or other incorporated company thenceforth subject to be forfeited, annulled and declared forever void by the legislature.—Act of 22nd of March, 1817, Sec. 5, 6 Sm. L. 441.

When Holder of Note May Sue on Note Unlawfully Issued.

Sec. 16. So much of any act of Assembly heretofore passed, as deprives or prevents the holder of any note, ticket or engagement of credit in the nature of a bank note, from recovering from any individual, bank or corporation, association or partnership, by whom, or by any of whose officers or agents the same has been made, signed or issued by reason of such note having been made, signed or issued, without or in contradiction to law, be, and the same is hereby repealed, and the holder of every such note shall have the same legal remedy for the recovery of the amount thereof from the party or parties, whether corporate, association, or partnership, or individual, who made, signed, or issued the same, as can by the provisions of this act, or by the existing laws of this Commonwealth, be had on a similar note, ticket or engagement of credit that has been lawfully issued.—Act of 22nd of March, 1817, Sec. 7, 6 Sm. L. 441.

Demand May be Made Upon Branch Offices.

Sec. 17. From and after the first day of May next, the several offices of discount and deposit within this Commonwealth shall, on demand made, pay in the lawful currency of the United States, any note or ticket of such offices respectively, or of the mother bank, when issued from such offices respectively, and on neglect or refusal to pay as aforesaid, shall be liable to the same penalties, and may be proceeded against in the same manner, as is hereinbefore provided, and any such note or ticket so as aforesaid issued, shall bear date at the office from which issued.—Act of 22nd of March, 1817, Sec. 9, 6 Sm. L. 441.

Judges and Certain State Officers Disqualified as Directors or Cashiers.

Sec. 18. No judge of any court, nor any person holding any office under this Commonwealth, in the accounting or Treasury Department, or in the land offices, or any person authorized to receive and account for public moneys of this Commonwealth, shall be capable at the same time of being a director or cashier of any bank.—Act 27th of January, 1819, Sec. 3, 7 Sm. L. 148.

Board of Directors May Call a General Meeting of Stockholders to Wind up Bank.—If So, Five Trustees to be Elected.

Sec. 19. The board of directors of any banking company incorporated by any law or laws of this Commonwealth, or twenty stockholders thereof, being together proprietors of one-tenth part of the capital stock actually paid in, may at any time call a general meeting of the stockholders of such company for the purpose of inquiring into the expediency of electing five trustees to close the concerns of the said institution, giving such notice of the same, as is required for general meetings of their stockholders under their act or acts of incorporation, and specifying in such notice the object or objects of such meeting; and if pursuant to such notice, a majority of the stockholders, being together proprietors of one-half or more of the capital stock actually paid in, shall assemble at the time and place required by said notice, and shall determine to close the concerns of said institution, they shall proceed to elect five trustees, which election shall be conducted in all respects in the same manner as the elections for directors are required to be conducted by the corporate provisions of such institution and the law "to regulate proxies," passed March twenty-eight, one thousand eight hundred and twenty.—Act of 1st of April, 1822, Sec. 1, 7 Sm. L. 541.

How General Meeting of Stockholders to be Called When Charter Forfeited.

Sec. 20. If any of the said banks have, or shall hereafter forfeit their charters, the board of directors or twenty stockholders thereof, being together proprietors of one-tenth of the capital stock, shall have power at any time after such forfeiture, to call a general meeting of the stockholders, giving such notice thereof as is required to be given for general meetings of stockholders, in the act incorporating such bank, specifying particularly in such notice the object of such meeting, which shall be to elect five trustees to close the concerns of such bank; and when the stockholders are so met, agreeably to such notice, they shall proceed to hold such election, which shall be conducted in the same manner as is provided for holding elections in the first section of this act.—Act of 1st of April, 1822, Sec. 2, 7 Sm. L. 541.

Terms, Powers and Duties of Trustees.

Sec. 21. The stockholders, previous to the election of trustees, shall determine the term for which such trustees shall, without a re-election, continue in office, which term shall not exceed one year from and after their election; and the trustees so elected, and those who may thereafter be elected agreeably to this act, shall, for the purpose of closing the concerns of such bank, have and possess all the privileges, powers and authorities which the directors thereof now have, or may have had previous to the forfeiture of the charter of such bank: Provided, That this act shall not be so construed as to authorize any such bank to declare any dividend of the net profits, or to issue any notes, or make any new loans: And provided also, That the acts and proceedings heretofore done, and performed by the board of directors of such bank, subsequent to the forfeiture of its charter, if the said acts and proceedings have been done and performed in the manner as they might or could have been lawfully done or performed previous to such forfeiture of charter, be, and the same are hereby confirmed and declared valid in law, with the same force and effect as if the said acts and proceedings had been done and performed previous to the forfeiture of the charter of such bank.—Act of 1st of April, 1822, Sec. 3, 7 Sm. L. 541.

Vacancies Supplied by Election of New Trustees.

Sec. 22. When any trustee or assignee elected or appointed agreeably to this act, by any of the banks aforesaid shall die, resign or remove out of the county where such bank is located, or shall become insolvent, in every such case the vacancies shall be supplied by a new election, of which election, and of the time and place when and where the same is to be held, the remaining trustees shall give such notice to the stockholders, as is provided in the first section of this act, and the said election shall be conducted in the manner provided by the said first section of this act.—Act of 1st of April, 1822, Sec. 6, 7 Sm. L. 541.

Liability of Banks to be Sued.—Suits How Conducted.

Sec. 23. When such trustees or a majority of them shall have accepted of said trust, any corporation thus electing trustees, shall be liable to be sued in its corporate name, before any court or magistrate in this Commonwealth having competent jurisdiction, by summons which may be served upon any of the trustees elected as aforesaid who shall have accepted of the trust which suit shall be conducted in all respects (after the service of the summons) agreeably to the provisions of "An act relative to suits brought by or against corporations," passed the twenty-second day of March, one thousand eight hundred and seventeen, and in the service of any execution issued against any institution, having elected trustees as aforesaid, the trustees who shall have accepted of the said trust or any of them shall be deemed and held to be the principal officers or officer of the said institution and the service of the execution on them or any of them, shall be deemed and held to be good and valid in law, in all courts and before all magistrates in this Commonwealth; and any corporation thus electing trustees to close the concerns of the corporation, shall be entitled to all the privileges in defending suits brought against said corporation, which are granted to corporations by the before recited act relative to suits brought by or against corporations: Provided, however, That a list of any trustees elected and who have accepted, as aforesaid, shall be filed in the prothonotary's office of the county immediately thereafter.— Act 1st of April, 1822, Sec. 7, 7 Sm. L. 541.

Powers to Make Loans.—Loans to Farmers, Mechanics and Manufacturers of the District.—Provisions for Loans to the State.

Sec. 24. The several banking companies enumerated in this act
shall make loans to the amount of one-fifth of their capital actually
paid in, for one year, to the farmers, mechanics and manufacturers
of the district in which the bank shall be established, if applied
for, on a sufficient surety being given by bond, mortgage, note, or
otherwise, at six per cent. per annum. And whenever the Legislature of the State may require it, each bank hereby chartered shall
loan to the Commonwealth any sum not exceeding five per centum
of its capital stock actually paid in, at an interest not exceeding five
per centum per annum, payable half yearly, for any time not exceeding the unexpired term of the charter of any such bank hereby
granted: Provided, That the money thus loaned to the State, shall
not be drawn from such bank so loaning, for the purpose of being
deposited in any other bank; but shall remain in the bank, subject
to the order of the State, at such times, and in such sums as the
State Treasurer may believe the exigencies of the State require:
Provided, That at least sixty days' notice shall be given by the
Governor to any bank, previous to any requisition for such loan or
loans.—Act of 25th of March, 1824, Sec. 8, 8 Sm. L. 236.

Notes Under Five Dollars Not to be Issued and Circulated.

Sec. 25. It shall not be lawful for any person or persons, or body
corporate, with the intention to create or put in circulation, or continue in circulation, a paper circulating medium, to issue, circulate
or directly or indirectly cause to be issued or circulated, any note,
bill, check, ticket or paper, purporting or evidencing, or intended
to purport or evidence, that any sum less than five dollars will be
paid to the order of any person, or to any person receiving or holding such note, bill, check, ticket or paper, or to the bearer of the
same, or that it will be received in payment of any debt or demand,
or that the bearer of the same, or any person receiving or holding
the same, will be entitled to receive any goods or effects of the value
of any sum less than five dollars; and * * * * it shall not be
lawful for any person or persons, or body corporate, to make, issue
or pay away, pass, exchange or transfer, or cause to be made, issued,
paid away, passed, exchanged or transferred, any bank note, bill,
ticket or paper, purporting to be a banknote, of the nature, character or appearance of a bank note, or calculated for circulation
as a bank note, of any less denomination than five dollars.—Act of
12th of April, 1828, Sec. 1, P. L. 323, 10 Sm. L. 159.

Penalty for so Doing, How Recovered and Disposition of it.

Section 26. Any and every person and persons and body corporate, offending against any of the provisions of the first section of this
act, shall forfeit and pay for every such offence the sum of five
dollars, to be recovered by any person suing for the same as debts
of like amount are by law recoverable, one-half for his own use, and
the other half to be for the use of the overseers, guardians or directors of the poor of the city, county, district or township within which

such offense shall have been committed.—Act of 12th of April, 1828, Sec. 2, P. L. 323, 10 Sm. L. 159.

Action May be Brought on Such Notes.

- Sec. 27. No such note, bill, check, ticket or paper mentioned in the first section of this act, shall be held or taken to be void or of null effect, by reason thereof; but all suits and actions may be brought and sustained on such note, bill, check, ticket or paper, anything herein contained to the contrary notwithstanding; and in such suits or actions, if the same shall be determined in favor of the plaintiff, judgment shall be rendered for the principal sum due on such note, bill, check, ticket or paper, together with interest thereon, at the rate hereinafter provided for, and full costs.—Act of 12th of April, 1828, Sec. 3, P. L. 323, 10 Sm. L. 159.

Drawers, Acceptors and Indorsers to pay Twenty Per Cent. Interest.

Sec. 28. The drawer and acceptor of any such note, bill, check, ticket or paper, and every person or body corporate who shall endorse or in any way put his or their name upon the same, shall be liable to pay to any holder thereof, together with the principal sum expressed therein, interest thereon, to be calculated at and after the rate of twenty per cent. per annum from the time when such note, bill, check, ticket or paper was first issued, and that without any demand upon the drawer or acceptor or any endorser or party to the same.—Act of 12th of April, 1828, Sec. 4, P. L. 323, 10 Sm. L. 159.

Persons Circulating Such Notes Liable for Interest at Twenty Per Cent.

Sec. 29. Any person or persons, or body corporate, who shall have paid away, passed, exchanged or transferred any such note, bill, check, ticket or paper, shall be liable to any holder thereof, and shall pay to him or her, together with the principal sum expressed therein, interest thereon, to be calculated at and after the rate of twenty per cent. per annum from the time when such note, bill, check, ticket or paper was first issued, and that without any demand on the drawer or acceptor or any endorser, or party to the same.—Act of 12th of April, 1828, Sec. 5, P. L. 323.—10 Sm. L. 159.

When Such Notes Shall be Deemed to Have Been Issued.

Sec. 30. In the trial or hearing of any suit or action which may be brought upon any such note, bill, check, ticket or paper, if the time when the same was first issued shall not be clearly proved, then the same shall be deemed and taken to have been first issued one year before the bringing of such suit or action, and interest shall be calculated thereon at the rate of twenty per cent. accordingly.—Act of 12th of April, 1828, Sec. 6, P. L. 323.—10 Sm. L. 159.

Banks May Purchase Stock of This Commonwealth But Not Individual or Corporate Stocks.

Sec. 31. The several banks of this Commonwealth are hereby authorized to negotiate loans to, or to purchase the stock of this Commonwealth from the officers or agents appointed under the authority of the State to effect such loans, or to sell such stock, but nothing in this act or any other law shall be construed to authorize any of said banks to make such purchases of any individual or corporation, except such as shall be taken in satisfaction of debts previously contracted in the course of its dealings: Provided, The amount of such loans made, or stock so held, shall not exceed one-third part of the actual capital stock of such bank or corporation: And provided also, That the said banks may sell out such stocks at any time their interest may require.—Act of 23rd of April, 1829, Sec. 1, P. L. 360.

Banks May Subscribe to State Loans.

Sec. 32. Any bank or banks incorporated by the laws of this Commonwealth are hereby authorized to offer for and subscribe to the whole or part of any loans or loans to this Commonwealth.—Act of 14th of April, 1835, Sec. 1, P. L. 439.

How Notice of Application for Charter to be Given by Publication; and Also for Renewals and Extensions.

Sec. 33. Whenever any citizen or association of citizens of this Commonwealth intend to make application to the Legislature for the creation, renewal or extension of any corporate body with banking or discounting privileges, it shall be their duty to cause a notice of such intended application, to be advertised in two newspapers, printed in the county in which such corporate body is, or is intended to be located, at least once a week in each paper for six months before the meeting of the then next Legislature, and also in one paper printed in the borough of Harrisburg, and the notice of such application shall specify the name and style, or the intended name and style, the location or intended location, the specific object for which created, and the amount of capital, or intended amount of capital, of such corporate body, and in the case of the renewal or extension of any such corporate body, such notice shall also specify the amount of increase of capital, or extension of privileges, if any be intended: Provided, That if there be only one paper printed in the county in which such corporate body is, or is intended to be located, the publication of such notice in one paper shall be deemed sufficient, but if there be no paper printed in such county, then the notice shall be given in a paper published in one of the nearest adjoining counties, and by at least one written or printed advertisement, put up in some public place in each township, in the county in which the corporate body is or is intended to be located.—Act of 1st of June, 1839, Sec. 1, P. L. 235.

Punishment for False Swearing to Statement.

Sec. 34. The wilful and deliberate false swearing by any officer or agent of any bank, or any other person, to or in relation to any statement or statements required by law to be made, or other duty enjoined by law, shall be deemed perjury in law, and punished as such, and the confinement within the penitentiaries of this State, which is hereby required to be part of the sentence in each such case, on conviction, shall not be less than one, nor more than six years.—Act of 3rd of April, 1840, P. L. 714.

Banks Prohibited From Issuing Certificates of Deposit of the Similitude of Bank Notes.—Proviso that Notes may be Issued Under Act of Fourth of May, 1841.

Sec. 35. It shall not be lawful for any bank in this Commonwealth to issue, or re-issue, any certificate in the similitude of a bank note, purporting to be receivable on deposit, special or general, under a penalty of five dollars for every certificate so issued or received, to be recovered as debts of like amount are by law recoverable, for the use of the person suing therefor; and the said bank shall be liable for any such issue already made, as if the same were made payable on demand, and were in the form of a bank note: Provided, That nothing contained in this act shall be so construed as to prevent the banks of this Commonwealth from issuing or reissuing the notes authorized by the act, entitled "An act to provide revenue to meet the demands on the treasury and for other purposes," passed the fourth of May, one thousand eight hundred and forty-one.—Act of 5th of May, 1841, Sec. 1, P. L. 357.

Tolls, Taxes, Etc., to be Paid in Gold, Silver or Notes of Specie Paying Banks Only.

Sec. 36. Hereafter no medium shall be received in the payment of tolls, taxes or other revenue of the Commonwealth, other than gold and silver or the notes of specie paying banks.—Act of 12th of March, 1842, Sec. 8, P. L. 68.

Issue of Such Notes to be Punishable by Indictment.

Sec. 37. It shall not hereafter be lawful for any banking institution or other corporation, or individual, to issue or put in circulation any note, bill, check or paper of any kind to circulate as currency, under the denomination of five dollars, except notes legally issued under the act of the fourth of May, one thousand eight hundred and forty-one, and upon conviction thereof of any president, cashier, clerk or other officer, of any corporation, or individual, before any court of quarter sessions, of issuing or putting the same in circulation, of which their name or signature to the said note, bill, check or other paper shall be evidence, the said president, cashier, clerk, or other officer or individual shall be fined in any sum not exceeding five hundred dollars, at the discretion of the said court, one-half for the use of the prosecutor, and the other half for the use of the county, and the said bank or corporation shall forfeit its charter.—Act of 24th of June, 1842, Sec. 2, P. L. 493.

Directors Ineligible the Fourth Consecutive Year.—Shall Not Be Directors of More Than One Bank at One Time.—Quo Warranto Will Lie.

Sec. 38. Hereafter bank directors of this Commonwealth shall be eligible for three years out of any four years; but no person shall be a director at the same time of more than one bank; and every person who has been or who shall hereafter be a director in one or more banks of this Commonwealth, for three years out of any four years, shall be ineligible (except the president, who shall always be eligible), as a director in any bank whatever, until the expiration of one year thereafter; and it shall be lawful for any stockholder to make application to the court of common pleas of the proper county for a writ of quo warranto, against every person violating the provisions of this section, the said writ to be heard and determined according to the provisions of "An act relating to writs of quo warranto and mandamus," passed fourteenth June, one thousand eight hundred and thirty-six; and every person so convicted, shall be removed from the office of director by a decree of the said court, and shall thereafter be ineligible as a director in any bank in this Commonwealth, and shall be fined in a sum not less than five hundred dollars, nor more than two thousand dollars, at the discretion of the court, and the vacancy or vacancies shall be filled as in the case of death.—Act of 18th of April, 1843, Sec. 8, P. L. 309.

Renewal of Loans to the State.

Sec. 39. The several banks whose loans to the Commonwealth, under the act of twenty-fifth of March, one thousand eight hundred and twenty four, entitled "An act to re-charter certain banks," which have fallen due, or shall hereafter fall due, be and they are hereby required to renew the same on the same terms, and in accordance with the several acts of incorporation; and the certificates of stock for said loans so falling or having fallen due, shall be delivered to the Auditor General and cancelled, and new certificates of stock therefor shall be issued, reimbursable at the expiration of their several charters.—Act of 20th of January, 1847, Sec. 1, P. L. 53.

Banks, Savings Institutions and Other Corporations to Publish Statements of Dividends or Profits Unclaimed.

Sec. 40. Each of the banks, savings institutions, loan companies and insurance companies, and each and every other of the companies, institutions or associations incorporated by or under any law of this Commonwealth, and legally authorized to declare and make dividends of profits amongst the stockholders thereof, shall, in the month of December of the present year, and annually thereafter, cause to be published, for four successive weeks, in one or more public newspapers, having the largest circulation, printed in the city or county in which such bank, savings institution, loan company, insurance company or other company, institution or association may be located, or in which its principal office or place of business may be situated, a true and accurate statement, verified by the oath or affirmation of the cashier or treasurer thereof, of all dividends or profits declared on its capital stock, which at the date of such settlement, shall have remained unclaimed by the person, co-partnership or corporation authorized to receive the same, for the period of three years then next preceding; which said statement shall set forth the names, and, if known, the residence and business of the persons, co-partnerships or corporations in whose favor said dividends or profits may have been declared, the amount of such dividends or profits, and the number of shares in the capital stock upon which the same has accrued.—Act of 6th of March, 1847, Sec. 1, P. L. 222.

Banks, Savings Institutions, Saving Fund Societies, Trust Companies and Other Corporations to Publish Annually a Statement of Unclaimed Deposits.

Sec. 41. Each of the said banks, savings institutions and loan companies and each and every saving fund society, insurance or trust company, or other company, institution or association, incorporated as aforesaid and legally authorized to receive deposits of money, shall, in the said month of December of the present year, and annually thereafter, cause to be published, in like manner, and for the same period, a statement, verified as aforesaid, of the names, and, if known, the residence and business of all persons, co-partnerships or corporations who have made deposits therein, or have balances due them, and who have not, within the three years then next preceding the date of said statements, either increased or diminished the amount of such deposits or balances, or received any interest thereon, with the dates when such deposits were made, or balances accrued, the amount thereof, and the amount of interest, if any, accruing thereon.—Act of 6th of March, 1847, Sec. 2, P. L. 222.

Penalty for Neglect to Publish Such Statements.—Dividends Less Than Five Dollars and Deposits Less Than Ten Dollars Accepted.

Sec. 42. If any such bank, savings institution, loan company, insurance company or other banking institution or association, incorporated as aforesaid, shall neglect or refuse to publish the statement hereinbefore required to be published, the same, and the cashier or treasurer thereof, in his individual capacity, shall be liable to the party in whose name such unclaimed dividend, profit, deposit or balance may stand, or to his, her or their legal representatives for the amount thereof, with the interest thereon, at the rate of twelve per centum per annum from the date of such dividend, profit, deposit or balance until paid, recoverable by action of debt as in other cases: Provided, That nothing herein contained shall be so construed as to require the publication of any such unclaimed dividends or profits, amounting to less than five dollars, nor such unclaimed deposits or balances amounting to less than ten dollars.—Act of 6th of March, 1847, Sec. 3, P. L. 222.

2

When Unclaimed Dividends and Deposits to Escheat.—May be Reclaimed by Owners.

Sec. 43. At the expiration of three years after the first publication of any particular dividend or profits, balance or deposit, with the interest that has accrued thereon, as provided for by the first and second sections of this act, such dividend or profit, balance or deposit, with the interest that has accrued, if not demanded within that time by the rightful owner or owners thereof, or their legal representatives, shall escheat to the Commonwealth, and shall be paid into the treasury thereof, without discount or deduction for commissions, fees or expenses of any description, by the cashier, treasurer or other proper officer of said bank, savings institution, loan company, insurance company, saving fund society or other company, institution or association, in which such dividend or profit, balance or deposit shall have remained without being demanded as aforesaid, or without being increased or diminished for the length of time aforesaid; and the said bank, savings institution, loan company, insurance company, saving fund society or other company, institution or association, as the case may be, shall thereupon be discharged from any obligation or liability to pay over such dividend or profit, balance or deposit, or interest thereon, to .the owner or owners thereof, that the said owner or owners, or their legal representatives, upon application to the State Treasurer for the time being, and producing satisfactory proof to that officer of his, her or their right to such dividend or profit, balance or deposit, with the interest thereon, paid into the treasury, as aforesaid, or any part thereof, shall receive from the Commonwealth, the amount he, she or they shall be found legally or equitably entitled to: Provided, That the expense of the publication or publications required by this act shall be paid out of such dividend or profit, balance or deposit so published.—Act of 6th of March, 1847, Sec. 4, P. L. 222.

Information Elicited by the Committee on Banks of Either House to be Recorded.

Sec. 44. All the facts and information which may be elicited by any examination which may be instituted by the Committee on Banks, of either the Senate or the House of Representatives, into the affairs of such banks or savings institutions as shall apply to the Legislature for a re-charter, or extension, or restoration of capital, shall be recorded in the form of interrogatories and answers, on the Journal, by the Clerk of the Senate or House of Representatives, as the case may be.—Act of 26th of January, 1849, Sec. 1, P. L. 21.

False Swearing to Interrogatories Propounded by the Committee to be Perjury.

Sec. 45. If any officer of a bank or savings institution, appearing before the Committee on Banks, of either the Senate or House of Representatives, or before any justice of the peace, or other person authorized by law to administer oaths, shall wilfully swear falsely to any interrogatories propounded by the Committee on Banks, or shall, after having been sworn or affirmed by the chairman, or any member thereof, to make true answers to the questions asked him, wilfully state anything that is false, respecting the condition, resources or liabilities of such institutions, or shall wilfully misrepresent any fact concerning their organization, indebtedness, means, or the administration of their affairs, he shall be deemed guilty of perjury, and be subject to prosecution and punishment therefor.—Act of 26th of January, 1849, Sec. 2, P. L. 21.

Officers of Banks Examined by the Committee not Entitled to Witness Fees.

Sec. 46. No fees or expenses shall be allowed to any president, cashier, or other officer appearing as a witness before either of the committees aforesaid.—Act of 26th of January, 1849, Sec. 3, P. L. 21.

CHAPTER 3.

BANKING ACT OF 1850.

Prefatory Remarks as to the Banking Laws Prior to the 16th of April, 1850.

Sec. 47. Prior to the passage of the Act of 1850 bands in the Commonwealth of Pennsylvania were incorporated by special acts of Assembly. A large number of such banks are still in existence with separate charters and, to a certain extent, under the special laws of their charters. However certain general laws were passed, a collection of which follows:

What Banks are Subject to the Act of 1850.

Sec. 48. Every banking corporation hereafter created by any special act of the General Assembly, and every bank hereafter rechartered, or the charter of which shall be hereafter extended or renewed by any such act of Assembly, shall be subject to the provisions of this act,—Act of 16th of April, 1850, Sec. 1, P. L. 477.

Division of Capital Shares to be Fifty Dollars Each.—How Subscriptions to be Taken.

Sec. 49. Whenever a special act of the general assembly shall be passed creating a new bank, the capital stock of such bank shall be divided into shares of fifty dollars; and the commissioners named in such act, or a majority of them, shall have power to open books for receiving subscriptions to the capital stock of such bank, at such times and places as they may deem expedient, notice of which shall be given by publication for three weeks in one or more newspapers published in the county where the books of subscription are intended to be opened; two or more of the commissioners shall attend at the time and place appointed in such notice, and shall permit all persons competent to enter into a contract, to subscribe to the capital stock of such bank; such subscription shall be made payable to the president and directors of the bank; the books shall be kept open for four hours in every juridicial day, for six days, if six days shall be necessary; and on the first of said days, any person competent by this act, may subscribe in his own name, or in the name of any other person competent as aforesaid, by whom he shall be authorized, for one or two shares; and on the second day, for any number not exceeding four shares; and on the third day, for any number of shares, not exceeding six; and on the fourth day, for any number not exceeding eight; and on the fifth, or any succeeding day, for any number of shares not exceeding two hundred, including such shares as shall have been subscribed on the previous days; if at the end of the six days the whole number of shares authorized by the special act be not subscribed, the commissioners may adjourn from time to time, and from place to place, until the whole number of shares shall be subscribed.—Act of 16th of April, 1850, Sec. 2, P. L. 477.

Payment on Each Share.

Sec. 50. All persons offering to subscribe, shall first pay to the attending commissioners the sum of five dollars on each share to be subscribed, out of which shall be defrayed the expenses of taking the subscription and other incidental charges, and the residue shall be paid over by the commissioners to the president and directors of such bank, as soon as the same shall be organized.—Act 16th of April, 1850, Sec. 3, P. L. 477.

Courts of Common Pleas to Appoint Commissioners in Case of Vacancies.

Sec. 51. Should any or all of the commissioners named in such special act, die, or neglect or refuse to act, the court of common pleas of the county in which the bank is to be located, may, on application, appoint other commissioners to supply their places.— Act of 16th of April, 1850, Sec. 4, P. L. 477.

Payments of Shares of Stock.

Sec. 52. The payment of the shares of the capital stock shall be made in gold, silver or notes of specie-paying banks of this Commonwealth, at the times and in the manner following, to wit: Five dollars on each share to the commissioners at the time of subscribing and twenty dollars on each share within sixty days thereafter; the residue to be paid in such instalments as by the by-laws of the corporation shall be directed.—Act of 16th of April 1850, Sec. 5, P. L. 477.

Issue of Letters Patent, Style and Privileges of the Same.—Corporate Powers.

Sec. 53. When not less than one-half of the shares into which the capital stock of such corporation may be divided shall have been subscribed for, and the sum of fifty per cent. has been actually paid on the amount so subscribed, which the commissioners are hereby authorized to receive, the commissioners, or a majority of them, shall certify to the Governor of this Commonwealth, under their hands and seals, and under their oaths or affirmations respectively, the names of the subscribers, and the number of shares subscribed by each, together with the amount so actually paid; and thereupon the Governor shall, by letters patent under his hand and the seal of the State, create and erect the said subscribers, their successors and assigns, and if the whole number of shares be not then subscribed, then also all those who shall afterwards subscribe, their successors and assigns, into one body politic and corporate, in deed and in law, by the name, style and title designated in the special act authorizing such bank, and shall so continue a body politic and corporate, for the term of fifteen years from and after the date of such letters patent and by the name and style aforesaid they shall be able to sue and be sued, implead and be impleaded, answer and be answered, in all courts of record, and elsewhere; and to purchase, have, hold, receive, possess, enjoy and retain, to them and their successors, lands, tenements, hereditaments, rents, goods and chattels of what kind, nature and quality soever, to an amount not exceeding in the whole the capital stock of such bank, except such as may be purchased in satisfaction of any judgment or decree in favor of the bank, or lands purchased upon which the bank may have a lien, or assigned to it as security for the payment of any debt, or received in discharge of any debt, and the same from time (to time) to sell, grant, demise, alien and dispose of; and also to make and to have a common seal, and the same to break, alter and renew at pleasure; and also to ordain and put in execution such by-laws, rules and regulations as shall be convenient and necessary for the good government of such bank: Provided, That they be not contrary to the Constitution and laws of this State or of the United States; and generally to do and execute all such acts, matters and things which a corporation may lawfully do, subject to the rules, regulations, restrictions and provisions in this act.—Act of 16th day of April, 1850, Sec. 6, P. L. 477.

Organization and Election of Officers.

Sec. 54. The commissioners aforesaid shall within thirty days after the said letters patent are obtained, give notice in one or more newspapers published in the city or county in which the bank is located, of the time and place by them appointed for the subscribers to meet and organize; at which time and place the subscribers shall, by a majority of their votes, choose by ballot thirteen directors to manage the business of such corporation until the next annual election, as hereinafter provided.—Act of 16th day of April, 1850, Sec. 7, P. L. 477.

Certificates of Stock.

Sec. 55. The directors shall deliver to the stockholders as soon as they shall have fully paid their subscription, certificates of the share or the shares held by each, signed by the president chosen as hereinafter directed, and countersigned by the cashier, and sealed with the common seal of the corporation.—Act 16th day of April, 1850, Sec. 8, P. L. 477.

Proceedings Upon Re-chartering, Extending or Renewing Charters Created by Special Acts.—Effect of Re-chartering.

Sec. 56. Upon the re-chartering or extending or renewing of the charter of any incorporated bank by any special act of Assembly, the directors of such bank shall, within six months thereafter, file in the office of the Secretary of the Commonwealth the written acceptance of the stockholders of such charter, if they shall accept the same at a general meeting to be called for that purpose; and thereupon the subscribers and stockholders, and their successors and assigns, shall, from and after the expiration of the then existing charter of such bank, be a body corporate and politic, by the same name, style and title as such bank had under its previous charter, and shall be invested with all the powers and privileges, and be subject to the restrictions enumerated in the sixth section of this act; and also to have, hold, receive, possess, enjoy and retain, to the subscribers and their successors, all the estate, property and effects of every kind which such bank shall be possessed of or entitled to at the time of the expiration of its former charter, and all rights respecting the same shall be vested in such bank so rechartered, as if the act incorporating the same had been continued in full force; and such banks may sue and be sued on all debts, claims or demands due or owing to and from such banks, and shall have the benefit and advantages, and be liable to all contracts and engagements entered into previous to the expiration of the former charter, as if the charter had not expired; and suits pending either for or against the bank, shall be proceeded in and adjudged in like manner as if the former acts incorporating the same were in full force, without the necessity of alleging the same in pleading.—Act of 16th day of April, 1850, Sec. 9, P. L. 477.

Fundamental Articles. Directors, How Chosen, Number and Who May be Directors.

Sec. 57. The following rules, restrictions, limitations and provisions shall form and be the fundamental articles of the constitutution of every bank which shall be hereafter incorporated, and of every incorporated bank hereafter re-chartered, or of which the charter shall be hereafter extended or renewed. The affairs of every such bank shall be conducted by thirteen directors, to be chosen annually by the stockholders; no person not a citizen of the United States, and a stockholder in his own right, shall be a director; no person shall, at the same time, be a director of any two banks; nor shall the Governor or any executive or judicial officer of this Commonwealth, city or county treasurer, or a member of the State Legislature, be a director.—Act of 16th day of April, 1850, Sec. 10, P. L. 477.*

Election of Directors.

Sec. 58. The election of the directors shall be by ballot and after the first election, as provided in the seventh section of this act, shall be held annually, on the third Monday of November, at such place within the city or county where the bank is located, as the directors for the time being shall appoint, notice of which shall be given thirty days previous thereto, in one or more newspapers published in the city or county in which the bank is located; and a fair and correct list of the stockholders shall always be kept up in the common hall of the bank, which shall be corrected quarterly, so as to exhibit, at those times, a true list of the actual stockholders; the directors shall assemble on the first Monday succeeding such election, and choose one of their number to be president of the bank; the directors shall continue in office one year, and until others be

---

*Number of directors made not less than five nor more than thirteen by act of 17th day of April, 1861, P. L. 341.

chosen; if it shall happen that the election of directors be not made on the day above prescribed, the corporation shall not for that reason be dissolved, but it may be lawful, on any other day within thirty days thereafter, three weeks' notice being given in the manner aforesaid, to hold an election in such manner as by the by-laws and ordinances shall be prescribed; and the directors shall, at their first meeting after such election, elect one of their number to be president; in case of the death, resignation or absence from the United States, or inability of the president or any director to act, the board of directors shall choose another to supply his place: Provided, That no person shall be eligible as a director for more than three years in any four, except the president, who shall always be eligible; partners, in business, of directors, shall be comprised in this restriction; and no two partners in business shall be directors at the same time: And provided, That the persons who may be directors of any bank hereafter re-chartered, shall, after the expiration of the former charter, continue directors of such bank until others are chosen according to the provisions of this act, and shall be subject to the duties imposed bv this act, and to its provisions.—Act of 16th day of April, 1850, Sec. 10, Art. 2, P. L. 477.*

Judges of Election to be Sworn or Affirmed and Shall Determine Whether Candidates for Directors Are Qualified and Shall Declare Results of Ballot.

Sec. 59. For the well ordering and conducting of the elections, the directors shall, previously thereto, appoint three shareholders, not being directors, to be judges of the election, who shall severally take and subscribe an oath or affirmation, before some officer authorized by law to administer oaths, well and truly, and according to law, to conduct such election; they shall determine whether the persons who have the greatest number of votes are qualified to be elected directors, and do come truly and plainly within the provisions of this act; and after the conclusion of the ballot, shall decide and declare who are elected directors for the ensuing year.—Act of 16th of April, 1850, Sec. 10, Art. 3, P. L. 477.

How Voting Depends Upon Number of Shares of Stock. Who May Vote.

Sec. 60. The number of votes to which each stockholder shall be entitled shall be according to the number of shares held in the proportion following, that is to say: For each share not exceeding two shares, one vote; for every two shares above two, and not exceeding ten shares, one vote; for every four shares above ten shares, and not exceeding thirty shares, one vote; for every ten shares above thirty shares, and not exceeding fifty shares, one vote; but no share, or number of shares, above fifty shall confer any additional right of voting and no share shall confer the right to vote which shall not have been holden three calendar months previous to the day of the election, nor unless it be holden by the person in whose name it appears absolutely and bona fide, in his own right or that of his wife, or as executor or administrator, trustee or guardian, or in the

---

*By act of 18th day of April, 1855, P. L. 258, a justice of the peace may become a bank director.

right of some corporation, co-partnership or society of which he or she may be a member, and not in trust for any other person; every person voting, except females, shall do so in their own proper person, and not by proxy: Provided, That this provision shall not prevent any guardian of minor children, or any bona fide trustee who holds stock in a fiduciary capacity, from voting upon such stock at any election.—Act of 16th of April, 1850, Sec. 10, Art. 4, P. L. 477.

Directors to Appoint Officers, Who Shall Give Bonds.—How Bonds to be Approved and Recorded.—Suit on Bonds Regulated.— Directors shall fix compensation of officers.—Officers not to vote as Proxies and Cashier Not to Engage in any Other Occupation. —Penalty for so Doing.—Exceptions.

Sec. 61. The board of directors shall have power to appoint a cashier and all other officers, clerks and other persons necessary for executing the business of the bank; and it shall be the duty of such board to require the cashier, tellers and other officers of the bank, severally to enter into a bond to the Commonwealth of Pennsylvania, (the cashier in any sum not less than one-fifth of the capital stock paid in, when the capital stock is not over two hundred thousand dollars; and when the capital stock is over two hundred thousand dollars and not greater than five hundred thousand dollars, the cashier shall give bond in not less than one-eighth of the capital stock; and when the capital stock is greater than five hundred thousand dollars and not over one million of dollars, the cashier shall give bond in not less than one-tenth of the capital stock; and when the capital stock exceeds one million of dollars, such bond shall not be less than one-twelfth of the capital stock), and the president, tellers and other officers in such sums as the board of directors may require, conditioned for the faithful execution of their duties; such bonds to be approved of by the court of common pleas (or district court) of the county in which the bank is located, and recorded in the office of the recorder of deeds, within ten days thereafter, of the proper county; any person aggreived by failure of any officer or clerk of the bank to comply with the condition of such bond, may commence and prosecute an action on the same in the manner provided for the suing on official bonds, in the act of fourteenth June, one thousand eight hundred and thirty-six, entitled "An act relative to bonds with penalties and official bonds;" they shall establish the compensation to be paid to the president, cashier and other officers of the bank, which, together with all other expenses, shall be defrayed out of the funds of the corporation; and it shall not be lawful for the president, cashier, teller or clerk of the bank to vote at any election for directors, as the attorney, proxy or agent of any stockholder; and that it shall not be lawful for the cashier of any bank to engage in any other profession, occupation or calling, either directly or indirectly, than that of the duties appertaining to the office of cashier, and if any cashier of the bank shall directly or indirectly engage in the purchase and sale of stocks, or in any other profession, occupation or calling other than that of his duties of cashier, such cashier, upon conviction thereof, in any court of criminal jurisdiction, shall be sentenced to pay a fine not exceeding five hundred dollars: Provided, That this section shall not be construed in such manner as to prevent any cashier from managing his own real estate or private property as heretofore, if such private property be not vested in mercantile, mechanical or manufacturing operations. —Act of 16th of April, 1850, Sec. 10, Art. 5, P. L. 477.*

Emoluments to Directors Regulated.

Sec. 62. No director, except the president, shall be entitled to any emolument, unless the same shall have been allowed by the stockholders, at a general meeting.—Act of 16th of April, 1850, Sec. 10, Art. 6, P. L. 477.

Stated Meetings of Directors and Quorum.—President Pro Tem. to be Appointed.

Sec. 63. The stated meetings of the directors shall be held at such times as the by-laws shall ordain, and special meetings may be held by particular appointments, or upon the call of the president; a majority of the whole number of the directors, of whom the president shall be one, shall form a board or quorum, for the transaction of any business; but ordinary discounts may be made by the president and four other directors; in case of sickness or necessary absence of the president his place may be supplied by a president pro tempore, to be appointed by the directors from among their number.—Act of 16th of April, 1850, Sec. 10, Art. 7, P. L. 477.

General Meeting of Stockholders.

Sec. 64. The board of directors, or any twenty stockholders thereof, being together proprietors of one-twentieth part of the stock, may at any time call a general meeting of the stockholders for purposes relative to the institution, giving at least thirty days' notice thereof in one or more newspapers in the city or county in which the bank is located, specifying in such notice the object or objects of such meetings.—Act of 16th of April, 1850, Sec. 10, Art. 8, P. L. 477.

Annual Meeting of Stockholders.

Sec. 65. A general meeting of the stockholders of the bank shall be held on the first Tuesday of November in every year, at which time the directors shall lay before them a general and particular statement of the affairs of such bank: Provided, That this shall not be so construed so as to compel the directors to lay before the stockholders a statement of the private account of any individual or individuals.—Act of 16th of April, 1850, Sec. 10, Art. 9, P. L. 477.

---

*By an amendment of the fifth article of the tenth section of the act of the 16th of April, 1850, a cashier of a bank will not be required to relinquish his office in consequence of coming into possession of property, gifts or inheritance invested in mercantile, mechanical or manufacturing purposes.—Act of 18th of April, 1855, P. L. 258.

The provisions of article five, section ten of the act of 1850 extended to all kinds of banks of this Commonwealth by act of April 18, 1856.

Stock to be Transferred as By-laws Ordain.—Stock Not to be Transferred or Dividend Thereon Paid Until Debt of Stockholder be Discharged or Secured.

Sec. 66. The stock of the bank shall be assignable and transferable on the books of the corporation only, and in the presence of the president or cashier, in such manner as the by-laws shall ordain; but no stockholder indebted to the bank for a debt actually due and unpaid, shall be authorized to make a transfer or receive a dividend until such debt is discharged, or security to the satisfaction of the directors given for the same.—Act of 16th of April, 1850, Sec. 10, Art. 10, P. L. 477.*

Rate of Discount.

Sec. 67. The rate of discount at which loans may be made shall not exceed one-half of one per centum for thirty days.—Act of 16th of April, 1850, Sec. 10, Art. 11, P. L. 477.

Declaration of Dividends.—Directors Personally Liable for Impairment of Capital.

Sec. 68. Dividends of so much of the profits as shall appear advisable to the directors of the bank, shall be declared at least twice a year, on the first Tuesday of May and November in every year, and paid to the stockholders on demand, at any time after the expiration of ten days therefrom; but such dividends shall in no case exceed the amount of the net profits actually acquired, so that the capital stock of the bank shall never be thereby impaired; and if the directors of the bank shall make any dividends which shall impair the capital stock of the bank, the directors consenting thereto shall be jointly and severally liable, in any action of debt, scire facias, or bill in equity, in their individual capacities, to such corporation, for the amount of the stock so divided; and each director present when such dividend shall be made, shall be adjudged to be consenting thereto unless he forthwith enter his protest on the minutes of the board and give public notice to the stockholders of the declaring of such dividend.—Act of 16th of April, 1850, Sec. 10, Art. 12, P. L. 477.

May Hold Lands Under Certain Circumstances.—Restrictions Upon Trading.

Sec. 69. It shall be lawful for such corporations to hold such lands, tenements and herditaments only as shall be requisite for their accommodation in the convenient transaction of their business, and such as shall be bona fide mortgaged or conveyed to them in satisfaction of debts previously contracted in the course of their dealings, or purchased at sales upon judgments of any person or body politic, where the same may be necessary to secure any debt, due to the said corporations; but all such lands, tenements and hereditaments,

---

*This section applies to banks of issue only, not to savings banks. (Merchants' Bank vs. Shouse, 102 Pa. 488.)

There is no lien upon stock at common law for indebtedness. (Merchants' Bank vs. Shouse, 102 Pa. 488.)

The bank may hold all stock owned by its debtor and refuse to transfer until the debt is paid. (17 S. & R. 285.)

except the banking house and lot, shall be disposed of within five years after such corporations are re-chartered, or after the same shall have come into their possession; not more than thirty thousand dollars shall be expended by any one of such corporations in procuring grounds and erecting suitable buildings for the banking house, except in the city and county of Philadelphia and city of Pittsburgh, which shall not exceed fifty thousand dollars; it shall not be lawful for such corporations, directly, or through the agency of any person or persons whomsoever, either in trust or confidence, to deal or trade with any profits, stocks, money or effects, in buying or selling any goods, wares, merchandise, whatsoever, but nothing herein contained shall be so construed as to prevent any such corporation from selling any public stock of which it may be possessed; such corporations shall not be at liberty to purchase any stock whatsoever to a greater amount than one-third of the capital stock actually paid in, and that in the stock or loans of this State and of the United States except in their own bank stock, and such stocks as shall be taken in satisfaction of debts previously contracted; such corporations shall not deal or trade in anything but bills of exchange, promissory notes, gold and silver and bullion, or in the sale of goods truly pledged for money lent and not redeemed in due time, or in goods which may be the produce of their lands.—Act of 16th of April, 1850, Sec. 10, Art. 13, P. L. 477.*

Bills Obligatory and of Credit Assignable by Endorsement.

Sec. 70. The bills obligatory and of credit, under the seal of such corporations, which shall be made to any person or persons shall be assignable by endorsement thereupon, under the hand or hands of such person or persons, and of his, her or their assignee or assignees, so as absolutely to transfer and invest the property and legal title thereof in each and every assignee or assignees successively, and to enable such assignee or assignees to bring and maintain an action thereupon in his, her or their own name or names; and bills or notes which may be issued by order of any of the said corporations, signed by the president and countersigned by the cashier thereof, promising the payment of money to any person or persons, his, her or their order, or to bearer, though not under the seal of such corporation, shall be binding and obligatory upon the same in like manner, and with like force and effect, as upon any private person or persons, if issued by him, her or them, in his, her or their private capacity or capacities, and shall be assignable and negotiable in like manner as if they were so issued by such private person or persons, that is to say: Those which shall be payable to any person or persons, his, her or their order, shall be assignable by endorsement, in like manner and with like effect, as foreign bills of exchange now are; and those which are payable to bearer shall be negotiable and assignable by delivery only; and all notes or bills at any time discounted by such corporation, or deposited for collection, and falling due at such bank, shall be and they are hereby placed on the same footing as foreign bills of exchange, so that the like benefits

---

*By act of 17tn of April, 1861, article 13 of tenth section of act of 1850 to be construed so that banks may receive notes of banks of other states.

shall be had in the payment and the like remedy for the recovery thereof against the drawer or drawers, endorser or endorsers, and their representatives, and with the like effect, except so far as relates to damages; any law, custom or usage to the contrary in any wise notwithstanding.—Act 16th of April, 1850, Sec. 10, Art. 14, P. L. 477.

Books, Papers, Etc., to be Subject to Inspection by Directors.

Sec. 71. The books, papers, correspondence and funds of the said several banks shall at all times be subject to the inspection of the directors, who 'shall keep fair and regular entries of their proceedings, in a book to be provided for that purpose; and on any question where two directors shall require it, the yeas and nays of the directors voting shall be inserted on their minutes, and those minutes shall at all times, on demand, be produced to the stockholders at a general meeting; and the minutes, books and papers shall be subject to the inspection of any committee who shall be authorized by the legislature to require the same.—Act 16th of April, 1850, Sec. 10, Art. 15, P. L. 477.

Duty of Auditor General to Make Exhibits for Legislature.

Sec. 72. It shall be the duty of the Auditor General to require the cashiers of the said banks, on some discount day to be designated by him, in every quarter of the then current year, one of which shall be in the month of November, to make and return to him the exhibits hereinafter provided for, which exhibits the Auditor General shall prepare in tabular form, and communicate the same to both branches of the legislature within ten days after their meeting. —Act of 16th of April, 1850, Sec. 11, P. L. 477.

Cashier to Prepare Exhibit Upon Requisition of Auditor General.

Sec. 73. It shall be the duty of the cashier of any such bank, for the time being, to prepare, upon the requisition of the Auditor General, a just and full exhibit of the affairs and condition of the bank on at least four different discount days of the then current year, to be designated by the Auditor General, one of which shall be in the month of November, so as to exhibit the entire amount of the assets of the bank, and every item thereof, under the separate heads; and also of the entire amount of the indebtedness and liabilities of the bank, and every item thereof, under separate heads setting forth, on the one side particularly, so as to give a full and proper view of all the assets belonging to the bank: First, the amount of gold and silver in the vaults of the bank; the amount of current notes, check and bills of other banks; the amount of uncurrent notes, checks and bills of other banks; the amount of any other obligations of other banks; the amount of bills and notes discounted, designating the amount under protest; the amount of the mortgages of the bank and the assessed value, for the preceding year, of the real estate bound by such mortgages; the amount of prior mortgages, judgments and other liens; the amount of the judgments held by the bank, and the assessed value for the preceding year, of the real estate bound by such judgments, the amount of prior judgments, mortgages and other liens; the amount of the real estate held and owned by the bank, and the assessed value, for the preceding year, of each separate piece or parcel of real estate owned by the bank, and its location; the amount due from other banks that are solvent, giving the name of each bank from which the same is due, together with the amount so due by each one of said banks; the amount due from insolvent banks, the names of such banks and the amount due from each one; the amount of public and corporate stocks and loans, the nature and kind of loans and stocks, designating particularly in what companies or corporations the stocks or loans are held, and the amount of stocks or loans of each company or corporation so held; the amount of bonds held, designating particularly the nature and character of the bonds held; the amount of treasury notes; the amount of claims against individuals or corporations that are disputed or in controversy; the amount of all other debts and claims either due or to become due; and the value of any other property of the bank, as the same stands charged on the books or otherwise; which said exhibit shall also set forth, on the other side, the debts and liabilities of the bank on the discount days designated by the Auditor General, specifying separately, under distinct heads, the various kinds of liabilities and indebtedness, the amount of capital stock actually paid in, the amount of the circulation, the amount of deposits, certificates of deposits, the amount due the Commonwealth, the amount due to corporations, the amount due to banks, the amount due to individuals, and the amount of claims against the bank remaining in controversy, and any other items of indebtedness or liabilities not embraced in the foregoing specifications.—Act of 16th of April, 1850, Sec. 12, P. L. 477.

Cashier to State Marketable Value of Assets.

Sec. 74. It shall moreover be the duty of the cashier, in preparing the exhibit required in the preceding section of this act, for the month of November preceding the meeting of the legislature, to state, in regard to each item and subdivision of the assets of the bank, what is, in the judgment of the cashier, the actual marketable cash value of each item of the same; the said amount of current notes of other banks on hand at the time the exhibit is made out; also the amount of uncurrent notes held by the bank.—Act of 16th of April, 1850, Sec. 13, P. L. 477.

Exhibit to be Verified by Oath of Cashier.

Sec. 75. The exhibit, agreeably to the twelfth and thirteenth sections of this act, shall be verified and accompanied with the oath or affirmation of the cashier of the said bank, duly attested before some officer authorized by law to administer oaths, to the following effect, namely: That he, the cashier, has carefully examined the books and muniments of the bank, and has compared the same with the said exhibit, and that he verily believes that said exhibit or statement presents a true, fair and full view of the actual condition of the bank; and, in addition to the above, the exhibit made for the discount day in the month of November preceding the meeting of the legislature shall be accompanied with the oath or affirmation of the cashier of the said bank, setting forth that he has inspected the several items of assets, or the evidence thereof, in the said exhibit referred to; and that he has, according to the best of his judgment and ability, valued each of said items of assets at the absolute cash price which it would produce at the time, and that in his judgment, the actual assets of the bank are intrinsically worth the amount of the valuation so made by him.—Act of 16th of April, 1850, Sec. 14, P. L. 477.

President, Directors, Cashier and Other Officer to be Sworn or Affirmed to Comply With Act.

Sec. 76. The president, directors, cashier and other officers of any such bank shall, before they enter on the duties of their several offices and stations, severally take an oath or affirmation, to be administered by some officer authorized by law to administer oaths or affirmations, to observe faithfully and honestly the provisions of this act and that they and each of them, during their continuance in office, will not knowingly violate, or sanction or willingly permit any of the provisions of this act to be violated, and that should any such violation take place without their concurrence known to them, that they will immediately communicate the facts to the Auditor General of the Commonwealth; the said oath or affirmation so to be taken, shall be subscribed and immediately delivered to the Auditor General to be filed in his office.—Act of 16th of April, 1850, Sec. 15, P. L. 477.

Official Misconduct and Penalty Therefor.

Sec. 77. If any president, director, cashier or other officer of any such bank shall, after having taken and subscribed the oath required by this act, wilfully violate any provision of this act, for which no other criminal punishment is specially provided in this act, he shall be taken and deemed to have committed a misdemeanor, and upon conviction in any criminal court in this Commonwealth, he shall suffer such punishment by fine not exceeding one thousand dollars and imprisonment in the county jail or penitentiary not exceeding three years.—Act of 16th of April, 1850, Sec. 16, P. L. 477.

Limit of Liabilities.

Sec. 78. The total liabilities of any such bank, exclusive of the capital stock, shall not, at any time, exceed three times the amount of the capital stock paid in; nor shall the debts of any kind due and to become due to the bank ever amount to more than four times the capital stock paid in; and the said banks shall neither loan nor discount when their circulation shall be equal, for thirty consecutive days, to three times the amount of specie State and United States loans, and notes of specie-paying banks in their possession belonging to said banks, and any balances standing to the credit thereof, in specie-paying banks, convertible into specie at the pleasure of the said banks.—Act of 16th of April, 1850, Sec. 17, P. L. 477.

Cashier to Make Return of Circulation.—Forfeiture of Charter for Violation of Seventeenth Section.

Sec. 79. The Auditor General may at any time require the cashier of any such bank to state and return, on oath or affirmation, the amount of the circulation of the bank for any consecutive period of thirty days, in the current year, which he may designate; and also, for the same period, the amount of specie, the State of Pennsylvania and United States loans and notes of specie-paying banks in its possession, belonging to the said bank, and the balance standing to its credit in specie-paying banks, convertible into specie at the pleasure of the bank; and also, the whole amount of its liabilities and debts due and to become due; and if, upon the return so made, it shall appear that any of the provisions of the seventeenth section of this act have been violated for the said period of thirty days so designated by the Auditor General, he shall give notice thereof to the Governor, who shall thereupon issue his proclamation, declaring the charter of the said bank to be forfeited.—Act of 16th of April, 1850, Sec. 18, P. L. 477.

Directors to Make Assignment in Case of Forfeiture of Charter.

Sec. 80. If the charter of any such bank shall be forfeited in manner provided in the preceding section, after proclamation made by the Governor, then the directors of said bank shall forthwith make and execute an assignment, in the manner provided in the twenty-seventh section of this act, and thereupoh proceedings shall be had in the manner provided in that section; if the directors of said bank should neglect or refuse to make the assignment provided for in this act, every director so neglecting, or refusing, shall be guilty of a misdemeanor, and, upon conviction in any criminal court in the Commonwealth, be imprisoned in the jail of the proper county for any period not exceeding two years, at the discretion of the court.— Act of 16th of April, 1850, Sec. 19, P. L. 477.

Embezzlement by Officers.

Sec. 81. If any president, cashier, director or any other officer or clerk of any such bapk shall fraudulently embezzle or appropriate to his own use, or to the use of any other person or persons, any money or other property belonging to said institution, or left with the same as a special deposit or otherwise, he or they, upon conviction of such offense, shall be fined in any amount not less than the sum so appropriated or embezzled, and sentenced to undergo imprisonment in the proper State penitentiary, to be kept in separate and solitary confinement at hard labor, for any term not exceeding five years: Provided, That this shall not prevent any person or persons aggrieved from pursuing his, her or their civil remedy against such person or persons.—Act of 16th of April, 1850, Sec. 20, P. L. 477.

Tax on Dividends.

Sec. 82. Said banks shall pay into the treasury of the State, in the manner now directed by law for the payment of a tax on dividends, as follows: On all dividends which do not exceed six per cent. per annum, eight per cent.; on dividends exceeding six per cent. and not exceeding seven per cent. per annum, a tax of nine per cent.; on dividends exceeding seven per cent. per annum, and not exceeding eight per cent. per annum, a tax of ten per cent.; on dividends exceeding eight per cent. per annum and not exceeding nine per cent., a tax of twelve per cent.; on dividends exceeding nine per cent. and not exceeding ten per cent., a tax of thirteen per cent.; on dividends exceeding ten per cent. and not exceeding eleven per cent., a tax of fifteen per cent.; on dividends exceeding eleven per cent. and not exceeding twelve per cent., a tax of seventeen per cent.; on dividends exceeding twelve per cent. and not exceeding fifteen per cent. a tax of twenty per cent.; on dividends exceeding fifteen and not exceeding twenty per cent., a tax of twenty-five per cent.; and on all dividends exceeding twenty-five per cent., a tax of thirty per cent.—Act of 16th of April, 1850, Sec. 21, P. L. 477.

Bills and Notes of Banks to be Payable at Banks.

Sec. 83. It shall not be lawful for any such bank to issue and put in circulation any bill or note of said bank payable at any other place than at said bank, or otherwise than payable on demand, and of a denomination less than five dollars; and any violation of this section by any officer of any such bank, shall be a misdemeanor, punishable, upon conviction, by a fine of not less than five hundred dollars, and imprisonment in the jail of the proper county not less than one year.—Act of 16th of April, 1850, Sec. 22, P. L. 477.

Discounts to Directors Restricted.

Sec. 84. No director of any such bank shall appear as drawer or endorser, or as both drawer and endorser, at any one time for a greater amount than three per cent. on the capital stock paid in; and the gross amount discounted for or loaned to all the directors and other officers of said bank, and to the houses or firms in which they may be interested directly or indirectly, shall not exceed at any one time the sum of six per cent. on the capital stock paid in. —Act of 16th of April, 1850, Sec. 23, P. L. 477.*

Failure to Redeem Notes to be Forfeiture of Charter.

Sec. 85. If any such bank shall at any time fail or refuse to redeem its notes and pay its liabilities in gold and silver coin, upon demand being made at the banking house of said bank during banking hours, such failure or refusal shall be deemed and held to be an absolute forfeiture of the charter of said bank.—Act of 16th of April, 1850, Sec. 24, P. L. 477.

---

*This section applies to all banking corporations created prior to the act of 13th May, 1876, except savings banks.—12 Pa. C. C. R., 42.

**Cashiers May be Required to Give Certificates of Deposit.—Interest
on Failure to Redeem.—Time of Demand to be Endorsed and
Penalty for Neglect or Refusal so to do.**

Sec. 86. It shall be the duty of the cashier of any such bank,
when required, to give a certificate of the time and the amount of
the deposit to every person making a deposit; and if any of the
said banks shall, at any time, refuse or neglect to pay on demand in
gold or silver, any bill, note or obligation issued by such banks,
according to the contract, promise or undertaking therein expressed,
or shall neglect or refuse to pay on demand in gold or silver, any
moneys received in such bank on deposit, except in the case of special deposits, when the contract is different, to the person or persons entitled to receive the same, then and in any such case, the
holder of any such note, bill, or obligation, or the person or persons
entitled to demand' and receive such moneys as aforesaid, shall be
entitled to receive and recover interest on the said notes, bills, obligations, certificates or moneys until the same shall be fully paid and
satisfied, at the rate of twelve per centum per annum, from the
time of such demand as aforesaid until the same is paid, and it shall
be the duty of the president or cashier of the bank, and he is hereby
required to make, at the time of demand being made for the payment of any note, bill or obligation, or any moneys deposited as
aforesaid, the payment of which in gold or silver shall have been
refused, an endorsement on the said note, bill, obligation, or certificate of deposit, setting forth the day and year when the payment
thereof was demanded, and subscribe his name thereto; and if the
said president or cashier shall evade, neglect, or refuse making such
indorsement at the time and in the manner hereinbefore required,
he shall forfeit and pay to the holder of such note, bill, obligation,
or certificate the sum of one hundred dollars, to be recovered in the
same manner as debts of like amount are by law recoverable: Provided, That nothing in this act shall be construed to prevent any
bank from redeeming its own notes with the notes of any other bank
when the demand is made on behalf of such other bank.—Act of
16th of April, 1850, Sec. 25, P. L. 477.

One-fifth of Amount of Demand to be Paid in American Gold Coin.

Sec. 87. Whenever any demand for specie shall be made by a
note-holder of any bank, subject to the provisions of this act, it shall
be the duty of the cashier or other officer of the bank upon whom
such demand is made, to pay one-fifth of the amount of such demand
in American gold coin, if the same shall be requested by the note-
holder making such demand: Provided, That the one-fifth of such
demand be not less in amount than five dollars.—Act of 16th of
April, 1850, Sec. 26, P. L. 477.

**Proceedings on Failure to Redeem.—Citation May Issue and How
Served.—Court to Decree General Assignment, Same to be Re-
corded.—Assignees to be Sworn and Give Security.—Corporate
Powers to Cease Except for Certain Purposes.**

Sec. 88. Upon application to any court of common pleas or district
court, of the proper county, or a single judge thereof in vacation,

on the oath or affirmation of any person, setting forth that he or she had presented to the proper officer or officers of such bank, located within said county, a note or notes, or certificates of deposit or other liability issued by the same, except notes issued by authority of the act of fourth May, one thousand eight hundred and forty-one, and demanded the payment thereof in gold or silver coin, which said bank had refused or failed to pay, it shall be the duty of said court, if in session, or a judge in vacation, to direct a citation to be issued by the prothonotary of said court, to the president, cashier or other officer of said bank, in the nature of a summons, which it shall be the duty of the sheriff or coroner of the proper county to serve forthwith, commanding the president, cashier, or other officer of the said bank to appear at the time and place designated by the said court or judge, not less than four nor more than eight days thereafter; in case none of the officers of the bank can be found, the service shall be made by posting a copy of the citation on the front door of the banking house during banking hours; and upon the hearing of the parties, if the said court or judge shall be satisfied of the truth of said complaint, and that the provisions of the twenty-fifth section of this act have been wilfully violated, then the directors of the bank shall make and execute, under their corporate seal, a general assignment of all the estate, real and personal, of the bank, to such person or persons, as they may select, subject to the approval of the court of common pleas, or district court of the proper county; the assignment shall be recorded in the office of the recorder of deeds of the proper county, within thirty days from the execution thereof; the said assignee or assignees, before entering on the duties of their office, shall take and subscribe an oath or affirmation to execute the trusts confided to them with fidelity, which oath or affirmation shall be filed in the office of the prothonotary of the proper county, and shall give such security as the said court may deem amply sufficient to secure the faithful execution of the said trust; they shall proceed to sell at public sale all the real and personal estate of said bank, and shall collect all the outstanding debts, and for this purpose may use the corporate name of the bank: Provided, however, That the said assignees shall receive in payment of debts due to said bank its own notes and obligations, and the checks of its depositors, at par; the said assignees shall, once in every six months, file an account of their receipts and disbursements in the office of the prothonotary of said court, verified by their oaths or affirmations; they shall, at least once in every six months, make a pro rata dividend of the balance in their hands among the creditors of the bank who shall in pursuance of public notice given in such manner and form as shall be directed by the court, have made claim and delivered up the evidence of their claims, if such evidence be in writing, to the said assignees, and receive from the said assignees a certificate, stating particularly the nature of the claim and the amount thereof; the said assignees shall be allowed such commission or compensation for their services as may be agreed upon in such assignment, with the approbation of the court, and shall be subject, except as herein otherwise provided, to the several provisions of the act of assembly, passed June fourteen, one thousand eight hundred and thirty-six, entitled "An act relating to assignees for the benefit of creditors and other trustees:" Provided, That the corporate powers of the bank shall, after the making of the assignment, cease and determine, except so far as may be necessary for the following purposes, to wit:

I. For the purpose of suing and being sued, and for continuing all suits and proceedings at law or in equity, pending for or against the bank.

II. For the purpose of making such assurances, conveyances and transfers, and doing all such acts, matters and things as may be necessary or expedient to make the said assignments, or the trusts thereof effectual.

III. For the purpose of citing the said trustees to account, and compelling them to execute the said trusts.

IV. For the choosing of directors for the purpose of receiving and distributing, amongst the stockholders of the said bank, such surplus as shall remain after discharging all the debts of the bank. —Act of 16th of April, 1850, Sec. 27, P. L. 477.

Attachment May Issue Against Bank's Property.—Trustees May Be Appointed by the Court.

Sec. 89. It shall be the duty of the said court, or any judge thereof, on application and proof as aforesaid, if it shall be deemed necessary for the protection of parties interested, to issue an attachment commanding the sheriff or coroner forthwith to seize and take possession of the banking house, books, moneys, deposits, papers and effects thereof, and to deliver the same to the trustees, when legally authorized to receive them; and if the directors shall not within ten days thereafter, make an assignment as hereinbefore provided, the trustees appointed by the court shall, by operation of the law, be vested with the same rights and powers as if such assignment had been made: Provided, That no person shall be appointed a trustee under this act who is a director or other officer of the bank, or who has been so one year previous thereto.—Act of 16th of April, 1850, Sec. 28, P. L. 477.

Majority of Stockholders May Direct an Assignment.

Sec. 90. It shall be lawful for the directors of every such bank, whenever it may be deemed expedient by a majority of the stockholders in number and interest, to wind up the affairs of such bank, to make a general assignment of all the estate, real and personal, of the bank, subject to the conditions and provisions relating to assignments by directors of banks provided in the twenty-seventh section of this act.—Act of 16th of April, 1850, Sec. 29, P. L. 477.

Banks not to Issue Notes Other Than Their Own.

Sec. 91. It shall not be lawful for any of the said banks to issue or pay out any bank notes other than those issued by itself payable on demand in gold or silver; notes of specie-paying banks of this State which are taken on deposit, or in payment of debts, at par at the counter of the bank where paid out, or notes of banks issued under the authority of the act of the fourth of May, one thousand eight hundred and forty-one, at the option of the person receiving the same; and any violation of this provision shall work an absolute forfeiture of its charter, and be proceeded in the manner provided in the twenty-seventh section of this act.—Act of 16th of April, 1850, Sec. 30, P. L. 477.*

Notes of Certain Denominations Prohibited.

Sec. 92. It shall not be lawful for any bank to create or put in circulation, any note, bill, check, ticket or paper purporting to be a bank note of any denomination between five and ten, ten and twenty, or twenty and fifty dollars.—Act of 16th of April, 1850, Sec. 31, P. L. 477.

Stockholders Individually Liable for Notes in Circulation in Proportion to the Amount of Stock Held.—How Such Liability to Be Enforced.

Sec. 93. The stockholders of every such bank, in addition to the corporate liability, shall be jointly liable to the creditors of said bank, being note-holders, in their individual capacities, for the amount of all notes issued; and the manner of enforcing such liability shall be as follows: In case the said bank shall violate the provisions of this act, so as to forfeit its charter, or becomes insolvent and in failing circumstances by reason of the mismanagement of its affairs, and is compelled to make an assignment under the provisions of this act, the assignees so appointed shall proceed to make a fair and equitable appraisement of the assets of the said bank of every description, at their cash value; and also to make a list of all the debts due by the said bank, and if it shall appear that the assets are insufficient to redeem the notes in circulation, the stockholders of the said bank shall be liable to make up such deficiency, in proportion to the respective amounts of stock held by each, at the time such assignment is made.—Act of 16th of April, 1850, Sec. 32, P. L. 477.

Assignees to Issue Sci. Fa. Against Stockholders.—Writ Not to Abate for Non-joinder or Mis-joinder.

Sec. 94. It shall be the duty of the assignees aforesaid to cause a scire facias, in the name of the Commonwealth of Pennsylvania, to be issued by the prothonotary of the court of common pleas, or district court of the county in which the bank is located, against all the stockholders of the said bank, reciting the amount of such deficiency, and requiring them to appear at the next court of common pleas or district court, in said county, and show cause why execution should not be issued against them for such amount; and such scire facias shall also set forth the proportions due from each of the said stockholders; and it shall be the duty of the sheriff of said county to serve the said writ upon all stockholders named in said writ residing within his bailiwick; and it shall be lawful for the court of common pleas, or a judge in vacation, to make such order

---

*The thirtieth section of the act of 1850 extended to all incorporated banking, saving fund, trust and insurance companies but they are not authorized to create any bank note.—See act of 6th of November, 1856.

in reference to giving notices to stockholders, non-residents of the county, and named in said writ, as the case may require: Provided, That the writ of scire facias shall not abate by reason of the non-joinder or mis-joinder of any stockholder, but any stockholder not named in the said writ of scire facias may, on motion to the court issuing the same, and upon due notice, as the said court shall direct, be made defendant in said proceedings, in the same manner as if originally named in such process and duly served therewith; and in case it shall appear that one or more persons in said writ named are not liable, under the provisions of this act it shall not vitiate the proceedings against the others.—Act of 16th of April, 1850, Sec. 33, P. L. 477.

Judgment and Execution Thereon.

Sec. 95. On the return day of said writ of scire facias, it shall be the duty of the said court to render judgment against the stockholders named in said writ for the several amounts for which they are respectively liable, if no sufficient cause shall be shown to the contrary, and to award writs of execution as in other cases; but if any suit be disputed it shall be lawful for the court to direct an issue to try the same.—Act of 16th of April, 1850, Sec. 34, P. L. 477.

Proceedings in Case of Insolvent Stockholder.

Sec. 96. If the amount assessed on the shares of any stockholder under the provisions of this act shall not be collected from such stockholder by reason of his insolvency, or his absence from the State, the sum remaining due on such assessment shall be recoverable against the person from whom the delinquent stockholder, at any time within one year previous to the assignment of the said bank, shall have received a transfer of the shares, or any portion of the shares then held by him; and any person having made such transfer, being made a party by an alias writ of scire facias, shall be liable in the same manner and for the same proportion that he would have been liable had he continued to hold the shares so transferred: Provided, That any person having made an assignment or transfer of his or her stock in the said bank, may discharge himself or herself from liability under this section, by showing that the transactions which caused the insolvency of said bank were made after such assignment or transfer, or such part thereof as he or she may show occurrred after such transfer or assignment.— Act of 16th of April, 1850, Sec. 35, P. L. 477.

Persons Holding Stock in the Names of Others Liable.

Sec. 97. Every individual who may own stock in his or her own name, or in the name of any other person or persons, at the time of such assignments, shall be deemed liable for his or her proportions, under the provisions of this act; but it shall be lawful for any stockholder of the said bank, either before or after process shall have been issued, to pay his or her proportionable share of liability to the assignees, and receive a full discharge from them; and the process shall be proceeded in only against the other stockholders who are liable.—Act of 16th of April, 1850, Sec. 36, P. L. 477.

The Term Stockholder Construed.

Sec. 98. The term stockholder, as used in the preceding sections of this act, shall extend to every person holding stock in his own name, and also to every equitable owner of stock appearing on the books of the said bank at the time of its insolvency in the name of another person, and to every person who shall have advanced the instalment or purchase money of any shares of stock standing in the name of any of his children under the age of twenty-one years; but no trustee appointed by a last will and testament, or by a court of competent authority, and no legal or equitable owner of stock, under the age of twenty-one years, shall be individually liable on account of the shares so held.—Act of 16th of April, 1850, Sec. 37, P. L. 477.

Powers of Courts to Compel Settlements by Assignees and Distribution to Creditors.

Sec. 99. The several provisions of the act of June fourteenth, one thousand eight hundred and thirty-six, entitled "An act relating to assignees for the benefit of creditors and other trustees," shall be held to apply to all assignments made by the said bank, except as hereinbefore provided; and the courts shall exercise all the powers therein given, in addition to the authority conferred by this act, to compel a settlement of the accounts of the assignees, and to do any other act necessary and proper to accomplish the purposes of the trust, and to compel the distribution of the moneys and assets in the hands or power of the said assignees amongst the creditors entitled, according to the just proportion due to each.— Act of 16th of April, 1850, Sec. 38, P. L. 477.

Distribution to Creditors Regulated.

Sec. 100. Said assignees shall pay out of the assets and property of the said bank, in case of an assignment, the debts and liabilities in the following order:

I. Noteholders.

II. Depositors.

III. All other creditors, except stockholders, who shall be last paid.—Act of 16th of April, 1850, Sec. 39, P. L. 477.*

Directors' Liability in Certain Cases of Insolvency.

Sec. 101. If the insolvency of the said bank be occasioned by the fraudulent conduct of the directors of the said bank, the directors by whose acts or omissions the insolvency was in whole or in part occasioned, and whether then in office or not, shall each be liable to the stockholders and creditors of the said bank for his proportional share of the losses, the proportion to be ascertained by dividing the whole loss amongst the whole number of directors liable for its re-imbursement.—Act of 16th of April, 1850, Sec. 40, P. L. 477.

---

*The thirty-ninth section of this act does not apply to savings institutions.—93 Pa., 408. Nor to the case where deposit depends upon special agreement.—1 Chester Co., 431.

Section does apply to an exchange bank where there is a running account with another bank.—6 W. N. C., 109. But not if there are periodical settlements.—6 W. N. C. 394.

When Insolvency to be Deemed Fraudulent.

Sec. 102. The insolvency of every bank hereafter incorporated shall be deemed fraudulent, unless its affairs shall appear, upon investigation, to have been fairly and legally administered, and with the same care and diligence that agents, receiving a compensation for their services, are bound by law to observe.—Act of 16th of April, 1850, Sec. 41, P. L. 477.

Term Insolvency Construed.—In case of Assignment, a Statement of Affairs to be filed in Court.—What Statement to Contain.

Sec. 103. The term insolvency used in this act shall be construed to apply to the said bank when it is compelled to make an assignment according to the provisions of this act; and it shall be thereupon the duty of the directors of the said bank, for the time being, within ten days after such assignment, to file in the office of the prothonotary of the court of common pleas or district court of the proper county, verified by oath or affirmation, a full statement of its affairs, containing:

I. An account of the capital stock of the bank, the amount paid in, and the amount of stock held by such corporation.

II. Quantity, description and value of the real estate of the said bank.

III. The shares of stock held by the bank, whether absolutely or as collateral security, with their number and value.

IV. The debts owing to said bank, and the amount of said debts that are collectible.

V. The amount of debts owing by said bank, with the amount of notes or bills in circulation, amount of deposits and all other liabilities, together with an account of its loans and discounts, and of specie on hand.

VI. A particular account of the losses of the corporation, and the cause of its insolvency.

VII. An accurate list of the names and residences, and the amount of stock held by each stockholder in said bank, at the time of and for one year prior to the time of the assignment.—Act of 16th of April, 1850, Sec. 42, P. L. 477.

Court to Appoint Auditors.—Duties of Auditors.

Sec. 104. If the court shall be in session when the statement is filed, the same shall be immediately presented to the court by the said directors for examination, and if the court shall not be in session at such time, then the statement shall be presented upon the first day of the session of the court thereafter; and it shall thereupon be the duty of the court to appoint three competent auditors, who shall be sworn or affirmed to make a strict investigation of the affairs of such bank, and of the accuracy and fairness of the statement thus presented to the court, and to perform their duties with fidelity.—Act of 16th of April, 1850, Sec. 43, P. L. 477.

Powers of Auditors.

Sec. 105. The auditors thus appointed shall have power to compel the production of the books and papers, and to subpoena and examine the directors and officers of such bank, and generally to have and exercise all the authority now conferred on auditors by existing laws and after having performed their duties, they shall report to the court the result of their investigation, and in case they report that the insolvency was fraudulent, it shall be their duty also, to ascertain and report the amount due from the several directors, according to the liabilities imposed by this act.—Act of 16th of April, 1850, Sec. 44, P. L. 477.

Court to Investigate Matters Reported by Auditors.

Sec. 106. Said court shall thereupon proceed to the investigation of the matters contained in said report, and shall determine whether the insolvency of such bank was fraudulent or otherwise, or, if they deem it necessary for the purpose of justice, they may direct an issue at the request of any person interested, to try the fact of fraudulent insolvency; and if the judgment of the court upon the report of the auditors, or upon the verdict rendered upon such issue, shall be that the insolvency of such bank was fraudulent, then and in such case, the said court shall proceed to decree against the directors the amount due from each according to their several liabilities; and the said court of common pleas or district court, for the purpose of carrying into effect the provisions of this act, shall have the same powers and authorities to obtain the appearance of persons, and to compel obedience to their orders and decrees and enforce execution thereof, as are by law vested in the said courts in cases of trust.—Act of 16th of April, 1850, Sec. 45, P. L. 477.

Taxes for Use of Commonwealth.

Sec. 107. In addition to the taxes imposed on the dividends of banks incorporated, subject to the provisions of this act, such banks shall pay a tax of four and one-half mills per annum, for the use of the Commonwealth on every dollar of the capital stock paid in; such tax shall be retained and deducted by the officers having charge of the bank from the dividends made or declared, and it shall be paid into the treasury of the Commonwealth, at the same time and in the same manner provided by existing laws in relation to taxes on bank dividends: Provided, That the capital stock of such banks shall not be subject to taxation for any other purpose than State purposes, or to any other tax of the capital stock under existing laws.—Act of 16th of April, 1850, Sec. 46, P. L. 477.

Notes to be Kept at Par in the Cities of Philadelphia and Pittsburg.

Sec. 108. That it shall be obligatory on the several banks of this Commonwealth to keep their notes respectively at par in the cities of Philadelphia and Pittsburg, to wit: Those located east of the Allegheny mountains, shall keep their notes at par in the city of Philadelphia and those located west of the Allegheny mountains, shall keep their notes at par in the city of Pittsburg; any bank failing to comply with the provisions of this section shall for such length of time as its notes may be under par as aforesaid, forfeit and pay to the State Treasurer for the use of the Commonwealth of Pennsylvania, at the rate of two mills per annum on every dollar of the average amount of the circulation of such bank for the preceding year; such forfeiture to be paid on or before the third day of November in each year; it shall be the duty of the cashiers of the several banks to state in their annual exhibits made to the Auditor General (Commissioner of Banking), the length of time that their notes have been under par as aforesaid: Provided, That no forfeiture or penalty shall be incurred under the provisions of this section until after the first day of August next.—Act of 16th of April, 1850, Sec. 47, P. L. 477.

Notes of Less Denominations Than Five Dollars Not to be Issued by Foreign Banks.

Sec. 109. From and after the twenty-first day of August, one thousand eight hundred and fifty, it shall not be lawful for any person or persons, corporation or body corporate, directly or indirectly, to issue, pay out, pass, exchange, put in circulation, transfer, or cause to be issued, paid out, passed exchanged circulated or transferred, any bank note, bill, certificate or any acknowledgment of indebtedness whatsoever, purporting to be a bank note, or of the nature, character or appearance of a bank note, or calculated for circulation as a bank note, issued, or purporting to be issued by any bank or incorporated company, or association of persons, not located in Pennsylvania of a less denomination than five dollars; every violation of the provisions of this section by any corporation or body corporate, shall subject such corporation or body corporate to the payment of five hundred dollars; and any violation of the provisions of this section by any public officer holding any office or appointment of honor or profit under the Constitution and laws of this State, shall subject such officer to the payment of one hundred dollars; and any violation of this section by any other person, not being a public officer, shall subject such person to the payment of twenty-five dollars, one-half of which, in each case above mentioned, shall go to the informer, and the other half to the county in which the suit is brought, and may be sued for and recovered as debts of like amount are now by law recoverable in any action of debt, in the name of the Commonwealth of Pennsylvania, as well for the use of the proper county as for the person suing.—Act of 16th of April, 1850, Sec. 48, P. L. 477.

Additional Penalty.—Grand Juries May Present Persons for Violations of This Act.

Sec. 110. In addition to the civil penalties imposed for a violation of the provisions of the last preceding section, every person who shall violate the provisions of that section, shall be taken and deemed to have committed a misdemeanor, and shall, upon conviction thereof, in any criminal court in this Commonwealth, be fined in any sum not less than one dollar, and not more than one hundred dollars; and the several courts of quarter sessions shall, in their charges to the grand jury, call their attention to this subject; and it shall be the duty of the several grand juries to make presentment of any person within their respective counties, who may be guilty of a violation of the provisions of the last preceding section; and it shall be the duty of the several constables and other peace officers within this Commonwealth to make information against any person guilty of such violation, and they shall be sworn so to do: Provided, That it shall not be necessary, in any civil suit or criminal prosecution under this section, and the last preceding section, to produce in evidence the charter of any bank, or articles of association of any company not located in this State.—Act of 16th of April, 1850, Sec. 49, P. L. 477.

Establishment of Branch or Agency Prohibited.—Infraction of Prohibition to Work a Forfeiture of Charter.

Sec. 111. Each and every bank of this Commonwealth, or any other State, is hereby prohibited from establishing, maintaining, or continuing, directly or indirectly, in the name of one or more individuals, in any manner or by any device whatever, either for its own sole benefit and profit of its officers or any of them in whole or in part, any branch or agency for the transaction of banking business, or the issuing out of or circulation of its notes at any other place than that fixed and named in its charter for its location and the transaction of its business, without the express authority of an act of Assembly of this Commonwealth to do so; and any and every fraction of this prohibition by any bank in this Commonwealth, after the passage of this act, shall be deemed and held to be a forfeiture of the charter of any and every bank so offending or acting contrary to the provisions of this section; and the fact of any bank in this Commonwealth so offending shall be ascertained, verified and determined in the same mode and manner as is provided in the twenty-seventh section of this act, in any case of any bank refusing or failing to pay its liabilities in gold and silver coin and the like proceedings shall be had in such case thereafter as is provided by this act; and during the period of continuance of any such branch or agency by any bank in this Commonwealth, such bank so offending shall in each year of such continuance, be subject to and pay quadruple the amount of all taxes chargeable on and to be paid by the same in the whole current year.—Act of 16th of April, 1850, Sec. 50, P. L. 477.

Actual Business Paper of Directors Offered by Holders Thereof Exempted From Restrictions of Twenty-third Section.

Sec. 112. The provisions contained in the twenty-third section of this act shall not be held to embrace actual business paper, bona fide drawn or made by any director in the regular course of his private business, and offered for discount by the holder or holders thereof.— Act of 16th of April, 1850, Sec. 51, P. L. 477.

Cashiers to Certify Lists of Unclaimed Dividends or Deposits.

Sec. 113. It shall be the duty of the cashier of any such bank, on the first Monday in January in each year, to cause to be forwarded to the Auditor General a certified list of the names of any persons having unclaimed dividends or deposits in such bank, which shall have remained unclaimed for three years, or the amount of which has neither been increased nor diminished for the period of three years then next preceding.—Act of 16th of April, 1850, Sec. 52, P. L. 477.

Power to Alter, Revoke and Annul Charters Without Injustice to Corporators.

Sec. 114. The Legislature reserves the power to alter, revoke or annul the charters of all such banks whenever, in their opinion, it may be necessary for the public welfare; in such manner, however, that no injustice be done to the corporations.—Act of 16th of April, 1850, Sec. 53, P. L. 477.

CHAPTER 4.

LEGISLATION RELATING TO BANKS FROM THE BANKING
LAW OF 1850 TO THE BANKING ACT OF 1876.

Cashiers and Solicitors of Banks in Philadelphia to be Elected by
the Directors Annually.—Director Not to be Solicitor.—Directors of Philadelphia Banks Must Have Been Stockholders Three
Months Before Election.

Sec. 115. The cashiers and solicitors in the several banks in the
county of Philadelphia shall be elected annually by the directors
of said banks at the same time and in the same manner that the
presidents thereof are now elected; and no person shall be eligible
as solicitor of any bank in the county of Philadelphia of which he
may, at the time, be a director, nor shall any person be eligible as
director of any bank in the county of Philadelphia who shall not
have been a stockholder thereof at least three calendar months
before the time of his election.—Act of 29th of March, 1851, Sec. 15,
P. L. 293.

Supplement to Act of 16th of April, 1850.—Repeal of 46th Section
of Said Act and 33rd Section of Act of 29th of April, 1844
Declared in Force as to Banks Under Act of 1850.—Capital
Stock of Such Banks Only Subject to Taxation for State
Purposes.

Sec. 116. The forty-sixth section of the act entitled "An act regulating banks," approved the sixteenth day of April, eighteen hundred and fifty, be, and the same is hereby repealed, and that the
thirty-third section of the act, entitled "An act to reduce the State
debt, and to incorporate the Pennsylvania Canal and Railroad Company," approved the twenty-ninth day of April, eighteen hundred
and forty-four, be, and the same is hereby declared to be in full
force and effect and as applicable to the several banks chartered or
re-chartered, or that may hereafter be chartered or re-chartered
under the provisions of the said act of eighteen hundred and fifty,
as though the said forty-sixth section of the same had never been
passed: Provided, That the capital stock of such banks shall not
be subject to taxation for any other than State purposes.—Act of
27th of April, 1852, Sec. 1, P. L. 443.

Cashiers of Banks Incorporated Previous to Act of 1850 to Have
Same Privileges as Those Incorporated Under Act of 1850.

Sec 117. That the cashiers of banks incorporated previous to the
passage of the act to which this is a supplement, shall have the

same privileges as are enjoyed by the cashiers of banks incorporated in accordance with the provisions of this act.—Act of 27th of April, 1852, Sec. 2, P. L. 443.

Liabilities of Any Bank in Pennsylvania.—How Estimated.

Sec. 118. The total liabilities of any bank in this Commonwealth. exclusive of the capital stock, shall not at any time exceed three times the amount of the capital stock paid in: Provided, That when the deposits shall exceed one-fourth of the capital stock, such excess shall not be counted as a liability in the meaning of the above prohibition, nor shall the debts due and to become due to any such bank, ever amount (to) more than four times the capital stock paid in, in loans to the Commonwealth excepted.—Act of 22nd of April, 1854, Sec. 1, P. L. 467.

Extension of Seventeenth and Eighteenth Sections of Act of 1850 to Banks Prior to 1850.

Sec. 119. The seventeenth and eighteenth sections of act of sixteenth of April, 1850, extended to banks prior to 1850 who accept the same.—Act of 22nd of April, 1854, Sec. 2, P. L. 467.

Supplement to Act of 16th of April, 1850.—Inheritance of Property Invested in Business Operations Not to Disqualify Cashiers.

Sec. 120. So much of the fifth article of the tenth section of the act to which this is a supplement, as prohibits cashiers from engaging in any other profession, occupation or calling, directly or indirectly, shall not be so construed as to require the cashier of any bank to relinquish the office in consequence of coming into possession of property, by gift or inheritance, invested in mercantile, mechanical or manufacturing operations.—Act of 18th of April, 1855, Sec. 1, P. L. 258.

Justices of the Peace Not Disqualified.

Sec. 121. So much of any law as prohibits judicial officers from being bank directors shall not be held to apply to justices of the peace.—Act of 18th of April, 1855, Sec. 2, P. L. 258.

Supplement to Act of 16th of April, 1850.—Amount of Cashier's Bond.

Sec. 122. The fifth article of the tenth section of the act to which this is a supplement is hereby amended so as to authorize the stockholders of any bank to determine, at any general or special meeting regularly convened for the purpose, the amount of the bond required from the cashier: Provided, That in all cases where the capital of any bank shall be five hundred thousand dollars or upwards, the amount of said bond shall not be less than fifty thousand dollars, and in no case shall the bond of any cashier be for a sum less than twenty thousand dollars.—Act of 7th of May, 1855, Sec. 1, P. L. 508.

Vice President and Assistant Cashier May be Elected by Directors.
—Ten Days' Notice of Election to be Given.

Sec. 123. It shall be lawful for the board of directors of any bank to elect a vice president and an assistant cashier, and to empower said vice president and assistant cashier to sign all checks, notes and other documents which require the signature of the president and cashier, or either, and to perform such other duties as the said board of directors may impose upon them: Provided, That the board of directors of any bank which shall elect the offcers hereby authorized, shall give ten days' notice thereof in at least one newspaper published in the city or county in which the bank is located.—Act of 7th of May, 1855, Sec. 2, P. L. 508.

Fifth Article of Tenth Section of Act of 16th of April, 1850 and Supplements Thereto Extended to all Banks of the Commonwealth.

Sec. 124. The provisions of article fifth, section tenth, of an act regulating banks, approved the sixteenth day of April, one thousand eight hundred and fifty, and the supplement thereto, approved the seventh day of May, one thousand eight hundred and fifty-five, be and the same are hereby extended to all the banks of this Commonwealth.—Act of 18th of April, 1856, Sec. 1, P. L. 403.

Thirtieth Section of Act of 16th of April, 1850 Extended to All Banks, Saving Fund, Trust and Insurance Companies.

Sec. 125. The thirtieth section of the act approved the sixteenth of April, one thousand eight hundred and fifty, entitled "An act regulating banks," be and the same is hereby extended to all incorporated banking, saving fund, trust and insurance companies, which said companies shall be subject to the provisions of the said section: Provided, That nothing herein contained shall authorize any savings bank, trust or other company, as aforesaid, to create any bank note or certificate in the similitude of a bank note: Provided further, That this act shall not go into effect until the first day of July next. —Act of 6th of November, 1856, Sec. 1, P. L. 1857, Page 797.

Bank, Saving Fund, Trust of Insurance Companies not to Purchase Bank Notes Less Than Par.—Penalty.

Sec. 126. No bank, savings fund, insurance or trust company shall, directly or indirectly, purchase, or be concerned in the purchase of the notes of any of the incorporated banks of this State, at less than their par value; and any and every of the officers of said institutions violating the provisions of this section, shall be deemed guilty of a misdemeanor, punishable upon conviction by a fine of not less than five hundred dollars nor more than one thousand dollars; one-half to be paid to the informer, and the other half to the use of the Commonwealth.—Act of 13th of October, 1857, Sec. 10, P. L. of 1858, Page 614.

Salary of Vice President.

Sec. 127. It shall be lawful for the duly elected vice presidents of any bank within this Commonwealth, to receive such salary as may be fixed upon by the board of directors of said bank.—Act of 13th of April, 1859, Sec. 1, P. L. 613.

May Receive Notes of Banks of Other States.

Sec. 128. Article thirteen of the tenth section of the act, entitled "An act regulating banks," approved April sixteenth, one thousand eight hundred and fifty, shall not be so construed as to prohibit the banks of this Commonwealth from receiving the notes of the banks of other states, at such rates of discount as may enable them, without loss, to send the same out of the State for conversion or redemption, and for such purpose only.—Act of 17th of April, 1861, Sec. 1, P. L. 341.

Stockholders May Fix the Number of Directors at Annual Meeting at not Less Than Five Nor More Than Thirteen.

Sec. 129. The stockholders of said banks, at their annual meeting, as required by law, may fix the number of directors to be elected, to conduct the affairs of said bank, at such number as they may then determine; said number shall not be less than five nor more than thirteen; and when the number of said directors shall be seven; or any less number, a majority then shall be necessary to constitute a quorum for business.—Act of 17th of April, 1861, Sec. 1, P. L. 341.

Loans to Directors Limited.

Sec. 130. No director of any bank shall be a borrower in said bank, at any one time, for a greater amount than five percentum on the capital stock paid in; and the gross amount loaned to all the directors and other officers of said bank, and to the houses or firms in which they may be interested, directly or indirectly, shall not exceed, at any one time, the sum of six per centum on the capital stock paid in.—Act of 17th of April, 1861, Sec. 1, P. L. 341.

Number of Votes to Which Shareholders Shall be Entitled.

Sec. 131. At all meetings of stockholders of said banks of this Commonwealth, and in conducting the elections for directors thereof, the stockholders shall be entitled to vote in proportion to the number of shares held by them respectively, as follows, that is to say: For every share of stock, not exceeding ten shares, the holder shall be entitled to one vote; for every two shares of stock, above ten, and not exceeding twenty additional shares, the holder shall be entitled to one vote; and for every five shares of stock above thirty, and not exceeding one hundred the holder shall be entitled to one vote; and for every ten shares above one hundred, one vote.—Act of 17th of April, 1861, Sec. 2, P. L. 342.

May Hold Property Taken for Debts Due.

Sec. 132. The banks of this Commonwealth may hold, for more than five years, property taken or received by assignment, execution or otherwise, in payment of debts to said banks.—Act of 17th of April, 1861, Sec. 2, P. L. 342.

Small Notes to the Extent of Twenty Per Cent. of Capital Paid in May be Issued.

Sec. 133. It shall be lawful for the incorporated banks of issue, or that may hereafter be incorporated under the provisions of any law of this Commonwealth, to issue and put in circulation notes of the denomination of one, two and three dollars, to an amount not exceeding twenty per cent. of the capital stock paid in: Provided, That the specie-paying banks may pay out, at the option of the receiver, the notes of such banks of this State as they may receive, in the course of their business, at par.—Act of 17th of April, 1861, Sec. 3, P. L. 342.

Embezzlement, Fraudulent Issue of Notes, Etc., by Officers.—False Entries with Intent to Deceive.—Penalty.

Section 134. Every president, director, cashier, teller, clerk or agent of any bank who shall embezzle, abstract or wilfully misapply any of the moneys, funds or credits of such bank, or shall fraudulently and without authority from the directors, issue or put in circulation any of the notes of such bank, or shall without such authority fraudulently issue or put forth any certificate of deposit, draw any order or bill of exchange, make any acceptance, sign any note, bond, draft, bill of exchange, mortgage or other instrument of writing, or shall make any false entry on any book, report or statement of the bank, with an intent in either case to injure or defraud such bank or to injure or defraud any other company, body corporate or politic, or any individual person, or to deceive any officer or agent appointed to inspect the affairs of any bank, shall be deemed guilty of a misdemeanor, and upon conviction thereof, shall be confined in the penitentiary at hard labor not less than one nor more than ten years.—Act of 1st of May, 1861, Sec. 36, P. L. 503.

Acts Punishing the Circulating of Certain Notes Suspended in Counties Herein Named.

Sec. 135. The fines and penalties imposed by the second section of the act of March twenty-second, one thousand eight hundred and seventeen, the first and second sections of the act of April twelve, one thousand eight hundred and twenty-eight, and all other laws of the Commonwealth, imposing or inflicting, fines and penalties, for issuing or circulating, or causing to be issued or circulated, any note, bill, check, draft, order, ticket or paper, intending the same to be used as a circulating medium, be and the same are hereby suspended, in said counties of Tioga, Potter, McKean, Lycoming, Bedford and Warren, for all violations of said laws, prior to the passage of this act, and that no fines or penalties shall be inflicted, or imposed upon any corporation, person or persons within said counties, for the aforesaid violations of the law: Provided, however, That if any person, or persons, having issued any such note, bill, check, draft, order, ticket or paper, shall neglect, or refuse to pay the same, when presented in the manner stipulated in said note, check, bill, draft, order, ticket or paper, said person, or persons, shall not be entitled to claim the benefit of this act, but shall remain liable to all the penalties imposed by existing laws.—Act of 31st of July, 1863, Sec. 1, P. L. of 1864, 1100.

Proceedings Against Officers and Directors of Fraudulent Insolvent Banks.

Sec. 136. Whenever any bank now, or that may hereafter be incorporated under any law of this Commonwealth, shall be declared fraudulently insolvent, either by the report of auditors, or the verdict of a jury, upon an issue formed by direction of the court, then, and in that case, the assignees of said bank shall prepare, or cause to be prepared, a bill in equity, in which the said assignees shall be plaintiffs, and those who were officers and directors of said bank, at the time of its assignment as also those who heretofore had been officers and directors of said bank, and by whose acts of omission, or commission, the fraudulent insolvency. in whole, or in part, of said bank, was caused, shall be defendants; in which said bill the plaintiffs shall make the necessary and proper charges against the defendants, setting forth the fraudulent insolvency of said bank, that the same was caused by the acts of omission, or commission, of the defendants, or some of them, particularly specifying the fraudulent acts complained of, and by whom committed, the amount of the oustanding and unredeemed paper issues of said bank, including its certificates of deposit, and how much of each, and shall pray that the said defendants, or such of them, by whose acts of omission or commission, the fraudulent insolvency of said bank was caused, shall be adjudged and decreed to pay to the plaintiffs a sum of money, equal in amount to all the outstanding and unredeemed paper issues and certificates of deposit of said bank.—Act of 12th of April, 1867, Sec. 1, P. L. 71.

Proceedings by Bill in Equity.

Sec. 137. Said bill shall be heard by the court of common pleas (or district court) of the county in which said bank is, or was, located; service of a copy of the bill upon the defendants named therein, or any of them, in any city or county of this Commonwealth, shall be a sufficient service thereof, so as to require the party or parties, so served to appear and answer, demur, or plead thereto; and if no such service can be had upon any of said defendants, then the same may be served as to them, by publication of a copy of said bill in such newspaper, or newspapers, as the court may direct, for six weeks previous to the return day; and if default is made, or if upon the hearing the facts, as set out in the bill, are established, said court shall enter a decree, as prayed for in said bill, and award the proper process to carry the same into effect: Provided, That upon final decree made, either party may remove the proceedings to the Supreme Court, as in other cases.—Act of 12th of April, 1867, Sec. 2, P. L. 71.

Tax on Stock of National Banks.

Sec. 138. All the shares or stock held by any person, in any bank, incorporated by or in pursuance of any law of the government of the United States, are hereby declared subject to taxation, in the hands of the holders of such shares, at the same rate as the shares of stock, of banks incorporated by or under any law of the Commonwealth of Pennsylvania are now taxable in the hands of the individual holders of such shares, and at no other or greater rate; that is to say, a tax of three mills upon every dollar of the value of such shares or stock shall annually be assessed, and collected in the manner herein provided.—Act of April 12th, 1867, Sec. 1, P. L. 74.

Appointment of Assessors and Their Duties.—How Tax to be Collected.—Compensation of Assessors.

Sec. 139. The Auditor General and State Treasurer are hereby authorized and directed, immediately upon the passage of this act, to appoint an adequate number of suitable persons, citizens of this Commonwealth, to ascertain the residence and assess the value of the shares of stock aforesaid, said assessors so appointed, shall proceed as soon as possible after their appointment, and after having taken and subscribed an oath, in due form of law, to execute the duties imposed upon them, with fidelity and impartiality, to visit all the banks incorporated by the United States, and located within the county or district for which the assessor is appointed, and obtain from the officers of said banks a full and complete list of the shareholders of each bank, with their residence, and the number and par value of shares of stock held by each person respectively; whereupon the assessor shall proceed to assess all of the stockholders, resident within the county or district for which he is appointed, and the actual value of the shares, or stock, held by each, and make a complete list of the same; which list shall be returned to the commissioners of the city or county in which said bank is located; and the amount of taxes due the Commonwealth upon such assessment shall be collected in the manner in which taxes upon other personal property are now collectible; each assessor, appointed as aforesaid, shall receive a commission of seven (7) per centum upon every dollar of tax due the Commonwealth, upon the assessment made by him; which commission shall be adjusted and allowed by the Auditor General and paid by the State Treasurer, upon the warrant of the Auditor General.—Act of 12th of April, 1867, Sec. 2, P. L. 74.

Appointment of Assessors to be Made Annually.

Sec. 140. After performing the duties hereinbefore specified, the powers and duties of the assessors, aforesaid, shall cease and determine; and the Auditor General and State Treasurer shall annually, in the month of January, appoint said assessors, and assign their respective districts, or counties; and the assessors shall make return to the commissioners aforesaid, within sixty days after their appointment, and be removable at the pleasure of the Auditor General and State Treasurer.—Act of 12th of April, 1867, Sec. 4, P. L. 74.

Appraisement of Stock of National Banks.

Sec. 141. No stock or share of any National bank shall be appraised higher than the current value of said stock in the market where such bank is located; and any stockholder shall have the right of appeal to the Auditor General, who shall have the power to adjust such assessment, by inquiring into the value of such stock, and either abate or increase the value of the same as may be just and proper.—Act of 2nd of April, 1868, Sec. 1, P. L. 55.

Notice of Valuation.—Entering of Appeals.

Sec. 142. It shall be the duty of the assessors, after they shall have completed their assessment of bank shares to make return thereof to the Auditor General, and give public notice of such valuation or assessment, by posting one copy of said notice in the banking room and one copy in the commissioners' office of the said county; and if any shareholder shall be dissatisfied with such valuation, he shall enter his appeal therefrom within thirty days from the date of putting up such notice.—Act of 2nd of April, 1868, Sec. 2, P. L. 55.

Duties of Assessors. -

Sec. 143. The assessors appointed in accordance with the provisions of the second section of the act to which this is a supplement, shall visit and obtain from the banks incorporated by the United States the lists of stockholders, and the number and par value of shares held by each, as directed in said section, and shall proceed to assess all of the shares of said stock, in said banks, at their actual value, and make a complete list of the same, with the names of the several stockholders and the number and value of shares of stock held by each, stating whether the stockholder be resident or nonresident of the county in which the bank is located; which list shall be returned to the commissioners of the city or county in which the bank is located, and a certificate thereof transmitted to the Auditor General.—Act of 2nd of April, 1868, Sec. 3, P. L. 55.

Taxes Assessed to be a Lien upon the Stock.

Sec. 144. The taxes assessed under this act shall be a lien upon the shares of stock of said bank from the date of levy, and in case of non-payment, the shares of stock of defaulting stockholders, with the accrued dividends, shall be subject to attachment or levy and sale for non-payment of tax thereon, in like manner as other personal property.—Act of 2nd of April, 1868, Sec. 4, P. L. 55.

Tax on Bank Stock.

Sec. 145. It shall be the duty of the cashier of every bank and savings institution, incorporated under the laws of this State, to collect annually from every shareholder of said bank or savings institution a tax of one per centum upon the par value of the shares held by said shareholder, and to pay the same into the State Treasury on or before the first day of July, in every year; and the said shares shall be exempt from all other taxation under the laws of this Commonwealth.—Act of 1st of May, 1868, Sec. 10, P. L. 108.

Taxation of Bank Stock.

Sec. 146. The provisions of an act, entitled "An act to increase the revenue of the Commonwealth by taxation of the shares of stock of the National banks," approved April twelve one thousand eight hundred and sixty-seven, and of a supplement to said act, approved April two, one thousand eight hundred and sixty-eight, are hereby extended from and after January one, one thousand eight hundred and seventy, to the several banks and savings institutions incorporated under the laws of this Commonwealth, and it shall be the duty of the several assessors appointed in one thousand eight hundred and seventy, in accordance with the provisions of said act of April twelve, one thousand eight hundred and sixty-seven, to assess the actual value of the shares of State banks and savings institutions located within their respective districts, and include the same in the returns made to the commissioners of the proper city or county, and to the Auditor General.—Act of 22nd of December, 1869, Sec. 1. (P. L. of 1870, 1373).

Rate of Tax on Stock of Banks and Savings Institutions.

Sec. 147. All shares of National banks, located within this State, and of banks and savings institutions incorporated by this State, shall be taxable for State purposes at the rate of three mills per annum upon the assessed value thereof, and for county, school, municipal and local purposes, at the same rate as now is or may hereafter be assessed and imposed upon other moneyed capital in the hands of individual citizens of this State.—Act of 31st of March, 1870, Sec. 3, P. L. 42.

Such Stock to be Exempt from Tax in Certain Cases.

Sec. 148. In case any bank or savings institution aforesaid shall elect to collect annually, from the shareholders thereof, a tax of one per centum upon the par value of all the shares of said bank or savings institution, and pay the same into the State Treasury, on or before the twentieth day of January in every year, the said shares, capital and profits shall be exempt from all other taxation under the laws of this Commonwealth; and the law regulating the compensation of county treasurers for receiving moneys for the use of the Commonwealth, and paying over the same, is hereby extended to the cashiers of said banks and savings institutions.—Act of 31st of March, 1870, Sec. 4, P. L. 42.

Extent of Liability of stockholders.

Sec. 149. From and after the passage of this act all stockholders in banks, banking companies, saving funds institutions, trust companies, and all other incorporated companies doing the business of banks or loaning and discounting moneys as such in this Commonwealth, shall be personally liable for all debts and deposits in their individual capacity to double the amount of the capital stock held and owned by each: Provided, That before such liability shall accrue, in case of banks already chartered, the stockholders shall at a regular or adjourned meeting, declare by resolution or otherwise their intention to accept the provisions of this act, and notice of their action shall, within thirty days thereafter, be filed in the office of the Auditor General and Secretary of the Commonwealth, setting forth at length their proceeding, declaring their intention to be bound by its provisions in the same manner and as fully as if the same had been a part of the original act by which they were incorporated.—Act of 11th of May, 1874, Sec. 1, P. L. 135.

Married Women and Minors May Have Separate Deposits Without Interference of Husband or Guardian.

Sec. 150. The board of trustees of any bank in this Commonwealth shall have full power, at their discretion to pay on application the check, proper receipt, or order of any minor or married woman, such money, or any part thereof as he or she may have deposited to his or her credit, or any interest or dividend accruing thereon, without the assent or approbation of the parent or guardian of such minor or the husband of such married woman, as the case may be; and it shall not be lawful for the parent or guardian of such minor, or the husband or creditors of the husband of such married woman to attach, or in any manner interfere with any deposit, interest or dividend thereon to such minor or married woman.—Act of 15th of May, 1874, Sec. 1, P. L. 193.

Unlawfully Obtaining Key or Combination to Bank Vault or Safe, etc.—Penalty.

Sec. 151. If any person shall by fraud, force, threats or menaces, or by seizing, gagging or tying compel or attempt to compel another to surrender the key or other appliance, or to divulge the combination, secret or other means used to open any bank, vault, safe or other depository of money, securities, or property; or if any person shall administer or attempt to administer to another, any stupefying or overpowering drug, matter or thing for the purpose of enabling such offender to obtain such key or other appliance, with intent, in any of the cases aforesaid, to steal such money, securities or property, or any portion thereof, every such offender shall be guilty of a felony, and being convicted shall be sentenced to pay a fine not exceeding ten thousand dollars and to undergo imprisonment at hard labor not exceeding twenty years.—Act of 8th of May, 1876, Sec. 1, P. L. 139.

CHAPTER 5.

BANKING ACT OF 1876—THE TITLE OF THE ACT OF 1876.
"AN ACT FOR THE INCORPORATION AND REGULATION
OF BANKS OF DISCOUNT AND DEPOSIT."

May be Incorporated.—Articles of Association and Contents.—Copy
to be Forwarded Attorney General.—He to Approve and Transmit Same to Auditor General.

Sec. 152. Corporations for carrying on the business of banking may
be formed under the provisions of this act by any number of persons,
not less than three, who shall enter into articles of association, which
shall specify the object for which the association is formed, and may
contain any provisions, not inconsistent with this act, which the association may desire to adopt for the regulation and conduct of its business and affairs; which articles shall be signed by the persons forming such association, and a copy of them shall be forwarded to the
Attorney General for his inspection and approval and if approved
by him he shall endorse his approval thereon, and transmit the same
to the Auditor General to be filed in his office.—Act of 13th of May,
1876, Sec. 1, P. L. 161.

Certificate to be Made by Corporators.—Contents thereof.—To be
Acknowledged, Filed and Recorded.—Certified Copies to be Evidence.

Sec. 153. The persons forming such associations shall, under their
hands, make a certificate, which shall specify:
First. Name (subject to the approval of the Auditor General).
Second. Location or place of business, particularly designating the
county, city, borough or village.
Third. Amount of capital stock and number of shares in which
divided.
Fourth. The names and places of residence of shareholders, and
number of shares held by each.
Fifth. A statement that such certificate is made to enable the persons named to form a corporation for banking purposes under this
act.
This certificate shall be acknowledged before a judge or notary public, which certificate, with acknowledgment certified and authenticated by the seal of such court or notary public, shall be transmitted,
after approval, by the Attorney General. of the articles of association as hereinbefore directed to the Auditor General to be filed, recorded and preserved in his office; copies of such certificate duly certificate by the Auditor General and authenticated by the seal
of office, shall be conclusive evidence in all courts of the Com-

monwealth of the existence of such corporation, and of every other matter or thing which could be proved by the production of the original certificate.—Act of 13th of May, 1876, Sec. 2, P. L. 161.

Auditor General to Certify Copy of Articles of Association to Governor.—Governor to Issue Letters Patent upon Receipt of Certificate from Auditor General.

Sec. 154. The Auditor General upon the receipt of the articles of association with the approval thereon of the Attorney General as aforesaid, and the certificate hereinbefore provided, shall certify a copy of such certificate to the Governor, who shall, upon receiving the same, cause letters patent, under the great seal of the Commonwealth, to be issued to said banking corporation.—Act of 13th of May, 1876, Sec. 3, P. L. 161.

Notice of Application for a Charter, for a Renewal of Charter or Increase of Capital to be Advertised Giving Name, Style, Location, Objects, Amount of Capital and Amount of Increase.

Sec. 155. Before application shall be made under the provisions of this act for the creation of any corporate body with banking or discounting privileges, or for the renewal of the charter or increase of capital thereof, the person forming the same shall cause a notice of such intended application to be advertised in two newspapers printed in the county in which such corporate body is intended to be located, at least once a week, for three months before such application shall be made; and the notice of such application shall specify the name and style, the location, the specific object for which created, the amount of capital, and in the case of the renewal or extension of any such corporate body, such notice shall also specify the amount of increase of capital stock, if any such increase be intended. If there be only one paper printed in the county in which such corporate body is intended to be located, the publication of such notice in one paper shall be deemed sufficient, but if there be no paper printed in such county, then the notice shall be given in at least one paper published in one of the nearest adjoining counties: Provided, That all persons having advertised in the year one thousand eight hundred and seventy-five, at least six months previous to the meeting of the present Legislature, their intention to apply for bank charters under the then existing laws, shall be deemed to have complied with the provisions of this section relative to giving public notice by advertising.—Act of 13th of May, 1876, Sec. 4, P. L. 161.

Amount of Capital, Value of Shares and how Transfered.—Liabilities of Shareholders.

Sec. 156. No corporation shall be organized under this act with a capital stock of less than fifty thousand dollars, divided into shares of not less than fifty dollars each, which shall be deemed personal property and transferable on the books of the corporation in such manner as may be prescribed by the by-laws and articles of association thereof; and every person to whom stock shall be transferred as aforesaid, shall, in proportion to the shares received, succeed to all the rights and liabilities of the prior holders thereof, and no change shall be made in the articles of association by which the rights, remedies or securities of the existing creditors of the corporation shall be impaired. The shareholders of any corporation formed under this act, shall be individually responsible, equally and ratably, but not one for the other, for all contracts, debts and engagements of such corporation to the amount of their stock therein at the par value thereof in addition to the par value of such shares.—Act of 13th of May, 1876, Sec. 5, P. L. 161.

Powers of Corporation so Formed.

Sec. 157. Every association formed under the provisions of this act, shall from the date of the letters patent issued thereto, be a body corporate, but shall transact no business, except such as may be incidental to the purpose of its organization, and shall have power to adopt a corporate seal, have succession by the name designated in its articles of association for the term of twenty years from the date of the letters patent, unless sooner dissolved under the provisions of its articles of association or this act; by its corporate name it may make contracts, sue and be sued, complain, prosecute and defend in any court of law and equity, or before any magistrate, as fully at natural persons, and process against such corporation may be served upon its president or cashier, or by leaving a copy thereof with one of the officers thereof, during the usual hours of business; it shall elect or appoint directors, and by its board of directors, appoint a president, vice president, cashier and other officers, define their duties, require bonds of them, fixing the penalty thereof, dismiss any of said officers at pleasure and appoint others to fill their places, and exercise under this act all such power as shall be necessary to carry on the business of banking, by loaning money, discounting, selling, buying or negotiating promissory notes, drafts, coin and bullion, bills of exchange and all other written evidences of debt and specialties, and transact all such other business as shall appertain to the business of banking, and its board of directors shall have power to designate and regulate the manner in which its stock shall be transferred, directors elected or appointed, officers appointed, its property transferred and general business conducted, and all the privileges granted by this act to associations organized under it, shall be by them exercised and enjoyed; the usual business of the corporation shall be transacted at an office or banking house in the place specified.—Act of 13th of May, 1876, Sec. 6, P. L. 161.

May Borrow and Lend Money, Discount Negotiable Paper, Hold Collateral for Loans and Pay Interest on Deposits to Foreign Correspondents Only.—Rate of Interest.

Sec. 158. All associations incorporated under the provisions of this act shall have the power and may borrow or lend money for such period as they may deem proper, may discount bills of exchange, foreign or domestic, promissory notes or other negotiable paper, and the interest may be received in advance, and shall have the right to hold in trust or as collateral security for loans, advances or discounts, estate, real, personal or mixed, including the notes, bonds, obligations or accounts of the United States, individuals or corporations, and to purchase, collect and adjust the same, and to dispose thereof for the benefit of the said corporation or for the payment of the debts as security for which the same may be held: Provided, That no interest shall be paid directly or indirectly for any money deposited with such association, except foreign correspondents or correspondents in other states on daily balances, and then at a rate not to exceed three per centum per annum.—Act of 13th of May, 1876, Sec. 7, P. L. 161.

May Purchase, Hold and Convey Real Estate for Certain Purposes.

Sec. 159. It shall be lawful for any association incorporated under this act to purchase, hold and convey real estate as follows:

First. Such as shall be necessary for its immediate accommodation in the transaction of its business.

Second. Such as shall be mortgaged to it in good faith as security for debts contracted previous to the execution of any such mortgage.

Third. Such as it shall purchase at sales under judgments, decrees or mortgages held by such corporation or shall purchase to secure debts due to said corporation.

Such corporation shall not purchase or hold real estate in any other case or for any other purpose than as specified in this section, nor shall it in any case hold the possession of any real estate under mortgage, or the title and possession of any real estate purchased by it, except such as may be necessary for its immediate accommodation in the transaction of its business, for a longer period than five years.— Act of 13th of May, 1876, Sec. 8, P. L. 161.

Payment of Capital Stock.—Payment to be Certified to Auditor General.

Sec. 160. Before any association incorporated under this act shall commence business, at least fifty per centum of its capital stock shall be paid in, and the remainder of the capital stock of such corporation shall be paid in instalments of at least ten per centum on the whole amount of the capital per month from the time it shall commence business, and the payment of each instalment shall be certified under oath to the Auditor General by the president and cashier of the corporation.—Act of 13th of May, 1876, Sec. 9, P. L. 161.

Increase of Capital Stock regulated.

Sec. 161. Any corporation formed under this act may provide in its articles of association for an increase of its capital stock from time to time as may be deemed expedient, subject however to the regulations of this act; that only such maximum increase shall be allowed as shall be provided for in the articles of association, unless a majority of the stockholders shall formally certify in writing to the Auditor General their consent to a greater increase, and no increase of capital shall be valid unless the same shall be actually paid in within one year from the date of the written consent as aforesaid to such increase, and notice of such payment transmitted to the Auditor General; and every corporation, by a vote of the shareholders owning two-thirds of its capital stock, may reduce such capital to any sum not below the minimum amount of capital required by this act for such corporations; before such decrease shall be allowed, notice thereof shall be given to the Auditor General and his approval thereto obtained.—Act of 13th of May, 1876, Sec. 10, 161.

Proceedings Against Delinquent Stockholders.

Sec. 162. If any shareholder or his assignee shall fail to pay any instalment on the stock held by him, when the same is required by the by-laws, the articles of association, the resolution authorizing such stock, or the provisions of this act, the directors of such corporation may allot the same to the other shareholders in the proportion they shall hold shares in the capital stock, or to those who shall desire to take the same; should such shareholders not take the stock of such delinquent shareholder, it shall be sold at public auction to any person who will pay the highest price therefor, and not less than the amount due thereon, and the excess, if any, shall be paid to such delinquent shareholders; before any such public sale shall be made, public notice thereof shall be published for not less than three weeks in a newspaper of general circulation in the city or county where such corporation is located, and if no newspaper is published in such county or city, then in a newspaper published nearest thereto; if no bidder can be found who will pay the amount due on such stock to the corporation and the expenses of sale, the amount previously paid shall be forfeited to the corporation, and such stock shall be disposed of as the directors may order within four months from the time of such forfeiture, and if not sold, it shall be cancelled and deducted from the capital of the corporation; and if such cancellation and deduction shall reduce the capital of the corporation below minimum of the capital required by this act, the capital stock thereof shall, within thirty days from the date of such cancellation, be increased to the requirements of this act; in default of such increase, such bank shall be adjudged to have committed an act of insolvency, and its business shall be closed as hereinafter provided in cases of insolvency.—Act of 13th of May, 1878, Sec. 11, P. L. 161.

Corporation to be Managed by Not Less Than Five Directors.—Cashier, Clerk or Teller Not to be Director.—Qualifications.

Sec. 163. The affairs of every corporation organized under this act shall be managed by not less than five directors, one of whom shall be president and another vice president; no cashier, clerk or teller, in any of the corporations organized under this act, shall be eligible as a director thereof; every director shall during his term of service, be a citizen of the United States and a citizen of Pennsylvania; each director shall own in his own right at least ten shares of the capital stock of the corporation of which he is a director; each director when appointed or elected, and before assuming the duties of his office, shall take an oath that he will, so far as a duty devolves upon him, diligently and honestly administer the affairs of such corporation, and that he is the bona fide owner in his own right of the number of shares of stock required by this act, subscribed by him or standing in his name on the books of the corporation, and that the same is not hypothecated or pledged in any way as security for any loan or debt, which oath shall be transmitted to the Auditor General to be filed and kept in his office.—Act of 13th of May, 1876, Sec. 12, P. L. 161.

Directors to be Elected Annually for Term of One Year.—How Vacancies to be Filled Until Annual Election.—Proceedings upon Failure to Elect at Time Fixed for Election.

Sec. 164. The directors of any corporation first elected or appointed, shall hold their places until their successors shall be elected and qualified; all subsequent elections shall be held annually on such day in the year as may be specified in the articles of association; and the directors elected on such day shall hold their places for one year and until 'their successors are elected and qualified; any director ceasing to be the owner of the requisite amount of stock, or who shall in any other way become disqualified, shall thereby vacate his place; any vacancy in the board shall be filled by appointment by the remaining directors, and any one so appointed shall act as a director until the next annual election; if for any cause an election for directors shall not be held at the time appointed, an election may be held on a subsequent day, at least thirty days' notice thereof having been given by advertisement in a newspaper published in the city or county where such corporation is located, or if no newspaper is published therein, then in the one published the nearest thereto if the articles of association do not fix the day on which the election shall be held, the day for election shall be designated by the directors in the by-laws; in case the directors fail to fix a day for the election as aforesaid, two-thirds in value of the shareholders shall designate a day for that purpose.—Act of 13th of May, 1876, Sec. 13, P. L. 161.

Election of Directors Regulated.

Sec. 165. In all elections for directors and otherwise each shareholder shall be entitled to one vote on each share of stock held by him; shareholders may vote by proxies executed in writing. No officer, clerk, teller or book-keeper of the corporation shall act as a proxy, and no shareholder whose liability is past due shall be allowed to vote; in all elections for directors of a corporation organized under this act, each shareholder may cast the whole number of his votes for one candidate or distribute them upon two or more candidates as he may prefer.—Act of 13th of May, 1876, Sec. 14, P. L. 161.

Directors Shall Keep a List of Shareholders, a Copy of Which Shall be Transmitted to Auditor General.

Sec. 166. The directors of every corporation under this act shall cause to be kept at all times a full and correct list of the names and residences of the shareholders and the number of shares held by each therein, in the office where its business is transacted, and such list shall be subject to the inspection of the shareholders and creditors of the corporation and the officer authorized to assess taxes under any state authority during business hours of each day in which business may be lawfully transacted; a copy of this list on the first Monday of June in each year, verified by the president and cashier, shall be transmitted to the Auditor General.—Act of 13th of May, 1876, Sec. 15, P. L. 161.

When Directors May Declare and Pay Dividends.—Liability of Directors for Making Dividends Impairing Capital.

Sec. 167. The directors of the corporations under this act may quarterly or semi-annually in each year, as they may see fit, declare a dividend of so much of the net profits of such corporations as they shall judge expedient, and pay the same to its stockholders on demand, at any time not exceeding fifteen days after such dividend is declared; but such corporation shall, before the declaration of a dividend, carry at least one-tenth of the net profits of the preceding quarter, if it is a quarterly dividend, and at least one-tenth of the net profits of the preceding half year, to its surplus fund until such surplus fund shall amount to twenty-five per centum of its capital stock; if the directors of the corporation shall make any dividends which shall impair the capital thereof, such directors consenting thereto shall be jointly and severally liable in an action of debt or bill in equity in their individual capacities to such corporation for the amount of stock so divided, and each director present or otherwise when such dividend shall be made, shall be adjudged consenting thereto unless he shall forthwith enter his protest on the minutes of the board and give public notice to the stockholders thereof.—Act of 13th of May, 1876, Sec. 16, P. L. 161.

Sworn Statement of Condition of Corporation to be Made on Each Dividend Day.—What Statement to Contain.

Sec. 168. On each dividend day the cashier shall make a full, explicit and accurate statement of the condition of the corporation as it shall be on each day previous to the declaring of such dividend, to be verified on the oath of the president and cashier, setting forth—

First. The amount of capital stock actually paid in and then remaining as the actual capital stock of the corporation.

Second. The balances and debts of every kind due to banks and bankers of this State or elsewhere.

Third. The amount due to time and call depositors separately.

Fourth. The total amount of debts and liabilities of every description and the greatest amount since the last previous statement, specifying the time when the same occurred.

Fifth. The amount on hand of bills, bonds, notes and other evidence of debts discounted or purchased by the corporation, gold, silver, coin, bullion and cash on hand, the amount specifically and particularly of suspended debts, the amount considered doubtful, the amount considered bad and the amount in suit or judgment.

Sixth. The value of the real and personal property held for the convenience of the corporations, specifying the amount of each, the amount of real estate taken for debts due the corporation, how taken and still held.

Seventh. The amount of the undivided profits of the corporation.

Eighth. The amount of the liabilities to the corporation by the directors or officers thereof, specifying the particular items and the gross amount thereof separately, as principal debtors, and as endorsers or sureties.

Ninth. The amount of liabilities to the corporation by the stockholders thereof, specifying the gross amout of such liabilities as principal debtors, and the gross amount as endorsers or sureties, which statement shall be entered at length in a book to be provided for that purpose.—Act of 13th of May, 1876, Sec. 17, P. L. 161.

Persons Necessary for Executing the Business to Agree With Corporation to Discharge Duty.—Must Give Bond for Faithful Performance of Duty.—Suit on Such Bond.

Sec. 169. Before the cashier, teller, book-keeper or other persons necessary for executing the business of the corporation shall enter upon their duties, they shall each enter into articles of agreement with the corporation for the proper discharge of his duty, in which it shall be provided, among other things, that he will give the business of the corporation his care and attention, rendering true accounts of all his transactions, never to use the moneys of the corporation in his private transactions nor to engage in private financial operations through his office as one of the officers of said corporation; and they shall each also enter into a bond to the Commonwealth of Pennsylvania in such amount as the board of directors may require, conditioned for the proper and faithful performance of his duties, the security of which bonds shall be approved by the court of common pleas of the county in which the corporation is located, and recorded within thirty days thereafter in the office for recording deeds in such county; any person aggrieved and suffering injury by the failure of any officer or clerk of the corporation to comply with the conditions of his bond, may commence and prosecute an action on the same in the manner provided for suing official bonds in the act approved June fourteenth, one thousand eight hundred and thirty-six, entitled "An act relative to bonds with penalties and official bonds."—Act of 13th of May, 1876, Sec. 18, P. L. 161.

Cashiers Not to Engage in any Other Occupation.—Penalty.

Sec. 170. No cashier of any corporation under this act shall engage in any other profession, occupation or calling, either directly or indirectly, than that of the duties appertaining to the office of cashier; and if any cashier of such corporation shall, directly or indirectly, engage in the purchase and sale of stocks or in any other profession or calling other than that of his duties as cashier, he shall be guilty of a misdemeanor, and upon conviction thereof in a court of criminal jurisdiction, be sentenced to pay a fine not exceeding five hundred dollars; nothing however in this section shall be construed as to prevent such cashier from managing his own real estate or private property as heretofore, if such property be not vested in mercantile, mechanical or manufacturing operations.—Act of 13th of May, 1876, Sec. 18, P. L. 161.

Embezzlement by Officers.—Criminally Liable and May be Fined and Imprisoned.—Liable by Civil Remedy.

Sec. 171. If any president, cashier, director, clerk, teller, agent or any, other officer of any corporation under this act, who shall fraudulently embezzle, abstract or wilfully appropriate to his own use or to the use of any other person or persons, or misapply any money or other property belonging to such corporation or left with the same as a special deposit or otherwise, he or they so offending, upon conviction thereof, shall be fined in any amount not less than the sum so appropriated or embezzled, and to undergo an imprisonment at separate and solitary confinement not $exceeding$ five years: Provided, Such conviction shall not prevent any person of persons aggrieved from pursuing their civil remedy against such person so convicted.—Act of 13th of May, 1876, Sec. 19, P. L. 161.

Books, Funds, Etc., to be Open to Inspection by Directors.—Minutes of Proceedings of Directors to be Kept.

Sec. 172. The books, funds, papers and correspondence of the several corporations under this act, shall at all times be subject to the inspection of the directors who shall keep fair and regular entries of their proceedings in a book provided for that purpose, and on any question when two directors shall require it, the yeas and nays shall be inserted on the minutes, which minutes shall at all times, on demand, be produced to the stockholders at a general meeting, and shall be subject, also, together with their other books and papers, to the inspection of any committee who shall be authorized by the Legislature to require the same.—Act of 13th of May, 1876, Sec. 20, P. L. 161.

Loans to Directors and Others Regulated.—Liability to the Corporation.—A Lien on Debtor's Stock.

Sec. 173. No director of any corporation under this act, shall receive as a loan from such corporation an amount greater than ten per centum of the capital stock actually paid in, and the gross amount loaned to all the officers and directors of such corporations, and to the houses or firms in which they may be interested directly or indirectly, shall not exceed at any time the sum of twenty-five per centum of the capital stock paid in; and no shareholder shall sell or transfer any shares in the capital stock held in his own right so long as he shall be liable, either as principal debtor, surety or otherwise, to the corporation, for any debt, without the consent of a majority of the directors, nor shall such shareholders, when liable to the corporation for any debt that is overdue and unpaid, be entitled to receive any dividend, interest or profit on such shares as long as such liabilities shall so continue overdue, but all such dividends, interest and profits shall be retained by such corporation to discharge such liabilities.—Act of 13th of May, 1876, Sec. 21, P. L. 161.

Cashier to Publish Every Six Months A Specific Statement of Condition of Corporation, Amount of Assets, Indebtedness and Liabilities.

Sec. 174. It shall be the duty of the cashier of every corporation, under this act, to publish once every six months, in two papers published in the county where such corporation is located, if so many are there published, if two are not published therein, then in one paper therein; if none are published therein, then in one published in one adjoining county, a statement of the condition of said corporation, which shall set forth the entire amount of its assets and every class of items therein, the entire amount of indebtedness and liabilities thereof, particularly specifying the same at the time of making such statement.—Act of 13th of May, 1876, Sec. 22, P. L. 161.

Bank Not to Take as Security for Loans a Lien on its Capital Stock. —To Hold its Own Stock for Certain Purposes.

Sec. 175. No corporation, under this act, shall take as security for any loan or discount, a lien on any part of its capital stock, but the same surety, both in kind and amount, shall be required of persons, shareholders and not shareholders; and no such corporation shall be the holder or purchaser of any portion of its capital, unless such purchase shall be necessary to prevent loss on a debt previously contracted in good faith on surety which at the time was deemed adequate for the payment of such debt, without a lien upon such stock, or in case of forfeiture of such stock for the non-payment of instalments due thereon, as provided in this act; and the stock so purchased shall in no case be held by the corporation so purchasing for a longer period than six months, if the same can be sold for what such stock cost the corporation.—Act of 13th of May, 1876, Sec. 23, P. L. 161.

Capital Stock Not to be Withdrawn as Dividends or Loans.—Dividends greater than Net Profits not to be Declared.—What are Suspended Payments.

Sec. 176. No corporation under this act shall, during the time it shall continue its operations, withdraw or allow to be withdrawn either in form of dividends, loans to stockholders, or in any other manner, any portion of its capital stock, except as hereinbefore provided; and if any losses shall at any time have been sustained by such corporation equal to or exceeding its undivided profits then on hand, no dividend shall be made, and no dividends shall be made by any such corporation, while in business operation, to an amount greater than its net profits then on hand, deducting therefrom losses, bad and suspended debts; and all debts due to such corporation, on which interest is due and unpaid for six months, unless the same shall be well secured or in process of collection, shall be considered bad and suspended debts within the meaning of this section.—Act of 13th of May, 1876, Sec. 24, P. L. 161.

Voluntary Liquidation.

Sec. 177. Any corporation under this act may go into liquidation and be closed by the vote of its shareholders, owning at least two-thirds of its stock, and whenever such vote shall be taken it shall be the duty of the board of directors to cause notice of this fact to be certified under the seal of the corporation to the Auditor General, and publication thereof made for at least three months in two news-papers, if so many are published, if two are not published, then one in the county in which such corporation is located, that it is closing up its affairs and notifying the creditors thereof to present their claims for payment; and it shall be the duty of the said directors, in the name of the corporation, to collect all its assets, apply the same first to the payment of the debts thereof and distribute the surplus, if any, to and among the shareholders in the proportion they hold the capital stock thereof.—Act of 13th of May, 1876, Sec. 25, P. L. 161.

What to be Deemed an Act of Insolvency.—Duties of Auditor General.

Sec. 178. If any corporation under this act shall refuse, after lawful demand, at its customary place of business, during usual business hours, to pay off its liabilities, for a period of ten days after such liabilities are due and payable, holders or owners thereof shall present in writing, a written demand for the payment thereof, at the place of business of such corporation, during usual business hours; and if payment thereof is refused because of the want of funds to pay the same, such holders may cause such written demand to be protested for non-payment, by a notary public under his official seal in the usual manner; and the Auditor General, on receiving and filing in his office such protest, shall forthwith give notice in writing to such corporation that if it omits to pay its liability aforesaid, with legal interest thereon and cost of protest, for thirty days after such notice, he will notify such corporation that it has committed an act of insolvency.—Act of 13th of May, 1876, Sec. 26, P. L. 161.

Agent to Investigate to be a Party.—When Receiver to be Appointed.

Sec. 179. The Auditor General after having notified such corporation that it has committed an act of insolvency, shall forthwith, with the concurrence of the Governor, appoint a special agent at a compensation not exceeding ten dollars per day and necessary traveling expenses, who shall make immediate inquiry into the truth of such information, and make report thereon to the Auditor General; and if the said special agent shall report to the satisfacion of the Auditor General that such corporation has suspended payment of its liabilities he shall forthwith apply to the court of common pleas of the propery county, if in session, or if in vacation, to the president judge of the district in which such corporation is located, to appoint a suitable receiver, who shall take immediate possession of the books, records, money, bills, bonds, notes, other evidence of indebtedness, and all the property of such corporation of every description, and hold the same for the creditors of such corporation.—Act of 13th of May, 1876, Sec. 27, P. L. 161.

Receiver to Give Bond When Appointed.—Assets How Distributed.

Sec. 180. The receiver appointed as provided for in the preceding section shall give bond in such sum and with such sureties as the said court or judges shall deem sufficient, and shall proceed under the direction of said court to settle up the affairs of such corporation, shall convert all its assets of every kind and description, if possible, without delay into money; the money so made to be applied:

First. To pay all the deposits of the corporation.

Second. To the payment and discharge of all the remaining liabilities of such corporation.

Third. The residue if any shall be distributed to the shareholders of the corporation in proportion to the stock by them respectively held.—Act of 13th of May, 1876, Sec. 28, P. L. 161.

Rights of Banks in Proceedings in Case of Insolvency.

Sec. 181. If any corporation under this act against which the Auditor General shall have instituted proceeding on account of any supposed act of insolvency as prescribed in this act, such corporation may apply to any court of competent jurisdiction for an injunction on said Auditor General to suspend all further proceedings against such corporation for insolvency, and such court after citing the Auditor General to appear and show cause why such writ should not be granted, the said court shall proceed to inquire if such corporation has actually suspended payment of its liabilities and continues such suspension, and for this purpose such court may direct an issue, if required by either party; and if after such inquiry, such court shall discover such corporation has not suspended and does not continue to suspend payment of its liabilities, shall make an order enjoining the Auditor General from all further proceedings against such corporation on account of the supposed act of insolvency on which such proceedings were instituted, and thereupon all the property and assets of such corporation shall be restored to it.—Act of 13th of May, 1876, Sec. 29, P. L. 161.

Not to Pay Interest on Call Deposits.

Sec. 182. The banks chartered under the provisions of this act shall not pay interest on call deposits, and any violation of this section shall work a forfeiture of the charter of the bank so paying interest.—Act of 13th of May, 1876, Sec. 30, P. L. 161. (Repealed by act of 10th of June, 1897, P. L. 138.)

Powers of Legislature to Revoke Charters Reserved.

Sec. 183. The Legislature reserves the power to revoke or annul the charters of all corporations organized under this act whenever in their opinion it may be necessary for the public welfare, in such a manner however that no injustice shall be done to the stockholders,

and such corporations shall be subject to all the laws of this Commonwealth regulating the taxation of banking corporations therein.
—Act of 13th of May 1876, Sec. 31, P. L. 161.

Existing Corporations May Come Under This Act.

Sec. 184. Any corporation now in existence, chartered under any of the laws of this State, making application to come under any of the provisions of this act, shall do so by coming under all the provisions of this act, and shall re-organize the said corporation to conform with this act.—Act of 13th of May, 1876, Sec. 32, P. L. 161.

Repeal.

Sec. 185. All general acts or parts of acts inconsistent with this act be and the same are hereby repealed.—Act of 13th of May, 1876, Sec. 33, P. L. 161.*

*The act substituting the Commissioner of Banking in the place of the Auditor General in regulating banks, etc., seems to apply to the cases where he is to act or intervene under the act of 1876.

CHAPTER 6.

LEGISLATION AS TO BANKS SINCE THE ACT OF 1876.

To Prevent and Punish for the Re-hypothecation of Stocks, Bonds or Other Securities Pledged for Money Lent or Borrowed.

Sec. 186. Be it enacted, etc., That it shall not be lawful for any person or persons, bank, savings fund, building association, or any corporation, to re-pledge or re-hypothecate any stocks, bonds or other securities, received by any of them for money lent and borrowed, during the continuance of the contract of hypothecation or pledging of such securities; and such re-pledging or re-hypothecation without the consent of the party pledging the same is hereby declared a misdemeanor, triable in the courts of quarter sessions, and on conviction thereof, any person or persons, or the officers of any corporation, violating the provisions of this act, shall be sentenced to a fine not less than five hundred nor more than five thousand dollars, and undergo an imprisonment for a period not exceeding five years, or both or either, at the discretion of the court before which such person shall be prosecuted.—Act of 25th of May, 1878, Sec. 1, P. L. 155.

Stock of Banking Companies May be Reduced.—Not to Affect Liability of Stockholders.

Sec. 187. The capital stock of any banking corporation created by the laws of this Commonwealth, may be decreased, from time to time, by the consent of the persons or bodies corporate holding the larger amount in value of the stock of such company: Provided, That no diminution of the capital stock of any company under this act, shall affect or destroy the liabilities of stockholders for the indebtedness of corporations where they are now liable under existing laws.—Act of 11th of June, 1879, Sec. 1, P. L. 133.

Meeting of Stockholders to be Called.—Notice of Meeting.

Sec. 188. Any banking corporation desirous of decreasing its capital stock as provided by this act, shall, by a resolution of its board of directors, call a meeting of its stockholders therefor, which meeting shall be held at its chief office or place of business in this Commonwealth, and notice of the time, place and object of such meeting, shall be published once a week for sixty days prior to such meeting, in at least two newspapers published in the county, city or borough where such office or place of business is situated.—Act of 11th of June, 1879, Sec. 2, P. L. 133.

Election to be Held.

Sec. 189. At the meeting called pursuant to the second section of this act, the stockholders present at said meeting shall vote for or against such decrease; said election shall be conducted by three judges, stockholders of said banking corporation, appointed by the board of directors to hold said election, and who shall respectively take and subscribe an oath or affirmation before any officer authorized by law to conduct such election to the best of their ability.—Act of 11th of June, 1879, Sec. 3, P. L. 133.

Ballots.—Voting on Shares Transferred, and by Proxy.—Statement to be Furnished Judges of Election.

Sec. 190. Each ballot shall have endorsed thereon the number of shares thereby represented; but no share or shares transferred within sixty days, shall entitle the holder or holders thereof to vote at such election or meeting, nor shall any proxy be received or entitle the holder to vote, unless the same shall bear date and have been executed within three months next preceding such election or meeting; and it shall be the duty of such banking corporation to furnish the judges at said meeting with a statement of the amount of its capital stock, with the names of persons or bodies corporate holding the same, and the number of shares by each respectively held, which statement shall be signed by one of the chief officers of such banking corporation, with an affidavit thereto annexed that the same is true and correct to the best of his knowledge and belief.—Act of 11th of June, 1879, Sec. 4, P. L. 133.

Election Return to be Filed With Secretary of Commonwealth, Also Certificate of Decrease of Capital Stock.—Penalty for Neglect so to Do.—Certificate to be Recorded and Certified to Auditor General.—Issue of New Certificates.

Sec. 190.* It shall be the duty of such banking corporation, if consent is given to such decrease, to file in the office of the Secretary of the Commonwealth within thirty days after such election or meeting, one of the copies of the return of such election provided for by the third section of this act, with a copy of the resolution and notice calling the same thereto annexed; and upon the decrease of the capital stock of such banking corporation made pursuant thereto, it shall be the duty of the president or treasurer of such corporation, within thirty days thereafter, to make return to the Secretary of the Commonwealth, under oath, of the amount of such decrease; and in case of neglect or omission so to do, such corporation shall be subject to a penalty of five thousand dollars, which penalty shall be collected on an account settled by the Auditor General and State Treasurer, as accounts for taxes due the Commonwealth are settled and collected, and the Secretary of the Commonwealth shall cause said return to be recorded in a book kept for that purpose, and furnish a certified copy of the same to the Auditor General; and thereupon, the directors of such corporation shall alter and change the par value of the shares thereof to conform to the decrease for which the largest number of votes shall have been cast at such election, and issue new certificates of stock representing the par value fixed by such election. signed by the proper officers of said corporation, and deliver the same to the shareholders entitled thereto on the surrender of their former certificates, which shall be cancelled by said officers before paying any dividend declared after such reduction.—Act of 11th of June, 1879, Sec. 5, P. L. 133.

Liability of Stockholders After Decrease of Capital Stock.

Sec. 191. The capital stock of any banking corporation created by the laws of this Commonwealth, may be decreased from time to time, subject to the provisions of the act of eleventh of June, one thousand eight hundred and seventy-nine, entitled "An act to provide for the manner of decreasing the capital stock of banking corporations: Provided, That such decrease of the capital stock of any such banking company shall not effect or destroy the liabilities of the stockholders for the indebtedness of such corporations, at the time of such decrease, where they are now liable under their charters, but that for all deposits received by banking corporations after such decrease, the stockholders shall only be liable for the indebtedness of such banking company as the charter provides.—Act of 22nd of June, 1883, Sec. 1, P. L. 155.

Proceedings to Decrease Capital Stock Subscribed When Part Has Been Paid In.

Sec. 192. Whenever any banking company shall have fixed and subscribed a certain capital, but have paid in only a portion of such capital, and have issued capital stock certificates for the amount thus fixed, to each stockholder subject to assessment for the unpaid portion, such banking company may decrease the capital of such banking company to the amount paid in, and thereupon call in all outstanding capital stock certificates and issue in place thereof new certificates, fully paid and non-assessable for any purpose except only taxation: Provided, That no banking company, doing a general banking business in this Commonwealth, shall decrease the capital stock of any bank having stock so issued to less than two hundred thousand dollars, nor shall any savings bank, trust company or other savings institution decrease the capital of any institution having stock so issued, to less than fifty thousand dollars: And provided further, That notice of said decrease shall be published in two or more newspapers, in the county in which said bank is located for four weeks prior to said decrease.—Act of 22nd of June, 1883, Sec. 2, P. L. 155.

State Banks May Become National Banks.

Sec. 193. Any bank incorporated or organized by the authority of this Commonwealth, which shall become an association for carrying on the business of banking under the laws of the United States, shall be deemed to have surrendered its charter, if it shall have complied with the requirements of this act: Provided, That every such bank shall, nevertheless, be continued a body corporate for the term of three years after the time of such surrender, for the purpose of prosecuting and defending suits by and against it, and of enabling it to close its concerns and to dispose of and convey its property; but not for the purpose of continuing under the laws of this Commonwealth the business for which it was established.—Act of 26th of April, 1889, Sec. 1, P. L. 56.

Notice to Stockholders of Vote to Become Such Association.

Sec. 194. When a bank, at a meeting of the stockholders, has voted to become such association, and its directors have procured the authority of the owners of two-thirds of the capital stock to make the certificate required therefor by the laws of the United States, the cashier shall publish notice thereof for thirty days in such newspaper as the meeting of the stockholders may direct, and sent like printed notice, by mail or otherwise, to each stockholder.—Act of 26th of April, 1889, Sec. 2, P. L. 56.

Stockholders Entitled to One Vote Each on the Question.

Sec. 195. At a meeting of the stockholders of any such bank as aforesaid, each stockholder shall be allowed to cast one vote for every share of such capital stock held by him or her, on the question whether or not the said bank shall become such an association as aforesaid, for carrying on the business of banking and of exercising the powers conferred by this act; and every stockholder who is absent may vote by proxy, made at any time after this act shall become a law; and any executor, administrator or trustee holding any such share or shares of such capital stock may vote personally or by proxy, without incurring any responsibility by such vote.—Act of 26th of April, 1889, Sec. 3, P. L. 56.

Court of Common Pleas May Appoint Auditors to Ascertain Market Value of Shares of Such Bank.—Notice of Meeting to be Given.

Sec. 196. The court of common pleas of the proper county is authorized to ascertain and determine, by the appointment of one or more auditors, not exceeding three, and shall certify to the president and directors of said bank what was the fair market value of the shares of such bank, at the time of paying the last dividend, and if within said thirty days any stockholder, who has not joined in giving such authority, notifies in writing the president or cashier of his desire to surrender his stock upon receiving the value thereof as so determined, such bank shall, within thirty days thereafter, pay such stockholder for his shares, according to such valuation, with interest from the time of paying said dividend, upon his surrendering his shares: Provided, That notice shall be given of the time of meeting of the auditor or auditors appointed under the provisions of this section, in one or more newspapers of the proper county, directed to the president, directors and stockholders of such bank.—Act of 26th of April, 1889, Sec. 4, P. L. 56.

How Fractional Shares Are to be Valued.

Sec. 197. When, in adjusting the shares of stock of any stockholder in a bank surrendering its charter under the provisions of this act, to the value of the shares of an association for banking under the laws of the United States, there shall be fractional shares of the stock of such surrendering bank, the value of such fractional shares shall be taken to be the same as shall have been ascertained to be the value of the shares of refusing stockholders in said bank; and in case there shall be no refusing stockholders, then the value shall be ascertained in the manner directed in relation to refusing stockholders, and, upon the payment of such value, with like interest as is directed to be paid to refusing stockholders, the owner of such fractional shares shall deliver the certificate thereof and transfer said fractional shares to such bank: Provided, That the directors of the bank and such stockholders may agree upon a sum as the value of such fractional shares and the payment thereof shall have the same effect as if the value had been ascertained in the mode hereinbefore mentioned.—Act of 26th of April, 1889, Sec. 5, P. L. 56.

How Capital Stock May be Reduced.

Sec. 198. The capital stock of such bank shall be reduced to the extent of the par value of the shares so surrendered, and may be further reduced to any amount fixed by authority of the owners of two-thirds the capital stock, by purchase and cancellation of shares, by reducing the par value of each share, or by both methods as the directors may determine: Provided That such bank may, if it deems it expedient, instead of reducing its capital stock to the amount so appraised, dispose of the same to any person or persons at the par value thereof without any reduction of capital.—Act of 26th of April, 1889, Sec. 6, P. L. 56.

Directors to Deliver Plates and Dies to Court of Quarter Session on Surrender of Charter.—Penalty for Neglect or Refusal.

Sec. 199. When the charter of any bank is surrendered, under the provisions of this act, the members of the board of directors last in office shall forthwith deliver up all their plates and dies to the court of quarter sessions in the county in which the bank has been established, and the court shall cause them to be disposed of in such manner as shall be deemed expedient, in order to prevent their use for any unlawful purpose. The members of the board who wilfully refuse or neglect so to do shall be deemed guilty of a misdemeanor and severally punished, on conviction in the proper court, by a fine not exceeding five hundred dollars.—Act of 26th of April, 1889, Sec. 7, P. L. 56.

Payment of Bank Tax Regulated.

Sec. 200. The bank tax imposed by the laws of this Commonwealth shall be paid by such bank up to the date of its becoming such association, in proportion to the time since the next preceding payment therefor.—Act of 26th of April, 1889, Sec. 8, P. L. 56.

Auditor General to Send Certificate to Governor.—Surrender of Charter.

Sec. 201. When a bank furnishes to the Auditor General satisfactory evidence, by the oaths or affirmations of the president and cashier, and by the exhibition of its books or otherwise, that all the requirements of this act have been complied with in relation to such bank, and that it has become a banking association, under the laws of the United States, the (Auditor General) shall certify the facts to the Governor, who shall cause notice thereof to be published in some newspaper in the county where such bank is located at least for three weeks. And the charter of the bank shall thereupon be deemed to be surrendered, subject to the provisions of the first section of this act.—Act of 26th of April, 1889, Sec. 9, P. L. 56.

Assets to Vest in New Association Without Transfer.

Sec. 202. When the charter of said bank shall be surrendered to the Commonwealth, under the provisions of this act, all the assets, real and personal, of the said bank, shall immediately, by act of law and without any conveyance or transfer, be vested in and become the property of the said association for carrying on the business of banking, formed as aforesaid.—Act of 26th of April, 1889, Sec. 10, P. L. 56.

New Association to be Liable for Obligations of the Bank.

Sec. 203. Nothing in this act shall be construed as releasing such association from its obligation to pay and discharge all liabilities incurred by the bank before becoming such association.—Act of 26th of April, 1889, Sec. 11, P. L. 56.

Charters Created or Renewed Not to Exceed a Term of Twenty Years.—Results of Vote to Renew Charter to be Certified to Secretary of Commonwealth.

Sec. 204. The charters of State banks created or renewed and extended under any special or general law of this Commonwealth, shall hereafter be renewed and extended for a term not exceeding twenty years, in the manner following, namely:

When the stockholders of any such State bank shall desire to apply for a renewal and extension of their charter, the board of directors of such bank, or any twenty stockholders thereof, being together proprietors of one-twentieth part of the number of all the shares of the said bank, may call a general meeting of the stockholders of the said bank, to be held at the banking house at a time to be fixed, for the purpose of considering and deciding the question of renewing and extending the charter of the said bank, giving at least thirty days' notice thereof in one or more newspapers published in the city or county in which the bank is located, specifying the object or objects of such meeting.

At such meeting the stockholders shall consider and vote for or against the proposition to renew and extend the charter, corporate rights and franchises of the said bank, for any period of years not exceeding twenty, each stockholder having the number of votes fixed by law.

If such stockholders or a number holding a majority of the shares of stock of the said bank, voting in person or by proxy, shall decide in favor of renewing and extending their charter, the result shall be certified by the board of directors to the Secretary of the Commonwealth, together with a statement of the condition of said bank, according to a form to be furnished by the Auditor General of the Commonwealth, on application to him, which statement shall be made by the president and cashier of the said bank under oath or affirmation.—Act of 26th of April, 1889, Sec. 1, P. L. 61.

Directors to Petition Governor After Filing of Certificate.—Contents of Certificate, Notice Thereof and Proof of Publication.—Petition, etc., to be Submitted to Attorney General.—His Certificate to the Governor.—To be Submitted to Auditor General.

Sec. 205. Upon the filing of such certificate with the Secretary of the Commonwealth, the board of directors shall present and file therewith a petition to the Governor, setting forth the corporate name of the said bank, the amount of its capital stock, the par value of its shares, the names of the directors, and of the president and cashier, the date of the special or general act creating, and of the last act (if any) renewing and extending its charter or the date of the patent of the Governor, when renewed and extended by patent, the time when the charter will expire, the proceedings of the stockholders to renew and extend, and the term or time of the renewal and extension prayed for, and that due notice of the intended application has been given according to law. The said notice shall be by publication, for at least three months, in two newspapers published daily (or weekly if there be no daily) in the city or town in which said bank is located, or if there be but one such paper published therein, then in the same, or if none such be published therein, then in two such newspapers published nearest thereto, proof of which publication shall be by the affidavit of the publisher before competent authority. On the filing of the said petition, together with the proof of the notice given, in the office of the Secretary of the Commonwealth, the same shall be immediately submitted to the Attorney General of the Commonwealth for examination, who shall forthwith examine the same, and without delay certify to the Governor, by certificate endorsed upon or annexed to the same, his opinion, whether the said petition is in proper form and conforms to the requisitions of the law, and if not, in what respect its non-conformity consists. If the said Attorney General shall certify that the petition is in proper form, and conforms to the laws of the State, the Governor shall at once submit the same to the Auditor General, who shall forthwith examine the same, and without delay certify upon the same or annexed to the said petition whether the said bank is in good financial standing and repute so far as he knows and believes, whether in the conduct of its affairs, so far as he officially knows, the said bank has conformed to the laws of the State, and if not, in what respect its non-conformity consists, and his opinion, whether the renewal and extension of its charter is or is not consistent with the interests of the public.—Act of 26th of April, 1889, Sec. 2, P. L. 61.

Auditor General and Attorney General May Object.—Banks May Except.—Court to Decide and Issue Mandamus.

Sec. 205.* If either the Attorney General or the Auditor General shall find objections to the petition of the said bank for a renewal and extension of its charter privileges and franchises, he shall state distinctly and clearly in his certificate to the Governor, the objections he finds thereto, and the said bank may by its attorneys, except to the said objectors, and thereupon may proceed by application for a writ of mandamus, in the proper court having jurisdiction, against said Attorney General or Auditor General, or each if necessary, to have the validity of the said objections determined by the said court, according to law, and if determined in favor of the said bank, the said court shall issue its writ of mandamus to the said Attorney General or Auditor General as the case may be, or against each if necessary, requiring him, or each of them, as the case may be, to issue his certificate in proper form in favor of the said bank, whereupon the Governor shall proceed to issue his patent of renewal and extension, in manner hereinafter provided.—Act of 26th of April, 1889, Sec. 3, P. L. 61.

If Auditor General and Attorney General Certify in Favor, Governor to Issue Patent.

Sec. 205.** If the Attorney General and the Auditor General shall certify as aforesaid, affirmatively in favor of the said bank, the Governor shall forthwith issue his patent under the Great Seal of the Commonwealth, setting forth briefly the premises, and declaring that the charter of the said bank is renewed and extended for the term of years prayed for in said petition, and then and thenceforth the said charter and the corporate rights and franchises of the said bank shall be in law renewed and extended accordingly: Provided, And it is hereby declared and enacted, that no such bank whose charter is so renewed and extended hereafter, shall be authorized to issue its own notes or bills for circulation, without first having them registered and countersigned by the proper officer of the State, according to law, nor shall such notes or bills for circulation be issued by the said bank, until ample security for the full amount thereof shall be deposited with the Auditor General of the Commonwealth for their redemption, according to law.—Act of 26th of April, 1889, Sec. 4, P. L. 61.

Officer of Insolvent Bank Receiving Money on Deposit Guilty of Embezzlement.—Penalty.

Sec. 206. Any banker, broker or officer of any trust or savings institution, national, state or private bank, who shall take and receive money from a depositor with the knowledge that he, they or the bank is at the time insolvent, shall be guilty of embezzlement and shall be punished by a fine in double the amount so received, and imprisoned from one to three years in the penitentiary.—Act of 9th of May, 1889, Sec. 1, P. L. 145.

State Banks Authorized to Pay Interest on Deposits.

Sec. 207. That banks, chartered under the provisions of the laws of Pennsylvania, be and they are hereby authorized to pay interest upon deposits payable on demand, and upon daily balances of deposits subject to check.—Act of 10th of June, 1897, Sec. 1, P. L. 138.

Repealing Clause.

Sec. 208. All acts and parts of acts inconsistent herewith are hereby repealed.—Act of 10th of June, 1897, Sec. 2, P. L. 138.

Amendment of the Eighth Section of the Act of Thirteenth of May, 1876, as to What Real Estate May be Held by Banks.

Sec. 209. That it shall be lawful for any association incorporated under this act to purchase, hold and convey real estate as follows:

First. Such as shall be necessary for its immediate accommodation in the transaction of its business.

Second. Such as shall be mortgaged to it in good faith as security for debts.

Third. Such as it shall purchase at sales under judgments, decrees or mortgages held by such corporation, or shall purchase to secure debts due to said corporation.

Such corporation shall not purchase or hold real estate in any other case or for any other purpose than as specified in this section, nor shall it in any case hold the possession of any real estate under mortgage, or the title and possession of any real estate purchased by it, except such as may be necessary for its immediate accommodation in the transaction of its business, for a longer period than five years.—Act of 19th of April, 1901, Sec. 1, P. L. 79.

Banks and Banking Companies to Improve Real Estate Held by Them.

Sec. 210. Be it enacted, &c., That it shall be lawful for any bank or banking company of this Commonwealth to improve any real estate it may now or hereafter hold for the accommodation and transaction of its business, by erecting new buildings, or by renewing or replacing any building or buildings thereon with such new or additional structures of such dimensions as its board of directors may from time to time deem expedient; and to use such portion thereof as may be suitable and convenient for the transaction of its business for that purpose; and to lease and let, from time to time, such portions or apartments of such building or buildings as it may not require for its banking business, and to receive rents for the use of the same: Provided, however, That no such bank or banking company shall, for the purposes aforesaid, reduce its surplus fund below fifty per centum of what its amount may be when such improvement, buildings, et cetera, may be commenced.

That all acts or parts of acts inconsistent with this act be and the same are hereby repealed.—Act of 21st of May, 1901, Sec. 1 and 2, P. L. 288.

Banks Authorized to Loan Money on Certain Securities.

Sec. 211. Be it enacted, &c., That banks chartered under the provisions of the laws of the Commonwealth of Pennsylvania be and they are hereby authorized to loan money on the security of bonds and mortgages, on unincumbered real estate situated in this State, not in excess of their time deposits, and to invest their funds, not exceeding twenty-five per centum of their capital stock, surplus and undivided profits, in the purchase of such mortgages; and may also purchase, for investment, any interest bearing bonds or other obligations of any corporation or individual.

All acts and parts of acts inconsistent herewith are hereby repealed.—Act of 10th of July, 1901, Sec. 1 and 2, P. L. 639.

Title of the Act of Seventeenth of February, 1906.

An act to regulate the deposits of State funds, to prescribe the method of selecting State depositories, to limit the amount of State deposits, to provide for the security of such deposits, to fix the rate of interest thereon, to provide for the publication of monthly statements of moneys in the general and sinking funds, to declare it a misdemeanor to give or take anything of value for obtaining the same, and prescribing penalties for violations of this act.

Selection of State Depositories by Revenue Commissioners and Banking Commissioner Jointly.—Restriction of Selection.

Sec. 212. Be it enacted, &c., That on and after the first day of June, one thousand nine hundred and six, the selection of the banks, banking institutions, or trust companies, in which the State moneys shall be deposited, shall be made by the Revenue Commissioners and the Banking Commissioner, jointly, or a majority of them; and for this purpose they shall meet once a month, or oftener at the call of the State Treasurer; but no selection shall be made of any institution not subject to National or State supervision, except as hereafter provided.—Act of 17th of February, 1906, Sec. 1, P. L. 45.

Written Application to Become Depositories.—Written Statement of Capital, Surplus, Etc., to be Verified by Oath.

Sec. 213. All banks, banking institutions, or trust companies desiring to become depositories of State moneys shall make written application to the State Treasurer for a deposit of State moneys, designating the amounts of deposits solicited, and accompanying their applications by a written statement of the amount of their capital actually paid in, the amount of their surplus, the number of their stockholders and whether their stock is well distributed, or largely held by a few individuals, and the length of time that said institution has been engaged in business under its charter, verified by the oath or affirmation of the president, cashier, or trust officers, as the case may be. Said State Treasurer shall present the same to the Revenue Commissioners and Banking Commissioner, acting jointly, for their consideration, within thirty days, and that where a selection of any bank, banking institution, or trust company as a depository of State moneys has been made by the Revenue Commissioners and the Banking Commissioner, or a majority of them, as aforesaid, without a previous application, as aforesaid, it shall be the duty of the depository so selected to furnish, on request, the information aforesaid, verified in the manner stated.—Act of 17th of February, 1906 Sec. 2, P. L. 45.

Selection of Private Banking Institutions.—Subject to Supervision and Examination.

Sec. 214. That the Revenue Commissioners and Banking Commissioner, or a majority of them, shall be and are hereby authorized to select as depositories for State funds private banking institutions, located and doing business in this Commonwealth: Provided, The same file a statement in writing, to the said Revenue Commissioners and the Banking Commissioner, that they will subject themselves to the same supervision, in all regards, as the other depositories named in the foregoing section, two. And provided further, That they will, in all regards, comply with the conditions required of any other depository; and after such selection of any private banking institution as a depository, the same shall be in all regards subject to such supervision and restrictions as other depositories selected by the Revenue Commissioners and Banking Commissioner, and be subject to examination by the State Banking Department and its examiners, at any time; and it shall be the duty of said Banking Department to make such examinations at any time after said private banking institutions become State depositories.—Act of 17th of February, 1906, Sec. 3, P. L. 45.

Limitation of Deposits.—Proviso.—Collections by Active Banks.

Sec. 215. That no bank, banking institution, or trust company shall receive a deposit of State moneys in excess of twenty-five per centum of its paid in capital and surplus; and no bank, banking institution, or trust company shall receive a deposit, or have at any one time an aggregate of deposits, in excess of three hundred thousand dollars ($300,000): Provided, That this section shall not apply to the institutions to be designated by the Revenue Commissioners and the Banking Commissioner, or a majority of them, as active depositories of State funds, subject to check daily by the State Treasurer. The active banks, so designated, shall be required to make all collections for the Commonwealth without cost or compensation, but at no time shall the combined deposits in the active banks exceed the total sum of five million dollars.—Act of 17th of February, 1906, Sec. 4, P. L. 45.

Banks Selected to Furnish a Bond in Favor of the Commonwealth.

Sec. 216. That all banks, banking institutions, and trust companies, selected as aforesaid, shall, upon the receipt of notice of such selection as depositories of State moneys, furnish a bond to secure payment of deposits and interest to the Commonwealth of Pennsylvania, with a proper warrant of attorney to confess judgment in favor of the Commonwealth, secured by a surety company or individual sureties, to be approved by the Revenue Commissioners and Banking Commissioner, or a majority of them, in double the amount of the deposit to be made, and, if corporate bonds are given, no one company shall be approved in an aggregate amount in excess of five times its capital, surplus and reserve.—Act of 17th of February, 1906, Sec. 5, P. L. 45.

Individual Sureties to Qualify.

Sec. 217. That whenever individual sureties are presented for approval, they shall qualify in an aggregate, over and above their individual liabilities, to three times the amount of the deposit; no one person to qualify for more than one-fourth of the total amount required.—Act of 17th of February, 1906, Sec. 6, P. L. 45.

Deposit of Securities in Lieu of Bonds of Sureties.

Sec. 218. That in lieu of the surety bonds of surety companies, or of individuals, as aforesaid, the deposit of State moneys may be secured by the deposit with the State Treasurer of United States, municipal, or county bonds, to be approved by the Revenue Commissioners and the Banking Commissioner, or a majority of them, in an amount, measured by their actual market value, equal to the amount of deposit so secured and twenty per centum besides. Said bonds to be accompanied by proper assignments or power of attorney to transfer the same, and said trust deposit of securities to be maintained, on request, at the amount aforesaid, in case of any depreciation in the value thereof.—Act of 17th of February, 1906, Sec. 7, P. L. 45.

Interest Rate Upon Deposits.—Active Depositories in Certain Counties.

Sec. 219. The interest rate to be paid by the depositories upon all State deposits shall be at the rate of two per centum per annum, and all distinctions between active and non-active depositories, as to interest rate, shall be abolished.

The Revenue Commissioners and the Banking Commissioner, or a majority of them, shall designate two banks or trust companies in Dauphin county, two banks or trust companies in Philadelphia county, and two banks or trust companies in Allegheny county, to be known as active depositories, in which shall be deposited a sufficient amount of the daily receipts of the State Treasury to transact the current business of the Commonwealth.—Act of 17th of February, 1906, Sec. 8, P. L. 45.

Powers and Duties of State Treasurer.—Withdrawals by State Treasurer.—His Liability.

Sec. 220. Nothing in the act contained shall be held to prevent the State Treasurer from withdrawing any or all of said funds, so deposited, for the purpose of paying the appropriations and obligations of the Commonwealth; and nothing herein contained shall in any way affect the duty of the State Treasurer to keep a correct and accurate account of all moneys received for the use of the Commonwealth, and pay out the same only on authority of law; but the said State Treasurer shall be, as heretofore, personally responsible for a faithful performance of his duties under the law, and for a proper

accounting of all moneys paid to him as State Treasurer; but he shall
not be held personally liable for any moneys that may be lost by reason of the failure or insolvency of any bank, banking institution or
trust company selected as aforesaid.—Act of 17th of February, 1906,
Sec. 9, P. L. 45.

Reduction, Change or Withdrawal of Deposits.

Sec. 221. The Revenue Commissioners and the Banking Commissioner, or a majority of them, in case they are of the opinion that
the credit of any of said depositories is impaired, the safety of the
State reposits imperiled, or for any other cause whatsoever, shall
have power and authority to require the State Treasurer to reduce,
change, or wholly withdraw, within thirty days, any deposit or deposits held by any such depository or depositories.—Act of 17th of
February, 1906, Sec. 10, P. L. 45.

Monthly Statement of State Treasurer to be Verified, Recorded and Published.

Sec. 222. The State Treasurer, on the first business day of each
month, shall render a statement of account to the Auditor General,
giving in detail the different sums which go to make up the grand
total of the amount on that day in the State Treasury, including
moneys appropriated to the sinking fund. Such statement shall include the names of banks, banking institutions or trust companies
with whom the public funds are deposited, with the various amounts
of such deposits, and shall be verified by oath or affirmation of the
State Treasurer, and recorded in a book kept for that purpose in the
Auditor General's office; and such record shall be open for the inspection of the Governor, heads of departments, members of the
Legislature, or any citizen of the State desiring to inspect the same;
and shall be correctly published in not more than six newspapers,
two of which shall be published at Harrisburg, to be selected by the
Auditor General, for general information; payment of publication
to be made from moneys in the State Treasury, not otherwise appro-
propriated.—Act of 17th of February, 1906, Sec. 11, P. L. 45.

Misdemeanor to Pay, Receive, Offer or Request for Use of State Money any Other Than Interest Payable to the State.

Sec. 223. It shall be a misdemeanor for any individual, whether a
State officer, representative of a State officer, or a bank officer, or any
representatives of a bank or bank officer, or office of any trust company, or representative of any such officer, or any go-between, to
pay, receive, offer, or request any money or valuable thing or promise
for the use of such State moneys, other than the interest payable
to the State; or for any person to secure, or assist in securing, a State
deposit for his or her own personal gain or benefit. Said misdemeanor shall be punishable by a fine of not less than five hundred
dollars and not less than one year's imprisonment for each offense.—
Act of 17th of February, 1906, Sec. 12, P. L. 45.

Repealing Clause.

Sec. 224. All acts or parts of acts inconsistent herewith be and
the same are hereby repealed.—Act of 17th of February, 1906, Sec.
13, P. L. 45.

CHAPTER 7.

CO-OPERATIVE BANKING ASSOCIATIONS.—TITLE OF ACT
FOR CO-OPERATIVE BANKING ASSOCIATIONS: "AN ACT
TO ENCOURAGE AND AUTHORIZE THE FORMATION OF
CO-OPERATIVE BANKING ASSOCIATIONS WHERE THE
PROFITS DERIVED FROM THE BUSINESS, AFTER PAY-
ING ALL LEGITIMATE EXPENSES, SHALL ACCRUE TO
THE DEPOSITORS AND BORROWERS OF THE ASSOCIA-
TION IN PROPORTION TO THEIR DEPOSITS OR LOANS.

Incorporated Upon Compliance with the Constitution.—To Have
Articles of Association.—How Net Profits to be Divided.

Sec. 225. Co-operative banking associations may be incorporated
under this act upon compliance with the requirements of section
eleven, article sixteen, State Constitution, when ten or more persons
of lawful age, citizens of this Commonwealth, who shall have associated themselves together by written articles of association for the
purpose of carrying on a co-operative banking business where the
profits derived from the business shall, after paying all legitimate
expenses, be divided pro rata among the depositors and borrowers
of the bank in proportion to their deposits or loans to each class,
one-half of the net profits; and a dividend not to exceed six per
centum per annum on original subscribed stock may be considered
legitimate expenses.—Act of 18th of May, 1893, Sec. 1, P. L. 89.

State Constitution.

Sec. 226. No corporate body to possess banking and discounting
privileges shall be created or organized in pursuance of any law
without three months previous public notice at the place of the intended location of the intention to apply for such privileges, in such
manner as shall be prescribed by law; nor shall a charter for such
privileges be granted for a longer period than twenty years.—Sec.
11, Article 16 of State Constitution.

Corporate Name.—Last Three Words to be "Co-operative Banking
Association."—Members Personally Liable for Debts if Proper
Name not Given.

Sec. 227. Such persons so associating may adopt any corporate
name indicating their co-operative character and which has not been
previously adopted by any other corporation formed under this act;
Provided, The last three words of such name shall be Co-operative
Banking Association, and it shall not be lawful to use in such name
either of the words "society" or "company," and that any violation
of this proviso by any corporation formed under this act shall ren-

6

der each member thereof personally liable for all its debts.—Act of 18th of May, 1893, Sec. 2, P. L. 89.

Where Articles to be Filed and Recorded.—May be Used in Evidence. —When Body to be Deemed Incorporated.

Sec. 228. Before any company formed under this act shall commence its business its articles of association shall be filed and recorded in the office of the Secretary of the Commonwealth, and two copies of said articles shall be made which the said Secretary of the Commonwealth shall certify by his official signature and the seal of this Commonwealth as being correct copies of said articles so filed and recorded; one of said certified copies shall be filed and recorded in the office of the clerk of the county in which the office of the association shall be located and the said clerk shall certify by his official signature and seal of his office that the said certified copy of said articles has been filed and recorded in his office, and the other certified copy of said articles shall be held by the association named therein, and the said articles or copies thereof, duly certified by either of the aforesaid officers, may be used as evidence in all courts and places of the incorporation of as well as for or against such association, and the said Secretary of the Commonwealth and the said county clerk shall be paid for said filing and recording and certifying at the rate of ten cents for each hundred words contained in said articles, and after such articles of association shall have been made, filed and recorded as herein required, the person signing the same and such other persons, partnerships or corporations who shall, from time to time, own or posses any share in the stock capital of such association, and their several successors and assigns, shall be deemed and taken to be a body corporate, and by the name and for the purposes mentioned in such articles of association.—Act of 18th of May, 1893, Sec. 2, P. L. 89.

Articles to be Signed, Etc.—What Articles to Contain.—Standing of Stockholders to be Approved by Superintendent of Banking Department.

Sec. 229. The articles of association shall be signed by the persons originally associating themselves together and shall be acknowledged by at least five of them before a notary public, and shall state distinctly, (a) the name by which this association shall be known, (b) the place in this State where its principal office is to be located, (c) the purpose or object for which it is formed, (d) amount of its stock capital, (e) the amount of each share of stock of such capital, such shares not to exceed ten dollars per share, and how such share may be paid for, (f) the amount of capital that will be actually paid in before commencing business; also amount of preferred stock to be assigned to stockholders who may hereafter earn stock from custom dividends, (g) whether, and if so, to what extent, loans or deposits of money are to be received for use in its business, (h), the terms upon which persons may become members, (i) on what days in January regular annual meetings of the members are to be held, (j) such other matters not repugnant to this act, as may be deemed proper and necessary, (k) the term of its existence not to exceed twenty years, (l) and names of first associates, their respective residences and the number of shares held by each of them. No such association shall commence business until the financial standing, responsibility and character of the original stockholders shall have been approved and certified by the Superintendent of the Banking Department of the Commonwealth.—Act of 18th of May, 1893, Sec. 3, P. L. 89.

Stock Capital to Consist of Amounts Outstanding to Credit of Members on Account of Shares.—Certificates to be Issued as Shares Fully Paid up or Earned. •

Sec. 230. The stock capital of any such association shall consist of the amounts standing to the credit of the members on account of the shares allotted to them, certificates of which shall be issued from time to time as shares shall be fully paid up or earned.—Act of 18th of May, 1893, Sec. 4, P. L. 89.

List of Stockholders, Amount of Stock Held by Each, Etc.—To be Posted in Principal Office.

Sec. 231. It shall be the duty of such company to exhibit in some conspicuous place in its principal office, at all times, a list of stockholders and the amount of stock held by each stockholder, the amount of stock subscribed or earned at the time of each last annual meeting; also the amount of preferred stock which shall not be liability stock, only as it becomes assigned to individual stockholders.—Act of 18th of May, 1893, Sec. 5, P. L. 89.

Duty of Auditors.—Contents of Statement to be Posted in Office of the Company.

Sec. 232. It shall be the duty of the auditors to audit all books, papers and vouchers of the company annually, or at any time when called upon in writing so to do by the president or any ten of the stockholders, or twenty of the depositors when joined by at least five of the stockholders, and each of these audits shall be rendered in writing which shall give a statement of the assets and liabilities of said company; also a detailed statement of the character and nature of all the notes and securities held by the association, and such statement shall be posted conspicuously in the office.—Act of 18th of May, 1893, Sec. 6, P. L. 89.

When Profit Shall be Paid to Stockholders.

Sec. 233. No profit shall be paid out to any stockholder until the total registered amount of stock shall be fully paid in cash, or earned from the net profits of the company.—Act of 18th of May, 1893, Sec. 7, P. L. 89.

Minors May Hold Shares in or Make Loans to or Deposits With Association.—Not to Hold Office in.

Sec. 234. It shall be lawful, if the by-laws so provide, for any minor to take and hold shares in, or to make loans or deposits of money to or with any such corporation, and for such association to pay any minor any moneys that may be due to him in respect of any shares, loans or deposits standing in his name, and his receipt therefor shall be in all respects valid in law, but such minor shall not be eligible to hold any office in such association though he may be subject to its by-laws and vote at any meeting of its members.—Act of 18th of May, 1893, Sec. 8, P. L. 89.

Depositors and Borrowers Not to Withdraw Dividends but Take Full Paid Stock in Lieu Thereof.—When to Become voting Members.

Sec. 235. Depositors and borrowers to whom dividends are due shall not withdraw the same, but shall take full paid stock in lieu thereof, until the registered and preferred stock of the company becomes fully paid up, and as each share of stock becomes fully paid up, this class of stockholders may become voting members, but each shareholder shall be entitled to but one vote on each share of stock.—Act of 18th of May, 1893, Sec. 9, P. L. 89.

Board of Directors, Number and Powers.—Loans of Association.

Sec. 236. The company shall be controlled by a board of six directors who shall serve for three years, two of which shall be elected annually, and provision shall be made at the first election to elect two to serve one year, two to serve two years, and two for three years. Said directors shall elect a president and secretary from their number, and said directors shall have full control of all employes and business of the association, subject to the by-laws, but no employe shall be a director. The by-laws shall provide rules and regulations for the loaning or discounting of the capital and deposits of the association and the nature of its securities, and no loan shall be made to any individual, firm or company, either singly or collectively, in excess of ten per centum of the deposits of the association at the time of making such loan, and any violation of this provision will render the person or cashier so making, liable upon his bond, and the directors sanctioning such a loan will render them individually liable, unless a protest be entered at the first monthly meeting subsequent to the making of such loan.—Act of 18th of May, 1893, Sec. 9, P. L. 89.

Auditors to be Elected Annually.—Notice of Election to be Given.

Sec. 237. Two auditors shall be elected annually by the stockholders from their number at their annual meeting in January, and one auditor shall be elected by the depositors from their number on the first Monday of each December, notice of which election shall be posted conspicuously in the bank room for at least three weeks prior to the election of such auditor, all of which shall serve for one year. —Act of 18th of May, 1893, Sec. 9, P. L. 89.

Liability of Members.—How and When to be Proceeded Against.

Sec. 238. The members shall be severally and jointly liable for all deposits, debts for labor, or service of any kind performed for such association, and for any other debts lawfully incurred under the provisions of this act; each of the members shall be liable to twice the amount of his subscribed or earned stock capital, and no more, but no suit shall be brought or any execution issued against any member individually until a judgment be first obtained for such deposits, labor, services, or other lawful debts against such association, and execution thereon be returned unsatisfied, in whole or in part, and in case any member shall be compelled to pay any such judgment, or any part thereof, beyond his pro rata liability therefor, he shall have the right to call upon all the members to pay their pro rata share of the same, or up to their pro rata liability therefor, and may sue them jointly, or severally, or any number of them, and recover in such action the ratable amounts due from the member or members so sued.—Act of 18th of May 1893, Sec. 10, P. L. 89.

Powers of Association.

Sec. 239. Any such association may take, hold lease and convey such real estate as may be necessary for the purpose of its organization, and may sue and be sued in its corporate name, and may submit any matter in dispute to arbitration, and shall have a common seal, which shall not be altered or imitated, and shall bear the corporate name of, together with such device or motto as may be adopted by such association, and such seal shall be impressed upon the articles of association.—Act of 18th of May, 1893, Sec. 11, P. L. 89.

Bond to be Given by Persons Appointed to Receive Money of Association.—Employees May be Required to Give Bond.

Sec. 240. Any person appointed to any position in any such association requiring the receipt, payment, management or use of money belonging to such association, shall, before entering upon the discharge of his duties, become bound with two or more good and sufficient sureties, or insurance bonds, in such sum and form as the directors shall require and approve; and the directors may also require from any other employes of such association, bonds with good and sufficient sureties for the faithful discharge of duties.—Act of 18th of May, 1893, Sec. 12, P. L. 89.

First Meeting and How it May be Called.—By-laws to be Made and Officers to be Elected.

Sec. 241. The first meeting of any such association may be called by a notice signed by any two of the associates who signed its articles of association, setting forth the time and place and objects of such meetings, such notice to be mailed to the address of each associate, at least four days clear prior to such meeting, and a majority of such associates at such meeting shall be competent to make all such by-laws as they may deem necessary for the proper management of the association, so that any such by-laws are not repugnant to or inconsistent with the provisions of this act, or any law of the State or United States, and to elect such officers as are heretofore provided by this act, and such officers shall hold office until their successors shall have been elected and installed.—Act of 18th of May, 1893, Sec. 13, P. L. 89.

How Articles and By-laws May be Amended or Extended.

Sec. 242. Any association may alter or amend its articles of association and may alter or rescind any by-laws or make any additional by-laws with the consent of the majority of its members present at a special meeting convened for such purpose, but the notice calling such meeting shall set forth fully and clearly the proposed alterations, amendment, recision or addition; and any alteration or amendment of the articles of association shall be approved, filed, recorded and certified in the same manner as the original articles of association.—Act of 18th of May, 1893, Sec. 14, P. L. 89.

CHAPTER 8.

TRUST COMPANIES.

Power of Certain Trust Companies Enlarged "To Receive Upon Deposit Valuable Property of Every Description.—To Act as Agent for Issuing Stocks, Bonds and Other Obligations and to Receive and Manage Sinking Funds.

Sec. 243. All companies incorporated under the laws of this Commonwealth, which are by their charters authorized to act as trustees, receivers, assignees, guardians and committees, be and they are hereby authorized:

First. To receive upon deposit for safe keeping jewelry, plate, stocks, bonds and valuable property of every description, upon such terms as may be agreed upon.

Second. To act as agents for the purpose of issuing or countersigning the certificates of stock, bonds or other obligations of any corporation, association, municipality, State or public authority and to receive and manage any sinking fund thereof on such terms as may be agreed upon.—Act of 11th of June, 1885, Sec. 1, P. L. 111.

Increase of Capital Stock and Amount Thereof.—Par Value May be Changed.

Sec. 244. Whenever such companies shall desire to increase their capital stock they may do so according to the forms prescribed by law: Provided, The amount of capital stock after such increase shall not exceed two million dollars, and may change the par value of the shares to one hundred dollars each.—Act of 11th of June, 1885, Sec. 2, P. L. 111.

Must First Accept Provisions of the New Constitution and File With Commissioner of Banking Certificates of Acceptance.

Sec. 245. Such companies before exercising any of the powers conferred by this act, shall first accept the provisions of the Constitution of this Commonwealth adopted December sixteenth, one thousand eight hundred and seventy-three and shall file with the Secretary of the Commonwealth a certificate of such acceptance in writing under their duly authenticated seal.—Act of 11th of June, 1885, Sec. 3, P. L. 111.

As amended by act of 11th of February, 1895, P. L. 4.

Increase of Powers of Trust Companies.

Sec. 246. Amendment of the fourth section of the act of the ninth day of May, 1889, supplementary to the twenty-ninth section of the act of 1874, giving trust companies power to act as assignees, receivers, guardians, executors, administrators, and to take, accept and execute trusts of every description not inconsistent with the laws of this State or of the United States, and to receive deposits of moneys and other personal property and issue their obligations therefor, to invest their funds in and to purchase real and personal securities and to loan money on real and personal securities.—Act of 29th of May, 1895, Sec. 1, P. L. 127.

Court May Order Money to be Deposited in Trust Company.

Sec. 247. Every court into which money may be paid by parties or be brought by order or judgment may, by order, direct the same to be deposited with any such corporation.—Act of 29th day of May, 1895, Sec. 2, P. L. 127.

How Surety Company Can Act as Surety and Guarantee.

Sec. 248. Whenever any bond, undertaking, recognizance or other obligation is, by law, or the charter, ordinances, rules or regulations of any municipality, board, body, organization or public officer, required or permitted to be made, given, tendered or filed with surety or sureties, and whenever the performance of any act, duty or obligation, or the refraining from any act, is required or permitted to be guaranteed, such bond, undertaking, obligation, recognizance or guarantee will be executed by a surety company qualified to act as surety or guarantor as hereinafter provided, and such execution by such company of such bond, undertaking, recognizance, obligation or guarantee shall be in all respects a full and complete compliance with every requirement of every law, charter, ordinance, rule or regulation, that such bond, undertaking, obligation, recognizance or guarantee shall be executed by one surety or by one or more sureties, or that such sureties shall be residents or householders or freeholders or either, or both, or possess any other qualification.—Act of the 26th of June, 1895, Sec. 1, P. L. 343.

Company Must be Qualified to Act as Surety Under Existing Laws. —Must Have Paid up Capital of $250,000.—Requisites to Qualify.

Sec. 249. Such company, to be qualified to so act as surety or guarantor, must be authorized under the laws of any State or country where incorporated; and its charter to guarantee the fidelity of persons holding places of public or private trust, and to guarantee the performance of contracts other than insurance policies, and to execute bonds and undertakings required or permitted in actions or proceedings or by law allowed, must comply with the requirements of the laws of this State applicable to such company in doing business therein, must have a paid up, unimpaired and safely invested capital of at least two hundred and fifty thousand dollars, must have at least one hundred thousand dollars invested in securities created by the laws of the United States, or by or under the laws of the State or country wherein it is incorporated, or in other safe, marketable and interest bearing stocks and securities, the value of which shall be at or above par and deposited with or held by the Insurance Commissioner or other corresponding officer of the State or country where such company is domiciled, or any State of the United States in which it is authorized to transact business, in trust for the benefit of the holders of the obligations of such company; its liabilities must not exceed its available assets, which said liabilities, however, shall be taken to be its capital stock, its outstanding debts and a premium reserved equal to fifty per centum of the annual premium on all outstanding risks in force; such company shall also, before transacting business in this State under this act, file with the Insurance Commissioner a certified copy of its charter or act of incorporation, a written application to be authorized to do business under this act, and a statement signed and sworn to by its president or one of its vice presidents and its secretary or one of its assistant secretaries, stating the amount of its paid up cash capital, particularly each item of investment, the amount of premium on existing bonds upon which it is surety, the amount of liability for unearned portion thereof estimated at fifty per centum of the annual premium on all outstanding premiums for one year or less, and pro rata for terms of more than one year, stating also the amount of its outstanding debts of all kinds; and if such company is incorporated under the laws of any other State or country than this State, it shall, in addition thereto, file a power of attorney appointing some resident of this State upon whom service process may be made as required by existing laws, whereupon, if the Insurance Commissioner be satisfied that such company is solvent and has the cash capital herein provided for and surplus assets in excess of its capital stock, its outstanding debts and the premium reserve specified, and that it has, in all respects, complied with and is qualified under this act, he shall issue to such company and to each of its agents in this State his certificate that it is authorized to become and be accepted as sole surety on all bonds, undertakings and obligations required or permtited by law or the charter, ordinances, rules or regulations of any municipality, board, body, organization or public officer, which said certificate shall be conclusive proof of the solvency and credit of such company for all purposes and of its right to be so accepted as such sole surety and its sufficiency as such. Such company shall also annually, in the month of January, file with the Insurance Commissioner a statement similar to that hereinbefore in this section provided for, and shall also furnish him with a certificate from the officer with whom the deposit herein mentioned is required to be made, describing such securities so deposited and the manner in which they are held by him, and stating that he is satisfied that such securities are fully worth one hundred thousand dollars, and also shall furnish the Insurance Commissioner with such other information touching the condition and credit as he may require, signed and sworn to as in this section required.—Act of 26th of June, 1895, Sec. 2, P. L. 343.

Deposit of Moneys for Which Sureties are Liable.—Withdrawal of Moneys.

Sec. 250. It shall be lawful for any party of whom a bond or undertaking is required to agree with his sureties for the deposit of any or all moneys for which said securities are or may be held responsible with a trust company authorized by law to receive such deposit, if such deposit is otherwise proper, and for the safe keeping of any and all other depositable assets for which said sureties are or may be held responsible with a safe deposit company authorized by law to do business as such, in such manner as to prevent the withdrawal of such moneys and assets, or any part thereof, except with the written consent of such sureties, or an order of the court made on such notice to them as such court may direct.—Act of 26th of June, 1895, Sec. 3, P. L. 343.

Company Cannot Deny Corporate Power.

Sec. 251. No company having signed such a bond, undertaking or obligation shall be permitted to deny its corporate power to execute such instruments or incur such liability in any proceeding to enforce liability against it thereunder.—Act of 26th of June, 1895, Sec. 4, P. L. 343.

Repealing Clause.

Sec. 252. All laws or parts of laws inconsistent herewith are hereby repealed.—Act of 26th of June, 1895, Sec. 5, P. L. 343.

An Act Amending the 29th Section of the Act of 29th of April, 1874, Giving Title Companies, Incorporated Thereunder, Additional Powers.—Additional Powers Granted to Insure Titles to Real Estate.—To Receive and Hold Property in Trust.—But Must Not Engage in Banking Business.—To Insure Fidelity of Persons, Etc.—To Act as Agents.—To Become Sole Surety.—To Take, Receive and Hold Certain Property.—To Purchase and Sell Real Estate.—To Secure Faithful Performance of Contracts.—To Become Sole Security for Certain Officers.—To Become Security for Clerks.—To Become Security for Payment of Damages for Lands Taken for Public Use.—To Become Security in Court Proceedings.—Proviso, Must Have a Paid-up Capital Stock of $125,000.—Certificate of Amount of Paid-up Capital Stocks.—Capital Liable for Faithful Discharge of Duties of Trust.—Authorized Depositories of Certain Trust Property.—Courts May Authorize Investigation of the Affairs of Such Company.—Shall Keep Trust Funds, Etc., Separate From Assets of Company.

Sec. 253, Clause I. Companies which may have heretofore, or which may hereafter be, incorporated under the provisions of this act for the insurance of owners of real estate, mortgagees and others interested in real estate from loss by reason of defective titles, liens and incumbrances, shall have the power and right—

1. To make insurances of every kind pertaining to or connected with titles to real estate, and to make, execute and perfect such and so many contracts, agreements, policies and other instruments as may be required therefor.

2. To receive and hold on deposit and in trust and as security estate, real and personal, including the notes, bonds, obligations of States, individuals, companies and corporations, and the same to purchase, collect, adjust and settle, sell and dispose of in any

manner, without proceeding in law or equity, and for such price and on such terms as may be agreed on between them and parties contracting with them: Provided, That nothing herein contained shall authorize said companies to engage in the business of banking.

3. To make insurance for the fidelity of persons holding places of responsibility and of trust, and to receive upon deposit for safe keeping, jewelry, plate, stocks, bonds and valuable property of every description, upon terms as may be agreed upon.

4. To act as assignees, receivers, guardians, executors, administrators, and to execute trusts of every description not inconsistent with the laws of this State or of the United States.

5. To act as agents for the purpose of issuing or countersigning the certificates of stock, bonds or other obligations of any corporation, association or municipality, State or public authority, and to receive and manage any sinking fund thereof on such terms as may be agreed upon.

6. To become sole surety in any case where, by law, one or more sureties may be required for the faithful performance of any trust, office, duty, action or engagement.

7. To take, receive and hold any and all such pieces of real property as may have been, or may hereafter be, the subject of any insurance made by such companies under the powers conferred by their charter, and the same to grant, bargain, sell, convey and dispose of in any such manner as they see proper.

8. To purchase and sell real estate and take charge of the same.

9· To act as security for the faithful performance of any contract entered into with any person, or municipal or other corporation, or with any State or government, by any person or persons, corporation or corporations.

10. To become sole security for the faithful performance of the duties of any national, State, county or municipal officer, and to execute such bonds or recognizances as may be required by law in such cases.

11. To become security for the faithful performance of the duties of any clerk or employe of any corporation, company, firm or individual.

12. To become security for the payment of all damages that may be assessed and directed to be paid for lands taken in the building of any railway, or for the purposes of any railway, or for the opening of streets or roads, or for any purpose whatever where land or other property is authorized by law to be taken.

13. To become security upon any writ of error or appeal, or in any proceeding instituted in any court of this Commonwealth, in which security may be required: Provided however, That nothing in this act shall be so construed as to dispense with the approval of such body, corporation, court or officer as is by law now required to approve such security: Provided however, That before exercising any of the powers hereby conferred, each such corporation shall have a paid up capital of not less than one hundred and twenty-five thousand dollars, an affidavit of which fact, made by the treasurer thereof, shall be filed in the office of the Secretary of the Commonwealth, and each such company, heretofore or hereafter incorporated, shall file in the office of the Secretary of the Commonwealth a certificate of its acceptance hereof, made by formal resolution

adopted at a regular or called meeting of the directors, trustees, managers or other proper officers thereof and certified under the corporate seal of such company, and a copy of such affidavit and of such resolution certified under the seal of the office of the Secretary of the Commonwealth shall be evidence of compliance with the requirements hereof.

Clause II. Whenever such companies shall receive and accept the office or appointment of assignees, receiver, guardian, executor, administrator, or to be directed to execute any trust whatever, the capital of said company shall be taken and considered as the security required by law for the faithful performance of their duties as aforesaid, and shall be absolutely liable in case of any default whatever.

Clause III. Any executor, administrator, guardian or trustee having the custody or control of any bonds, stock, securities or other valuables belonging to others, shall be authorized to deposit the same for safe keeping with said companies.

Clause IV. Whenever any court shall appoint said companies assignees, receiver, guardian, executor, administrator, or to execute any trust whatever the said court may, in its discretion, or upon the application of any person interested, appoint a suitable person to investigate the affairs and management of the company so appointed, who shall report to such court the manner in which its investments are made and the security afforded to those by or for whom its engagements are held, and the expense of such investigation shall be defrayed by the said company; or the court may, if deemed necessary, examine the officers of said company under oath or affirmation as to the security aforesaid.

Clause V. The said companies shall keep all trust funds and investments separate and apart from the assets of the companies, and all investments made by the said companies as fiduciaries shall be so designated as that the trust to which such investment shall belong shall be clearly known.—Act of 27th of June, 1895, Sec. 1, P. L. 399.

Company Must Furnish Affidavit of Paid Up Capital Stock Before it Shall be Entitled to Benefits of Act.

Sec. 254. Any company entitled to the benefits of this act and desirous of availing itself of the same, shall furnish the affidavit as to paid up capital required by the said supplementary act, and conform to all other conditions and requirements thereof applicable to companies organized under the provisions of the said act, approved the twenty-ninth day of April, Anno Domini one thousand eight hundred and seventy-four, and the aforesaid supplement thereto.—Act of 27th of June, 1895, Sec. 2, P. L. 399.

When Trustee Required to Give Bond as Such, to be Allowed the Expense of Bond of Company in His Account.—Maximum Amount of Charges.

Sec. 255. Any receiver, assignee, guardian, committee, trustee, executor or administrator, required by law or by the order of any court to give a bond as such, may include as a part of the lawful expense of executing his trust such reasonable sum paid a company. authorized under the laws of this State so to do, for becoming his

surety on such bond as may be allowed by the court in which he
is required to account, not exceeding, however, one per centum per
annum on the amount of such bond.—Act of 24th of June, 1895,
Sec. 1, P. L. 248.

Repeal.

Sec. 256. This act shall take effect immediately, and that all
acts and parts of acts inconsistent herewith are hereby repealed.—
Act of 24th of June, 1895, Sec. 2, P. L. 248.

Authorizing the Taking of a Trust Company as Sole Security.—
Qualifications.

Sec. 257. Whenever any person individually, or in any public or
private trust, who is now or hereafter may be required or permitted
by law to make or execute and give a bond, or undertaking with security, conditioned for the faithful performance of any duty or for the doing or not doing of anything in said bond or undertaking specified, any head of a
department, judge of the supreme court or prothonotary thereof,
judge of the court of common pleas, or prothonotary thereof, judge
of the orphans' court, register of wills, sheriff, magistrate or any
other officer who is now or shall be hereafter required to approve the
sufficiency of any such bond, or undertaking, may, in the discretion of
such officer, accept such bond or undertaking, and approve the same
whenever the conditions of such bond or undertaking are guaranteed by a company duly authorized by the insurance department of
this State to do business in this State, and authorized to guarantee the fidelity of persons holding positions of public or private
trust; and such company may become sole surety in any case where,
by law, one or more sureties may be required for the faithful performance of any trust or duty: Provided, however, That where such
bond or undertaking shall involve the safe keeping or faithful application of the assets of any fiduciary, such head of department, judge
or other officer shall make such order or decree as shall assure the
retention of such assets within this Commonwealth, in such manner
as such head of department, judge or other officer may direct, until
disposition thereof be made according to law.—Act of 25th of June,
1885, Sec. 1, P. L. 181.

Repeal.

Sec. 258. All acts or parts of acts inconsistent herewith are hereby
repealed.—Act of 25th of June, 1885, Sec. 2, P. L. 181.

Officers Like Private Persons to Make Oath When Corporation
Charged With Execution of Trust.

Sec. 259. In all cases where a corporation is or shall be charged
with the execution of any trust, the president, vice-president, trust
officer, secretary, treasurer or actuary of such corporation, shall
make the usual oath or affirmation directed to be taken by private
persons in such other like cases.—Act of 16th of February, 1877,
P. L. 3.

CHAPTER 9.

BUILDING AND LOAN ASSOCIATIONS.

Power to Purchase Adjoining Lands for Certain Purposes.

Sec. 260. Should any of the associations now or hereafter incorporated deem it necessary or expedient to purchase adjoining lands for the purpose of squaring their grounds in conformity with the streets running through or touching their lands, they are hereby fully authorized to make such purchases, and are invested with all the powers as regards the sale and conveyance in fee simple of the same given by this act, over the grounds squared by such purchases. —Act of 7th of March, 1853, Sec. 3, P. L. 155.

Investments by Building and Loan Associations.

Sec. 261. The act relative to investments by building associations, approved May eighth, one thousand eight hundred and fifty-five, shall be so construed as to extend to saving fund associations incorporated by the courts of common pleas, under an act entitled "A supplement to an act to prevent waste in certain cases within this Commonwealth," passed the twenty-ninth day of March, one thousand eight hundred and twenty-two, to land and building associations, etc., approved April twenty-second, one thousand eight hundred and fifty: Provided, That no company, incorporated under the last received act, or any supplement thereto, shall invest its capital stock, assets or moneys in the purchase or discount of any promissory note, bill of exchange or other negotiable paper, nor the stock of any incorporated company, nor receive moneys on deposit, other than the regular contributions of the members thereof.—Act of 8th of May, 1857, Sec. 1, P. L. 437.

Incorporation of Building Associations in Philadelphia.

Sec. 262. On the petition of any twelve or more citizens of Pennsylvania, the court of common pleas of the county of Philadelphia shall have all powers conferred by the acts relating to loan and building associations, to incorporate them and their associates as a perpetual corporation, for the purposes following, to wit: To purchase, hold and build upon and sell in fee simple, houses and lots in the city of Philadelphia, and also to make loans on bonds and mortgages to others to build and improve, and the same to sell and assign, and to borrow moneys upon bonds and mortgages or otherwise for said purposes; and in making sales or leases or loans on mortgages, it shall be lawful for such corporation, and borrowers of them, to agree upon, and insert in the deeds of conveyance, a condition against the use of any granted or leased premises for the sale of any intoxicating liquors, or unlawful immoral purposes, the carrying on any noxious or unhealthful business, with right of re-entry for breach of such condition: Provided, That no corporation chartered under this act shall have a greater capital than one-half million of dollars, and shall stipulate by their articles to devote their capital to improve or promote the improvement of parts of said city most needing physical, healthful and moral reform, which shall be defined and prescribed in its charter and not exceed eight main squares, and shall apply all their profits, over their expenses, and a return of eight per centum per annum to the shareholders to and for the construction of substantial stone, or brick or iron habitations for homes for respectable persons of limited means, either as lessees or purchasers: And provided, That the said court shall be satisfied of the benevolent purposes of the petitioners; and that the legislature may at any time repeal this act, and such charters, if the powers hereby granted should be found prejudicial to the community, but in manner to do no injustice to the corporators.—Act of 18th of February, 1869, Sec. 1, P. L. 201.

May Bring and Maintain Suits.—Officers to Represent the Corporation.

Sec. 263. All building, saving and loan associations may bring and maintain suits, and carry on those already brought, in their corporate names, on all judgments, bonds, mortgages, notes or other evidences of debt or obligations due them, or for monthly dues, interest or any demand owing to them, and proceed to judgment and execution, notwithstanding their charter may have expired; and the officers last elected, or the survivors of them, shall be the officers to represent said corporations for such purpose; and if no officers survive, the stockholders may elect others under their by-laws.—Act of 26th of April, 1869, Sec. 1, P. L. 1223.

Power to Collect Debts After Expiration of Charter Restricted.

Sec. 264. This act shall only be construed so as to enable said associations to collect up and divide their assets and wind up their affairs, and not to allow them to transact new business: Provided, That this act shall only apply to the city of Philadelphia.—Act of 26th of April, 1869, Sec. 2, P. L. 1223.

Corporate Powers, Etc.

Sec. 265. Building and loan associations incorporated under the provisions of this act, shall have the powers, and from the date of the letters patent creating the same, when not otherwise provided in this act, be governed, managed and controlled as follows:

I. They shall have the power and franchise of loaning or advancing to the stockholders thereof the moneys accumulated, from time to time, and the power and right to secure the repayment of such moneys, and the performance of the other conditions upon which the loans are to be made, by bond and mortgage or other security, as well as the power and right to purchase or erect houses, and to sell, convey, lease or mortgage the same at pleasure to their stockholders, or others for the benefit of their stockholders, in such manner also that the premiums taken by the said associations for the preference or priority of such loans, shall not be deemed usurious and so also that in case of non-payment of instalments, premiums or interest by borrowing stockholders, for six months, payment of principal, premiums and interest, without deducting the premium paid, or interest thereon, may be enforced by proceeding on their securities according to law.

II. The capital stock of any corporation created for such purposes, by virtue of this act, shall at no time consist in the aggregate of more than one million dollars, to be divided into shares of such denomination, not exceeding five hundred dollars each, and in such number as the corporators may, in the application for their charter, specify: Provided, That the capital stock may be issued in series, but no such series shall at any issue exceed in the aggregate five hundred thousand dollars, the instalments on which stock are to be paid at such time and place as the by-laws shall appoint; no period-ical payment of such instalments to be made exceeding two dollars on each share, and said stock may be paid off and retired as the by-laws shall direct; every share of stock shall be subject to a lien for the payment of unpaid instalments and other charges incurred thereon under the provisions of the charter and by-laws, and the by-laws may prescribe the form and manner of enforcing such lien; new shares of stock may be issued in lieu of the shares withdrawn or forfeited; the stock may be issued in one or in successive series, in such amount as the board of directors or the stockholders may determine; and any stockholder wishing to withdraw from the said corporation shall have the power to do so, by giving thirty days' notice of his or her intention to withdraw, when he or she shall be entitled to receive the amount paid in by him or her, less all fines and other charges; but after the expiration of one year from the issuing of the series, such stockholder shall be entitled, in addi-tion thereto, to legal interest thereon: Provided, That at no time shall more than one-half of the funds in the treasury of the corpora-tion be applicable to the demands of withdrawing stockholders, with-out the consent of the board of directors, and that no stockholder shall be entitled to withdraw, whose stock is held in pledge for security. Upon the death of a stockholder, his or her legal repre-sentatives shall be entitled to receive the full amount paid in by him or her, and legal interest thereon, first deducting all charges that may be due on the stock; no fines shall be charged to a deceased member's account, from and after his or her decease, unless his legal representatives of such decedent assume the future payments on the stock.

III. The number, titles, functions and compensation of the officers of any such corporation, their terms of office, the times of their elec-tions, as well as the qualifications of electors, and the ratio and manner of voting, and the periodical meetings of the said corpora-tion, shall be determined by the by-laws, when not provided by this act.

IV. The said officers shall hold stated meetings, at which the money in the treasury, if over the amount fixed by charter as the full value of a share, shall be offered for loan, in open meeting, and the stockholder who shall bid the highest premium for the prefer-ence or priority of loan, shall be entitled to receive a loan of not more than the amount fixed by charter as the full value of a share, for each share of stock held by such stockholder: Provided, That a stockholder may borrow such fractional part of the amount fixed by charter as the full value of a share as the by-laws may provide; good and ample security, as prescribed by the by-laws of the corporation, shall be given by the borrower, to secure the repayment of the loan; in case the borrower shall neglect to offer security, or shall offer security that is not approved by the board of directors, by such time as the by-laws may prescribe, he or she shall be charged with legal interest, together with any expenses incurred, and the loss in premium, if any, on a resale, and the money may be resold at the next stated meeting; in case of non-payment of instalments or interest by borrowing stockholders, for the space of six months, payment of principal and interest, without deducting the premium paid or interest thereon, may be enforced, by proceeding on their securities according to law.

V. A borrower may repay a loan at any time, and in case of the repayment thereof before the expiration of the eight years, after the organization of the corporation, there shall be refunded to such borrower one-eighth of the premium paid for every year of the said eight years then unexpired. Provided, When the stock is issued in separate series the time shall be computed from the date of the issuing the series of stock on which the loan was made.

VI. No premiums, fines, or interest on such premiums, that may accrue to the said corporation, according to the provisions of this act, shall be deemed usurious; and the same may be collected as debts of like amount are now by law collected in this Commonwealth.

VII. No corporation or association created under this act shall cease or expire, from neglect on the part of the corporators to elect officers at the time mentioned in their charter or by-laws; and all officers elected by such corporation shall hold their offices until their successors are duly elected.

VIII. Any loan or building association incorporated by or under this act, is hereby authorized and empowered to purchase at any sheriff's or other judicial sale, or at any other sale, public or private, any real estate upon which such association may have or hold any mortgage, judgment, lien or other incumbrance, or ground rent, or in which said association may have an interest, and the real estate so purchased, or any other that such association may hold or be entitled to at the passage of this act, to sell, convey, lease or mortgage, at pleasure, to any person or persons whatsoever, and all sales of real estate heretofore made by such associations to any person or persons not members of the association so selling, are hereby confirmed and made valid.

IX. All such corporations shall have full power to purchase lands and to sell and convey the same, or any part thereof, to their stockholders or others in fee simple, with or without the reservation of ground rents, but the quantity of land purchased by any one of said associations hereafter incorporated, shall not, in the whole, exceed fifty acres; and in all cases the lands shall be disposed of within ten years from the date of the incorporation of such associations respectively.

X. All land and building associations are hereby authorized to make sale of, and assign or extinguish, to any person or persons, the ground rents created as aforesaid.—Act of 29th of April, 1874, Sec. 37, P. L. 73.

May Convey Lands After Expiration of Charter.

Sec. 266. All deeds of conveyance of lands situate within this Commonwealth made by any savings fund, building or loan association after the term for which it was incorporated shall have expired, shall be as good and effectual, and have the same force and effect for passing title to the lands so conveyed as though executed during the period of its chartered existence.—Act of 17th of April, 1876, Sec. 1, P. L. 41.

Purchases and Sales by Building and Loan Associations Confirmed.

Sec. 267. All purchases of land heretofore made by building and loan associations, incorporated by virtue of any law of this Commonwealth, and also all sales of the same made by them to their stockholders or others are hereby confirmed, and the titles of said associations and their vendees are hereby declared good and valid, to all intents and purposes; and the said associations, their successors, or assigns, may sell, convey or lease, at pleasure, at any time within five years from the passage of this act, the undisposed-of portions of real estate so hereto purchased.—Act of 17th of June, 1878, Sec. 1, P. L. 214.

Payment of Premiums on Prior Loans.—Interest in Advance May be Deducted in Lieu of Premiums.

Sec. 268. It shall be lawful for any mutual savings fund, or building and loan association now incorporated or hereafter to be incorporated, in addition to dues and interest, to charge and receive the premium or bonus bid by a stockholder for preference or priority of right to a loan in periodical instalments; and such premium or bonus so paid in instalments shall not be deemed usurious, but shall be taken to be a payment as it falls due, in contradistinction to a premium charged and paid in advance; and in so far as said premium or bonus so charged and paid, in addition to dues and interest, shall be in excess of two dollars for each periodical payment, the same shall be lawful, any law, usage or custom to the contrary notwithstanding. It shall also be lawful for any mutual savings fund or building and loan association to charge and deduct interest in advance, in lieu of premiums for preference or priority of right to a loan: Provided, That the certificate of incorporation of each association hereafter to be incorporated, and the certificate provided in section nine of this act for those heretofore incorporated, shall set forth whether the premium or bonus bid for the prior right to a loan shall be deducted therefrom in advance or paid in periodical instalments, or whether interest in advance shall be deducted from the loan in lieu of premium or bonus.—Act of 10th of April, 1879, Sec. 1, P. L. 16.

Voluntary Withdrawals Regulated.

Sec. 269. Stockholders withdrawing voluntarily, shall receive such proportion of the profits of the association or such rate of interest as may be prescribed by the by-laws, any law or usage to the contrary notwithstanding; but payment of the value of stock, so withdrawn, shall only be due when the funds now by law applicable to the demand of withdrawing stockholders are sufficient to meet and liquidate the same, and then only in the order of the respective times of presentation of the notices of such withdrawals, which must have been presented in writing at a previous stated meeting, and have been then and there endorsed as to times of presentation by the officer designated by the by-laws of the association.—Act of 10th of April, 1879, Sec. 2, P. L. 16.

Involuntary Withdrawals Provided For.

Sec. 270. The by-laws may provide for the involuntary withdrawal and cancellation at or before maturity of shares of stock not borrowed on: Provided, That such withdrawal and cancellation shall be pro rata among the shares of the same series of stock: And provided further, That not less than legal interest shall be credited and allowed to each share so withdrawn and cancelled.—Act of 10th of April, 1879, Sec. 3, P. L. 16.

Re-payment of Loans.

Sec. 271. A borrower may repay a loan at any time, and in case of the repayment thereof before the maturity of the shares pledged for said loan, there shall be refunded to such borrower (if the premiums, bonus or interest shall have been deducted in advance) such proportions of the premiums, bonus or advance interest bid as the by-laws may determine: Provided, That in no case shall the association retain more than one one-hundredth of said premiums or bonus for each calendar month that has expired since the date of the meeting upon which the loan was made, or if interest in advance, it shall retain only the interest due on the loan up to the time of settlement: And further provided, That such borrower shall receive the withdrawing value of the shares pledged for said loan, and the shares shall revert back to the association.—Act of the 10th of April, 1879, Sec. 4, P. L. 16.

Payments of Instalments, Premiums, Etc.—How Enforced.

Sec. 272. In case of non-payment of instalments of stock, premiums, dues or interest, by borrowing stockholders, for the space of six months, payment of the same, together with the full principal of the loan, may be enforced by proceeding on their securities according to law; and the moneys so recovered shall be paid into the treasury of the association for such uses (loans or otherwise) as may be deemed proper by the association; and if the said moneys so recovered, together with the withdrawal value of the shares of such defaulting borrower shall exceed the amount it would have required according to the preceding section, to have voluntarily repaid the loan, together with all the expenses incurred by the association, such excess shall be repaid to such defaulting borrower.—Act of 10th of April, 1879, Sec. 5, P. L. 16.

Fines Regulated and Limited.

Sec. 273. Fines or penalties for the non-payment of instalments of dues, interest and bonus or premium, shall not exceed two per centum per month on all arrearages.—Act of 10th of April, 1879, Sec. 6, P. L. 16.

Married Women May Hold Stock.—Their Right as Stockholders.

Sec. 274. It shall be lawful for any married woman of full age to hold stock in any of said savings fund, building or loan associations; and as such stockholder she shall have all the rights and privileges of other members, including the right to borrow money from said associations and bid premiums therefor, and shall also have the right and power to secure such loan by transferring her said stock or other securities to said association, from which the same was borrowed, or by executing bond and mortgage upon her separate real estate to secure said loan: Provided, however, That the husband of such married woman join in the execution of such bond and mortgage; and such married woman shall also have the right to sell, assign and transfer her said stock or withdraw the same, without joining the husband in such transfer or withdrawal; and it shall be lawful for any such savings fund, building or loan association to collect such loan made to such married woman, including the dues, interest, premium and fines, as loans made by such associations to other members are now by law collected, and such stock or interest in such stock, shall not be liable for the debts of any husband of such married woman.—Act of 10th of April, 1879, Sec. 7, P. L. 16.

Bonus of Tax Due to Commonwealth Under Certain Acts Not to Apply to Building Associations.

Sec. 275. The bonus or tax due to the Commonwealth upon the capital stock of corporations, as provided for by act of first of May, one thousand eight hundred and sixty-eight, or by any other act, shall not apply to or be due from mutual savings fund, or building and loan associations; nor shall the registry for corporations, prescribed by the first section of the act of first of May, one thousand eight hundred and sixty-eight, the first section of the act of twenty-fourth of April, one thousand eight hundred and seventy-four, and the twenty-sixth section of the act of twenty-ninth of April, one thousand eight hundred and seventy-four, apply to or be required of mutual savings fund, or building and loan associations.—Act of 10th of April, 1879, Sec. 8, P. L. 16.*

Existing Associations Entitled to Benefits of Act. Mode of Procedure.

Sec. 276. Mutual savings fund, or building and loan associations, heretofore incorporated under the provisions of any law, shall be

---

*Act of June 7, 1879, P. L. 112, repealing Sec. 8.

entitled to all the privileges, immunities, franchises and powers conferred by this act, upon filing with the Secretary of the Commonwealth a certificate of their acceptance of the same in writing, under the duly authenticated seal of said association, which certificate shall also prescribe their mode or plan of charging premiums, bonus or advance interest, as set forth in the first section of this act; and upon such acceptance and approval thereof by the Governor, he shall issue letters patent to said corporation reciting the same.—Act of 10th of April, 1879, Sec. 9, P. L. 16.

Repeal.

Sec. 277. All laws or parts of laws inconsistent with the provisions of this act are hereby repealed.—Act of 10th of April, 1879, Sec. 10, P. L. 16.

Exemption From Taxation for State Purposes.

Sec. 278. Mutual loan and building associations shall be exempt from the provisions of each and every law imposing taxes for State purposes on their capital stock or mortgages, and other securities for moneys loaned to their own members; but the real estate owned by said association shall be subject to the same rates of taxation as the real estate of other corporations and persons: Provided, however, That the right of the Commonwealth to collect taxes already accrued is hereby reserved.—Act of 22nd of May, 1883, Sec. 1, P. L. 38.

May Borrow Money on Collateral and Loans to Stockholders.

Sec. 279. In addition to the corporate powers conferred on building and loan associations by the thirty-seventh section of the act of April twenty-ninth, one thousand eight hundred and seventy-four, they shall have the right, when applications for loans by the stockholders thereof shall exceed the accumulations in the treasury, to make temporary loans of such sum or sums of money to meet such demands, not exceeding in the aggregate of such loan at any time fifteen thousand dollars ($15,000), at a less rate of interest than six per centum, and secure the payment of the same by note, bond or assignment of its judgments and mortgages as collateral; said loans to be repaid out of the accumulations in the treasury, as soon as sufficient is paid in and there is no demand therefor by borrowing stockholders.—Act of 2nd of June, 1891, Sec. 1, P. L. 174.

Additional Powers Conferred.—Limit of Temporary Loans.

Sec. 280. In addition to the corporate powers conferred on building and loan associations by the thirty-seventh section of the act of twenty-ninth of April, one thousand eight hundred and seventy-four, they shall have the right, when a series of stock has matured, or when applications for loans by the stockholders thereof shall exceed the accumulations in the treasury, to make temporary loans of such sum or sums of money to meet such demands, not exceeding in the aggregate of such loan at any one time twenty-five per centum of the withdrawal value of the stock issued by said association at a rate of interest less than six per centum, and secure the payment of the same by interest bearing order, note or bond as collateral; said loans to be repaid out of the accumulations in the treasury as soon as sufficient is paid in and there is no demand therefor by borrowing stockholders.—Act of 25th of June, 1895, Sec. 1, P. L. 303.

An Act Taxing Certain Stocks of Building and Loan Associations for State Purpose.—Amount of Tax and How Payable.—Provisions as to Domestic and Foreign Corporations.—Duty of Banking Department.

Sec. 281. Upon all full paid, prepaid and fully matured, or partly matured stock in any building and loan association incorporated under the laws of this State, or incorpoarted under the laws of any other State and doing business within this State, and upon which annual, semi-annual, quarterly or monthly cash dividends or interest shall be paid, there shall be paid a State tax equal to that required to be paid upon money at interest by the general tax laws of this State; and such tax shall be deducted from the cash dividend or interest so provided for by the secretary or treasurer of such corporation and paid to the State Treasurer. And every such domestic corporation shall annually make return to the Auditor General, at the time other returns for taxation are required to be made, of the amount of its stock outstanding entitled to receive cash dividends or interest, and every such foreign corporation shall, in reports required to be made by them to the Banking Department, make report of the amount of its stock held by residents of this State, entitled to receive cash dividends or interest, and said Banking Department shall, at the time other returns for taxation are required to be made, certify to the Auditor General the amount of such stock each of said foreign corporations had outstanding at the time of its last report to said Banking Department; and upon said sum such foreign corporation shall pay the tax above required to be paid to the State Treasurer upon demand, and failure to make such payment within thirty days after such demand shall have been made, shall subject such corporation to the forfeiture of its right to transact business in this State: Provided however, That nothing in this act shall be taken to require the payment of any tax upon any unmatured stock of building and loan associations upon which periodical payments are required to be made or upon such stock after it has matured and is in process of payment.—Act of 22nd of June, 1897, Sec. 1, P. L. 178.

Repeal.

Sec. 282. All laws or parts of laws inconsistent herewith or supplied hereby are hereby repealed.—Act of 22nd of June, 1897, Sec. 2, P. L. 178.

Regulating Foreign Mutual Savings Fund or Building and Loan Associations Doing Business Within This Commonwealth, and Prescribing an Annual License Fee to be Paid by Such Associations.

Sec. 283. Be it enacted, &c., That from and after the first day of September, one thousand nine hundred and one, no mutual savings fund, building, building and loan, or co-operative loan association or corporation, or other association, company or corporation, by whatsoever name it may be called, claiming to have the right under its charter to take premiums for the preference or priority of loans, incorporated under the laws of any other State or foreign government, shall do any business within this Commonwealth without having fully complied with the requirements of this act, and without first having received a certificate from the Commissioner of Banking, certifying that it has fully complied therewith, and authorizing it to do business in this Commonwealth; and no person shall act as agent, solicitor or local treasurer of any such association, company or corporation, within this Commonwealth, in any manner whatsoever relating to the sale of stock of such association, company or corporation, soliciting subscriptions or receiving payments therefor, soliciting applications for loans or receiving payments on account of dues, fines or premiums upon stock or loans or in any manner relating to the business usually transacted by such association, company or corporation, until such association, company or corporation shall have received such aforesaid certificate from the Commissioner of Banking, and until such agent, solicitor or local treasurer shall himself have received a certificate from said Commissioner, authorizing him to act on behalf of such association, company or corporation: Provided, That any such association, company or corporation, doing business within this Commonwealth prior to the first day of September, one thousand nine hundred and one, and having prior to said date stock and loans, or either thereof, outstanding in this Commonwealth, may continue, either directly or through its agents, to collect instalments, interest, dues and premiums thereon; but the issuing of any new stock, soliciting subscriptions therefor, placing new loans, or soliciting applications therefor, or receiving payments on account of instalments, dues, fines, interest or premiums upon such new stock or loans, or transacting any other business within this Commonwealth other than such as relates to stock issued or loans made prior to said date, shall be deemed a violation of this section.—Act of 11th of May, 1901, Sec. 1, P. L. 153.

Requisites and Regulations for Beginning Business.—Provisions for Discontinuance of Business.—Duties of Trust Companies Acting as Depositories.

Sec. 284. No association, company or corporation described in the first section of this act shall be authorized by the Commissioner of Banking to do business within this Commonwealth until it shall satisfactorily appear to said Commissioner that such association, company or corporation is solvent, and has deposited with some trust company of this Commonwealth, to be approved by said Commissioner, the sum of at least one hundred thousand dollars in bonds of the United States, of the State of Pennsylvania, or of cities, counties, boroughs or school districts of this Commonwealth, as security for the creditors and shareholders thereof residing in this Commonwealth. None of the securities so deposited shall be withdrawn by any such association, company or corporation without the permission of said Commissioner, in writing and under the seal of his office, and no such withdrawal shall be permitted which will reduce the amount so deposited to less than the sum of one hundred thousand dollars. Exchanges of such bonds may be made, from time to time, with the approval of the Commissioner of Banking; and if any of said bonds are called in for payment, the proceeds thereof shall remain in the hands of the depositary until other bonds of the classes above mentioned shall be substituted, in like amount, for the bonds so paid, whereupon such depositary shall, with the permission in writing of the said Commissioner, pay over such proceeds to the association, company or corporation depositing said bonds. When any such association, company or corporation shall desire to discontinue its business within this Commonwealth, it may apply to the court of common pleas of Dauphin county, by petition, setting forth its resources and liabilities within and without this Commonwealth, and particularly its liabilities to creditors and shareholders within this Commonwealth; and thereupon, after due hearing, of which hearing the Commissioner of Banking shall have such notice as the said court may determine, the said court may make such order as will permit the withdrawal of said bonds or a part thereof, and will at the same time fully protect the rights of all creditors and shareholders of such association, company or corporation residing in this Commonwealth. Trust companies, acting as depositories under this section, shall pay over the income of the bonds deposited with them, as aforesaid, to the association, company or corporation depositing them, and shall make report in writing, signed and sworn to by the president or treasurer thereof, to the Commissioner of Banking, semi-annually, on the first day of January and the first day of July in each year, setting forth the amounts and kinds of bonds deposited with them, as aforesaid, and by what association, company or corporation the same have been deposited; and for failure to make such report within thirty days after the time fixed, as aforesaid, for making such reports, such trust company shall be liable to a penalty of fifty dollars, to be recovered in the name of the Commonwealth as other penalties are by law recoverable, and the amount so recovered shall be paid into the State Treasury. The trust company selected by any such association, company or corporation as its depository of bonds, under this section, may be changed from time to time by such association, company or corporation, with the approval in writing of the Commissioner of Banking.—Act of 11th of May, 1901, Sec. 2, P. L. 153.

Application to Commissioner of Banking for Certificate to do Business.—Regulations as to Certificate.

Sec. 285. Any association, company or corporation described in the first section of this act, desiring a certificate authorizing it to do business within this Commonwealth, shall present to the Commissioner of Banking its application, under its seal, therefor, accompanied by a statement, subscribed and sworn or affirmed to by its president or other principal officer and its treasurer, setting forth, in such form and in such detail as the said Commissioner may prescribe, its resources and liabilities; and said Commissioner may, before issuing such certificate, require such further information, under oath or affirmation, as he may deem necessary for the purpose of fully ascertaining the solvency of such association, company or corporation; and such application shall be further accompanied by a fee of one hundred dollars, which fee said Commissioner shall, immediately upon the issuing of such certificate, pay into the State Treasury. No such association, company or corporation shall receive such certificate, authorizing it to do business within this Commonwealth, or do business therein, until it has filed with said Commissioner a written stipulation under its seal, agreeing that any legal process affecting such association, company or corporation, served on the Commissioner of Banking or a person designated by him, or an agent designated in said stipulation to receive service of process for said association, company or corporation, shall have the same effect as if actually served on such association, company or corporation within this State; and if such association, company or corporation should cease to maintain such agent in this State, so designated, such process may thereafter be served on the Commissioner of Banking or on the person designated by him; but so long as any liability of such stipulating association, company or corporation to any resident of this State continues, such stipulation shall not be revoked or modified, except that a new one may be substituted, for the purpose of designating a different person to receive such service of process; and the term process, as used herein, shall include all process whatever, whether mesne or final, and all rules, notices, order or decrees in any judicial proceeding whatsoever, within this Commonwealth. And any such process may be served in any county of this Commonwealth in which the president or other principal officer, secretary, treasurer, or general manager, of such association, company or corporation, or the Commissioner of Banking, the person designated by said Commissioner, or the agent designated in said stipulation to receive service of process for such association, company or corporation, resides or may be found; and for the purpose of effecting such service, the sheriff, constable, or other officer to whom such process is directed, may deputize the sheriff, constable, or other officer, in the county in which such president or other principal officer, secretary, treasurer or general manager, the person designated by the Commissioner of Banking, or the agent designated in said stipulation, resides or may be found, or of the county in which the office of the Commissioner of Banking is located, to serve the same; and the fees of the officer serving such process shall be the same as are by law allowed for the service of similar process in other cases together with mileage allowed by law in such cases, the distance to be computed from the residence of the officer serving or executing such process, and no further.—Act of 11th of May, 1901, Sec. 3, P. L. 153.

Certificates to be Issued by Commissioner of Banking to Agents, Solicitors and Local Treasurers.

Sec. 286. Any association, company or corporation, described in the first section of this act and authorized to do business within this Commonwealth may, from time to time, designate to the Commissioner of Banking, in writing and under its seal, any agents, solicitors or local treasurers whom it desires to have authorized to do business for it within this Commonwealth; and thereupon the said Commissioner shall issue a certificate to each of said agents, solicitors or local treasurers, authorizing him to act on behalf of such association, company or corporation. A fee of one dollar shall be paid to the Commissioner of Banking for every such certificate. Each certificate issued under this section shall expire at the end of one year from its date, and may, upon the payment of a like fee, be renewed from year to year, until said Commissioner has been notified that the authority of such agent, solicitor or local treasurer has been revoked by the association, company or corporation appointing him. All fees collected by the Commissioner of Banking under this section shall be paid by him into the State Treasury.—Act of 11th of May, 1901, Sec. 4, P. L. 153.

Association to Pay Annual License Fee of One Hundred Dollars.
—Collection in Case of Refusal to Pay.

Sec. 287. Every association, company or corporation described in the first section of this act and authorized to do business within this Commonwealth shall, annually, upon the first Monday of May, pay into the State Treasury a license fee of one hundred dollars; and in case of neglect or refusal by any such association, company or corporation to pay the same, as aforesaid, into the State Treasury, at the time aforesaid, the Auditor General shall settle an account against such association, company or corporation for the amount due and payable by it as aforesaid, and shall proceed to collect the same, in the same manner and under the same penalties as are provided for the collection of taxes and penalties under existing laws. —Act of 11th of May, 1901, Sec. 5, P. L. 153.

Court May Revoke Certificate for Insolvency or Fraud.—Discretion of Court to Act in Such Case.—Certificates to Agents and Officers Also to be Revoked.

Sec. 288. Whenever it shall appear to the Commissioner of Banking that any association, company or corporation, described in the first section of this act and authorized to do business within this Commonwealth, is insolvent or is conducting its business fraudulently, or is in any manner doing business contrary to the laws of this Commonwealth governing domestic building and loan associations, it shall be the duty of said Commissioner to communicate the facts to the Attorney General, whose duty it shall then be to apply to the court of common pleas of the county of Dauphin, or in vacation to any of the judges thereof, for an order requiring said association, company or corporation to show cause why its certificate, authorizing it to do business within this Commonwealth, should not be revoked. Upon the return of said order, the said court shall hear the allegations and proofs of the respective parties, and if it shall thereupon appear that said association, company or corporation is insolvent or is conducting its business fraudulently, the said court shall make an order revoking such certificate; but if it shall appear that such association, company or corporation is doing business contrary to law, but without any fraudulent intent, the said court may either revoke such certificate or make such other order as to it may seem meet and proper. Immediately upon the granting by said court of any order revoking the certificate authorizing any such association, company or corporation to do business within this Commonwealth, it shall be the duty of the Commissioner of Banking to revoke all certificates granted to agents, solicitors or local treasurers of such association, company or corporation, and to notify, in writing, such agents, solicitors and local treasurers of such revocation.—Act of 11th of May, 1901, Sec. 6, P. L. 153.

Penalty for Doing Business Without Certificate.—Misdemeanor to Do Business After Revocation.

Sec. 289. Any association, company, or corporation described in the first section of this act, doing business within this Commonwealth without having first received from the Commissioner of Banking a certificate authorizing it so to do, or, having received such certificate, doing business within this Commonwealth after five days from the date of mailing a notice of the revocation of such certificate by the Commissioner of Banking to the principal office of such association, company or corporation, shall be subject to a penalty of five hundred dollars for each month or fraction thereof during which such illegal business is transacted, to be recovered, in the name of the Commonwealth, either by an action of assumpsit or by foreign attachment, and shall be prohibited from doing business within this Commonwealth until such penalty is, or penalties are, fully paid. Any person violating the provisions of the first section of this act, or any person acting as agent, solicitor or local treasurer of any such association, company or corporation after its certificate authorizing it to do business within this Commonwealth has been revoked, and knowing that the same has been revoked, shall be guilty of a misdemeanor; and upon conviction thereof shall be sentenced to pay a fine of not less than fifty dollars nor more than five hundred dollars, and upon conviction of a second offence shall be sentenced to pay a like fine and undergo an imprisonment not exceeding one year, or either, in the discretion of the court.—Act of 11th of May, 1901, Sec. 7, P. L. 153.

From Whom Bids of Premium or Bonus May be Received.—Former Bids Validated.

Sec. 290. It shall be lawful for any mutual savings fund or building and loan association, now incorporated or hereafter to be incorporated, to receive bids of premium, or bonus, for the preference or priority of loan, in writing, whether from members, or from persons who are not members, but intend to become such if loans are obtained by them, or to receive such bids from others duly authorized, in writing, by members or by persons intending to become such, so to bid: Provided, That such bids shall be received only in open meetings, as bids are now required by law to be received. And the directors of such associations may establish rules and regulations, not inconsistent herewith, for the receiving of such bids and the allotment of loans to the persons making or authorizing such bids; and all such bids heretofore accepted by any such association, and loans made thereon, are hereby confirmed and made valid; and no premium or bonus heretofore collected, or which may be hereafter payable on such loans, shall be deemed usurious by reason of the fact that any such bid was made or authorized in writing.—Act of 4th of June, 1901, Sec. 1, P. L. 403.

Repealing Clause.

Sec. 291. All laws or parts of laws inconsistent with the provisions of this act are hereby repealed.—Act of 4th of June, 1901, Sec. 2. P. L. 403.

CHAPTER 10.

SAVINGS INSTITUTIONS AND SAVINGS BANKS.

Regulation of Savings Institutions and Loan Companies.—Not to Receive More Than 6 Per Cent. Interest.—Not to Pay Loans or Discounts in Certificates Payable at a Future Day.—Nor to Issue Such Certificates except for Bona Fide Deposits.—Penalty for Violation of This Section.—Not to Issue Certificates of Deposit to Persons Indebted to Them.—Officers and Stockholders to be Individually Liable Therefor in Certain Cases.

Sec. 292. Every person holding one or more shares of the capital stock of the Philadelphia Savings Institution, shall be a member of said institution, entitled to all the rights, privileges and franchises of a member, and every person who shall become a member by virtue of this act, shall cease to be a member whenever such person shall cease to hold one or more shares of said stock. And also, that the fourth acticle of the third section of an act, entitled "An act to re-charter certain banks," passed the twenty-fifth day of March, one thousand eight hundred and twenty-four, directing the mode of voting for directors, be extended to this said institution. It shall not be lawful for the said Philadelphia Savings Institution, or for any other savings institution or loan company within this Commonwealth, to charge or receive as interest, commission or otherwise, from any person or persons, either directly or indirectly, for any loan or discount, more than at the rate of six per centum per annum on the sum loaned or discounted. Nor shall it be lawful for the said Philadelphia Savings Institution, or for any other savings institution or loan company, to offer or give in payment of any loan or discount by them made, or deposit withdrawn, any certificate or other paper, payable at a future day; but shall pay all loans, discounts and deposits in current money; nor shall it be lawful for the said Philadelphia Savings Institution, or for any other savings institution or loan company to issue certificates of deposit or other papers, as representatives of value, payable at a future day, for any other than deposits of money bona fide made with them, and all such certificates shall be for the amount of the deposits so made, and for the time for which they have actually been deposited. And if any member, director or officer of the said Philadelphia Savings Institution or of any other savings institution or loan company, shall advise or consent to any violation of the provisions of this section, or shall knowingly suffer them to be violated, shall forfeit and pay, for each offence, the sum of one hundred dollars, to be recovered in action of debt, in any court of competent jurisdiction, to the use of any person suing for the same. It shall not be lawful for the said Philadelphia Savings Institution, or for any other savings institution or loan company, to issue any certificate of deposit, or other paper issued, payable at a future day, to any person who shall be indebted to the institution or company, either as principal or security. And if any stock holder of the Philadelphia Savings Institution, or of any other savings institution or loan company shall advise or consent to, or if any member, director or officer thereof shall advise or consent to, or by neglect of duty, shall suffer any issue of notes, certificates or other paper, purporting to be for the payment of any money, other than those for bona fide depositors, for the term they were made, as aforesaid, all such stockholders, members, directors and officers, so advising or consenting to, or suffering to be done, shall be severally liable for the payment of all such notes, certificates or other papers.—Act of 27th of June, 1839, Sec. 1, P. L. 515.

Cashiers or Treasurers of Savings Institutions Subject to General Laws.

Sec. 293. All general laws relative to cashiers of banks shall be deemed and held applicable to the cashiers or treasurers of savings institutions.—Act of 22nd of April, 1854, Sec. 4, P. L. 468.

Act of 16th of April, 1850.—Sec. 30 Extended to Banking, Saving Fund, Trust and Insurance Companies.

Sec. 294. The thirtieth section of the act, approved the sixteenth of April, one thousand eight hundred and fifty, entitled "An act regulating banks," be and the same is hereby extended to all incorporated banking, saving fund, trust and insurance companies, which said companies shall be subject to the provisions of the said section: Provided, That nothing herein contained shall authorize any savings bank, trust or other company as aforesaid, to create any bank note or certificate in the similitude of a bank note.—Act of 6th of November, 1856, Sec. 1, in P. L. 1857, 797.

Limitation of Surplus Funds.—Division Among Depositors.

Sec. 295. No incorporated saving fund institution or bank, not having any capital stock, and doing business exclusively for the benefit of the depositors, shall accumulate or retain, out of net earnings, or otherwise, a surplus or contingent fund which shall exceed fifteen per centum of its liabilities; and it shall be the duty of the managers or directors of such corporation, at the expiration of every year hereafter, to divide pro rata among the depositors, whose accounts shall remain open on the first day of December in that year, the amount of such excess so ascertained in that year, if any.—Act of 17th of April, 1872, Sec. 1, P. L. 62.

Limitation of Actions for Deposits.—Unclaimed Deposits to be Paid Into the Treasury.—Remedy of Depositors.

Sec. 296. Where any depositor with any saving fund, savings institution or savings bank whatsoever, or his legal representatives, shall omit to make any demand for the amount deposited by him, or for any part thereof, for the space of thirty years after the last deposit or payment was made by or to him, or his said representatives, no action or suit shall thereafter be brought or maintained by him or them for the amount of such deposit, against such corporation, but the same shall be paid over instead to the State Treasurer for the use of the State: Provided, That no one now having any such right of action shall be so barred until the expiration of one year from the passage of this act: And provided, That it shall be lawful for such depositor, or his legal representatives, at any time after the amount of his deposit shall have been paid over into the treasury of (the) Commonwealth as aforesaid, to institute and prosecute an action of debt therefor, against the State Treasurer, for the time being, in the court of common pleas for Dauphin county; and on the recovery of judgment in such action, it shall be lawful for the court to issue thereon a writ commanding such State Treasurer, or his successor in office, to cause the amount thereof, with costs, but without interest, to be paid to the party entitled in the judgment, out of any unappropriated moneys in the hands of the State Treasurer, or if there be no such money unappropriated, then out of the first moneys that shall be received by him, and to enforce obedience to such writ by attachment as is provided by law in respect to actions against counties and townships.—Act of 17th of April, 1872, Sec. 2, P. L. 62.

Return of Unclaimed Deposits of Saving Fund Institutions or Banks.

Sec. 297. It shall be the duty of the treasurer or cashier of every incorporated saving fund institution, or bank in this Commonwealth on or before the first day of November, in each year after the present, to make returns to the Auditor General of the amount of all such unclaimed deposits as referred to in the previous section of this act, with the names and residences of the depositors, so far as known, and before the first day of January then next ensuing, pay over the amounts so returned to the State Treasurer, whose receipt therefor shall be a full and sufficient discharge to such saving fund institution or bank from any further liability to any such depositors.—Act of 17th of April, 1872, Sec. 3, P. L. 62.

Certificates of Stock to be Issued.—Transfers.

Sec. 298. All savings banks having a capital stock are hereby authorized and required to issue certificates of their said stock to all the stockholders, properly signed by the president, secretary or treasurer of said savings bank, which certificates transferred by the party holding the same, or his duly authorized attorney, in the presence of the president, secretary or treasurer, shall be a valid and legal transfer of all the said stock.—Act of 17th of April, 1872, Sec. 4, P. L. 62.

Charters May be Extended for Twenty Years.—Notice.—Meeting.—
When Certificate to Issue.—To be Subject to the Constitution.
—Saving Institution or Saving Bank Having no Capital Stock
Renewing Charter Not to be Bank of Discount Nor to Loan
Money Received on Deposit Except Upon Mortgages, Liens on
Real Estate or as Provided.—Rate of Discount.

Sec. 299. Provident institutions, savings institutions and savings
banks, banks of discount, and saving banks and trust companies, not
being banks of issue, chartered under the laws of the Commonwealth of Pennsylvania, may renew and extend their charters, corporate rights and franchises for the period of twenty years in manner following, namely: When the board of trustees or board of
directors of any such institutions or savings banks, or bank or
banks of discount, or savings banks and trust companies, not being,
banks of issue, shall deem it expedient to have such charter, corporate rights and franchises renewed and extended, and shall so
decide at a meeting called to consider the subject, they shall give
notice by publication for three months in two newspapers published
in the city or town where said institution or savings bank or banks,
or bank of discount, or savings banks and trust company, not being
banks of issue, is located, that at a specified time the stockholders,
where there are stockholders, and the directors, managers or trustees, where there are no stockholders, of such institutions or savings
bank or banks, or banks of discount, or savings banks and trust
companies, not being banks of issue, will meet at the office or place
of business of such institution or savings bank or bank or bank of
discount or savings bank or trust company, not being banks of
issue, and vote for or against the proposition to renew and extend
said charter, corporate rights and franchises.

If a majority in interest of said stockholders or directors, managers or trustees, where there are no stockholders, shall decide in
favor of such renewal and extension, said action shall be certified to
the Secretary of the Commonwealth, together with a statement of
the condition of such institution, upon a blank to be furnished by
the Auditor General upon application made, said statement to be
made by the cashier, secretary or president, under oath, attested by
at least three of the board of directors, trustees or financial board
of said institution, and a copy of its charter and all special acts of
Assembly relating to said institution or bank or bank of discount,
savings bank and trust company, not being banks of issue, who shall
refer the same to the Governor, Attorney General and Auditor General upon a certificate being given by them or a majority of them,
that such renewal is not inconsistent with the public interests and
thereupon the said Secretary of the Commonwealth shall issue a
certificate, under the seal of said Commonwealth, that the charter,
corporate rights and franchises of said provident institution, savings
institution, or savings banks or banks of discount, or savings banks
and trust companies, not being banks of issue, are duly renewed and
extended for a period of twenty years: Provided, That said provident institutions, savings institutions or savings banks, or banks of
discount, or savings banks and trust companies, not being banks
of issue, shall thereafter hold its charter, subject to the provisions
of the constitution of the State: Provided also, That no provident

institution, savings institution or savings bank, having no capital stock, renewing or extending its charter, corporate rights and franchises under the provisions of this act, shall thereafter be allowed the privileges of a bank of discount, nor be allowed to loan any money received on deposit, except upon first mortgage or lien upon real estate within this Commonwealth, upon the bonds or securities of the United States or of this State, or upon county, city, borough, township or school bonds of any county, city, borough, township or school district, or any other good and valid securities: And provided, That no bank re-chartered under the provisions of this act shall charge a greater rate of discount than six per centum per annum. —Act of 10th of May, 1889, Sec. 1, P. L. 185, amending act of 30th of June, 1885, Sec. 1.

Act for the Formation of Savings Banks.

Sec. 300. Corporations for the encouragement of saving money, intended to be savings banks, may be formed under the provisions of this act by any number of persons not less than thirteen, two-thirds of whom shall reside in the county where the proposed corporation shall be located, who shall enter into articles of association, which shall specify the object for which the association is formed, and may contain any provisions not inconsistent with this act which the association may desire to adopt for the regulation and conduct of its business and affairs, which articles shall be signed by the persons forming such association, and a copy of them shall be forwarded to the Attorney General for his inspection and approval, and if approved by him he shall endorse his approval thereon and transmit the same to the Auditor General to be filed in his office.—Act of 20th of May, 1889, Sec. 1, P. L. 246.

What Certificate of Association Shall Set Forth.—Certificate to be Acknowledged.—Approved by Attorney General and Filed in the Auditor General's Office.—Evidence.

Sec. 301. The persons forming such associations shall, under their hands, make a certificate which shall specify:

1st. Name (subject to the approval of the Auditor General).

2d. Location or place of business, particularly designating the county, city, borough or village.

3d. Names, residence, occupation and postoffice address of the proposed corporators.

4th. A declaration that each member of such association will accept the responsibilities and faithfully discharge the duties of a trustee in such institution, when authorized according to the provisions of this act.

This certificate shall be acknowledged before a judge or notary public, which certificate and acknowledgment certified and authenticated by the seal of such court or notary public, shall be transmitted, after approval by the Attorney General, to the Auditor General, to be filed, recorded and preserved in his office. Copies of such certificate duly certified by the Auditor General and authenticated by the seal of office, shall be conclusive evidence in all the courts of the Commonwealth of the existence of such corporations and of every other matter or thing which could be proved by the production of the original certificate.—Act of 20th of May, 1889, Sec. 2, P. L. 246.

Duties of Auditor General, Preliminary to Forming an Association.

Sec. 302. It shall be the duty of the Auditor General and he shall have the power in regard to any certificate of association so filed by him, as hereinbefore provided, to ascertain from the best sources of information at his command—

1st. Whether greater convenience of access to a savings bank will be afforded to any considerable number of depositors by opening a savings bank at the place designated in such certificate.

2d. Whether the density of the population in the neighborhood designated for such savings bank and in the surrounding country affords a reasonable promise of adequate support for the enterprise.

3d. Whether the responsibility, character and general fitness for the discharge of the duties appertaining to such trusts, of the persons named in such certificate, are such as to command the confidence of the community in which such savings bank is proposed to be located.—Act of 20th of May, 1889, Sec. 3, P. L. 246.

Letters Patent.

Sec. 303. The Auditor General upon receipt of the articles of association with the approval thereon of the Attorney General as aforesaid, and the certificates hereinbefore provided, shall certify a copy of such certificate to the Governor, who shall, upon receiving the same, cause letters patent, under the great seal of the Commonwealth, to be issued to said savings institution or savings bank..—Act of 20th of May, 1889, Sec. 4, P. L. 246.

Notice of Intended Application.

Sec. 304. Before application shall be made, under the provisions of this act for the creation of any corporation, notice of such intended application shall be advertised in two newspapers of general circulation in the county in which such corporated body is located, or intended to be located, at least once a week for three months before such application shall be made, and the notice of such application shall specify the name, style, location, specific object for which created. If there should be only one paper printed in the county in which such corporate body shall be located, the publication of such notice in one paper shall de deemed sufficient, but if there be no paper printed in such county, then the notice shall be given in at least one paper published in one of the nearest adjoining counties. —Act of 20th of May, 1889, Sec. 5, P. L. 246.

Corporate Powers.—Service of Process Against the Corporation.— Trustees and Their Powers.

Sec. 305. Every association formed under the provisions of this act shall, from the date of the letter patent issued thereto, be a body corporate and shall transact no business except such as may be incidental to the purpose of its organization, and shall have power to

8

adopt a corporate seal and have succession by the name designated in its articles of association perpetually from the date of the letters patent unless sooner dissolved under the provisions of the articles of association, or by the provisions of any act of Assembly. Such bodies corporate may make contracts, sue and be sued, complain, prosecute and defend in any court of law or equity, and before any magistrate, as fully as natural persons, receive money on deposit, invest the same, and further transact the business of a saving bank as hereinafter provided, and process against such corporation may be served on its president or cashier, or by leaving a copy thereof with one of the officers thereof during the usual hours of business.

It shall elect or appoint trustees, and by its board of trustees appoint a president, vice president, cashier and other officers and define their duties, require bonds of them, fixing a penalty therein, dismiss any of the said officers at pleasure and appoint others to fill their places, and exercise, under this act, all such power as may be necessary to carry on the business of the corporation.—Act of 20th of May, 1889, Sec. 6, P. L. 246.

Extension of Time by Auditor General.—In Case Bank Fails to Organize Within One Year.

Sec. 306. Any savings bank so incorporated that shall not organize and commence business within one year after this certificate of authorization of the same has been filed, as hereinbefore provided, shall forfeit its rights and privileges as a corporation under this act; but the Auditor General may, for satisfactory cause to him shown, extend the term within which such organization may be affected, and such business commenced, but not for a longer period than one year, and the order so extending such terms shall be under his hand and seal of office.—Act of 20th of May, 1889, Sec. 7, P. L. 246.

Association May Purchase, Hold and Convey Certain Real Estate.

Sec. 307. It shall be lawful for any association incorporated under this act to purchase, hold and convey real estate as follows:

First. Such as shall be necessary for its immediate accommodation in the transaction of its business.

Second. Such as shall be mortgaged to it in good faith as security for debts contracted previous to the execution of any such mortgage.

Third. Such as it shall purchase at sales under judgments, decrees or mortgages held by such corporation, or shall purchase to secure debts due to said corporation.—Act of 20th of May, 1889, Sec. 8, P. L. 246.

Names, Residence and Address of Its Officers to be Furnished to Auditor General Before Receiving Deposit.—Persons Named in Certificate to be First Trustees.

Sec. 308. Before any savings bank or institution for the encouragement of saving, intended to be incorporated under this act shall be authorized to receive deposits, such corporation shall transmit to the Auditor General the name, residence and postoffice address of each of the officers and trustees, and the place where its business is to be carried on, designating the same by street and number when practicable. The persons named in the certificate for incorporation, issued pursuant to the provisions of this act, shall be the first trustees of such corporation, and shall have the entire management and control of all the affairs of the corporation subject to the provisions of this act.—Act of 20th of May, 1889, Sec. 9, P. L. 246.

Change of Location.

Sec. 309. And it shall be lawful for any such savings fund, with the approval in writing, under the seal of the Auditor General, to change its location within the limits of any city or town wherein it may be established; and in affecting such change of location, such corporation owning a banking house and lot may purchase such additional plot as the corporation may require, and such banking house and lot, previously owned and occupied, shall be sold.—Act of 20th of May, 1889, Sec. 10, P. L. 246.

Trustees and Other Officers.—Powers of Board of Trustees.—Liability of Trustees for Losses.

Sec. 310. The business of every such corporation shall be managed and directed by a board of trustees of not less than thirteen, who shall elect from their number a president and two vice presidents, and shall elect or appoint from their number, or otherwise, such other officers as they may see fit; and all vacancies in such board by death, resignation or otherwise, shall be filled by the board of trustees as soon as practicable, at a regular meeting after such vacancies occur.

This board of trustees shall have power to make by-laws, rules and regulations for the election of officers and fixing their duties, the appointment of committees, and generally for transacting, managing and directing the affairs of the corporation; provided such by-laws, rules and regulations are not repugnant to, nor inconsistent with the provisions of this act and of the Constitution and laws of the Commonwealth or of the United States.

If the insolvency of said savings fund be occasioned by the fraudulent conduct of the trustees aforesaid, the trustees, by whose acts or omissions the insolvency was in whole or in part occasioned, shall each be liable to the depositors and creditors thereof for his proportional share of the losses, the proportion to be ascertained by dividing the whole loss among the whole number of directors liable for its reimbursement.—Act of 20th of May, 1889, Sec. 11, P. L. 246.

Duties of Trustees as to Funds of the Corporation.

Sec. 311. No trustee of any such corporation shall have any interest whatever, direct or indirect, in the gains or profits thereof, nor shall directly or indirectly receive any pay or emolument for his services except as hereinafter provided; and no trustee or officer of any such corporation shall directly or indirectly, for himself, or as the agent or partner of others, borrow any of its funds, deposits or in any manner use the same, except to make such current and necessary payments as are authorized by the board of trustees, nor shall any trustee or officer of any such corporation hereafter become an endorser or surety, or become in any manner an obligor for moneys loaned by or borrowed of such corporation.—Act of 20th of May, 1889, Sec. 12, P. L. 246.

How Office of Trustee May be Become Vacant.

Sec. 312. Whenever a trustee of any savings bank shall hereafter become a trustee, officer, clerk or employe in any other savings bank, or upon his borrowing, directly, or indirectly, any of the funds of the savings bank of which he is a trustee, or becoming a surety or guarantee for any money borrowed of, or a loan made by, such savings bank, or upon his failure to attend the regular meetings of the board, or to perform any of the duties involved upon him as trustee, for six successive months without having been previously excused by the board for such failure, the office of such trustee shall thereupon immediately become vacant; but the trustee vacating his office by failure to attend meetings or to discharge his duties may, in the discretion of the board, be eligible to a re-election.—Act of 20th of May, 1889, Sec. 13, P. L. 246.

Trustees to Require Bonds of Officers and Agents.—And Fix Their Salaries.

Sec. 313. The trustees of any such corporation shall have the power to require from the officers and agents of the corporation such security, to be fixed and approved by the court of common pleas of the county in which said savings bank or institution is located, for their fidelity and the faithful performance of their duties, as shall be deemed necessary, fix the salaries of such officers and agents, subject to the provisions of this act.—Act of 20th of May, 1889, Sec. 14, P. L. 246.

Deposits.

Sec. 314. It shall be lawful for any corporation, incorporated under this act, to receive on deposit any sum or sums of money that may be offered by any person or persons or by any corporations or societies, and to invest the same, credit and pay interest thereon. The sums so deposited, together with the dividends or interest credited thereon, shall be repaid to such depositors respectively, or to their legal representatives, after demand in such manner and at such times, and after such previous notices, and under such regulations as the board of trustees shall prescribe; which regulations shall be printed in the pass-books or other evidences of deposit furnished by the corporation; and shall be evidence between the corporation, and depositors holding the same of the terms upon which deposits therein acknowledged are made; and every such corporation shall have the right to limit the aggregate amount which any one person or persons, or societies may deposit, to such sum as they may deem it expedient to receive, and may in their discretion, refuse to receive a deposit, and may also at any time, return all or any part of any deposit, nor shall the aggregate amount of such deposits to the credit of any one individual or corporation at any one time exceed five thousand dollars, exclusive of accrued interest.—Act of 20th of May, 1889, Sec. 15, P. L. 246.

Deposit in Name of a Minor or Married Woman.—Deposit in Trust for Another.

Sec. 315. Whenever any deposit shall be made by or in the name of any person who is a minor, or a female, being or thereafter becoming a married woman, the same shall be held for the exclusive right and benefit of such depositor, free from the control or lien of all persons whatsoever except creditors, and it shall be paid, together with the dividends or interest thereon, to the person in whose name the deposit shall be made, and the receipt or quittance of such minor or female shall be a valid and sufficient release and discharge for such deposits, or any part thereof to the corporation.

Whenever any deposit shall be made by any person in trust for another, and no other or further notice of the existence and terms of a legal and valid trust shall be given in writing to the bank, in the event of the death of the trustee the same, or any part thereof, together with the dividends or interest thereon, may be paid to the person for whom such deposit was made.—Act of 20th of May, 1889, Sec. 16, P. L. 246.

Authorized Investments for the Trust Funds.

Sec. 316. It shall be lawful for the trustees of any saving bank to invest money deposited therein only as follows:

First. In the stocks or bonds of interest bearing notes, or the obligations of the United States, or those for which the faith of the United States is pledged to provide for the payment of the interest and the principal.

Second. In the stocks or bonds of the Commonwealth of Pennsylvania bearing interest.

Third. In the stocks or bonds of any State in the Union that has not within ten years previous to making such investments, by such corporation, defaulted in the payment of any part of either principal or interest of any debt authorized by any legislature of such State to be contracted.

Fourth. In the stocks or bonds of any city, county, town or village of any State of the United States, issued pursuant to the authority of any law of the State, or in any interest bearing obligation issued by the city or county in which such bank shall be situated.

Fifth. In bonds and mortgages or unincumbered improved real estate, situate in this State.—Act of 20th of May, 1889, Sec. 17, P. L. 246.

Temporary Investment of Current Receipts.—Duty of Auditor General and Examiners as to Investments.

Sec. 317. It shall further be lawful for any such corporation to deposit temporarily in banks or trust companies, as provided in the last preceding section of this act, the excess of current daily receipts over the payments, until such time as the same can be judiciously invested in the securities named: and whenever it shall appear to the Auditor General or to any of the examiners duly authorized to visit and inspect these saving funds, that the trustees of any such corporation are violating the spirit or intent of the provisions of this act, by keeping permanently uninvested all or an undue proportion of the money received by them, it shall be his or their duty to report the facts to the Attorney General, who shall proceed against such corporation as provided by law.—Act of 20th of May, 1889, Sec. 18, P. L. 246.

Loans on Notes and Bills of Exchange Forbidden.—Loans on Real Estate.

Sec. 318. It shall not be lawful for the trustees of any savings bank or institution incorporated under this act, to loan the money deposited with them, or any part thereof, upon notes, bills of exchange or drafts, or to discount any such notes, bills of exchange or drafts.

And in all cases of loans upon real estate, a sufficient bond secured by a mortgage thereon, shall be required of the borrower, and all the expenses of searches, examinations, certificates of title or appraisal of value and of drawing, perfecting and recording papers shall be paid by such borrower.—Act of 20th of May, 1889, Sec. 19, P. L. 246.

Buildings on Lands Given as Security to be Insured.—Expenses of Effecting Insurance.

Sec. 319. Whenever buildings are included in the valuation of any real estate upon which a loan shall be made by any such corporation, they shall be insured by the mortgagor in such company or companies as the trustees shall direct, and the policy of insurance shall be duly assigned or the loss made payable as its interest may appear, to such corporation, and it shall be lawful for such corporation to renew such policy of insurance from year to year, or for a longer or shorter time, in case the mortgagor shall neglect to do so, and may charge the amount paid to the mortgagor. And all the necessary charges and expenses paid by such corporation for such renewal or renewals shall be paid by such mortgagor to such corporation, and shall be a lien upon the property so mortgaged, recoverable with interest from the time of payment as part of the money secured to be paid by such mortgage.—Act of 20th of May, 1889, Sec. 20, P. L. 246.

Not to Deal or Trade in Personal Property.

Sec. 320. It shall be unlawful for any corporation incorporated under this act, directly or indirectly, to deal or trade in real estate, or in any goods, wares, merchandise or commodities whatever, except as authorized by this act and except such personal property as may be necessary in the transaction of its business.—Act of 20th of May, 1889, Sec. 21, P. L. 246.

Regulation of Interest on Deposits.—Allowance of Interest at Declaration of Dividends.—Change in Rate of Interest.

Sec. 321. It shall be the duties of the trustees of ever such corporation to regulate the rate of interest or dividends, not to exceed five per centum per annum upon the deposits therewith, in such manner that the depositor shall receive, as nearly as may be, all the profits of such corporation after deducting necessary expense and reserving such amount as the trustees may deem expedient as a surplus fund for the security of depositors, which, to the amount of fifteen per centum per annum of their deposits, the trustees of any such corporation are hereby authorized gradually to accumulate and hold to meet any contingency or loss in its business, from the depreciation of its securities or otherwise: Provided however, That the trustees of any such corporation may classify its depositors according to the character, amount and duration of their dealings with the corporation, and regulate the interest or dividends allowed in such manner that each depositor shall receive the same ratable proportion, with interest or dividends as all others of its class. It shall be unlawful for the trustees of any savings bank to declare or allow interest on any deposit for a longer period than the same has been deposited, and no dividends or interest shall be declared, credited or paid, except by the authority of a vote of the board of trustees, duly entered upon their minutes, whereon shall be recorded the yeas and nays upon each vote, and whenever any interest or dividend shall be declared and credited in excess of the interest or profits earned and appearing to the credit of the corporation, the trustees so voting for such dividends shall be jointly and severally liable to the corporation for the amount of such excess, so declared and credited. And it shall be the duty of the trustees of any such corporation, whose surplus amounts to fifteen per centum of its deposits, at least once in three years to divide, equitably, the accumulation beyond such authorized surplus as an extra dividend to depositors in excess of the regular dividends hereinbefore provided. A notice posted conspicuously in the bank of a change in the rate of interest shall be equivalent to a personal notice.—Act of 20th of May, 1889, Sec. 22, P. L. 246.

Annual Report to Auditor General.—Report to be Verified by Affidavit.—Penalty for Failure to Make Report.

Sec. 322. Every corporation incorporated under this act shall, before the thirty-first day of December of each year, report to the Auditor General of the State in writing, in such form as he shall prescribe; which report shall state the amount loaned upon bonds and mortgages, with a list of such bonds and mortgages and the location of the mortgage premises, that have not previously been reported, and also a list of such previously reported as have since been paid wholly or in part, or have been foreclosed, and the amount of such payments respectively, the cost, par value and estimated market value of all stock investments, designating each particular kind of stock, the amount loaned upon the pledge of securities, with a statement of securities held as collateral for such amounts, the amount invested in real estate, giving the cost of same, the amount of cash on hand and on deposit in banks or trust companies, with the names of such banks or trust companies and the amount deposited in each and such other information as the Auditor General may require. Such report shall also state all the liabilities of such saving corporation on the day of the date of such statement, the amount due to depositors, which shall include any dividend to be credited to them for the twelve months ending on that day, and any other debts or claims against such corporation, which are or may be a charge upon its assets.

Such report shall also state the amount deposited during the year previous and the amount withdrawn during the same period, the whole amount of interest or profits received or earned, the amount of dividends credited to depositors, together with the amount of such annual credit of interest and the amount of interest that may have been credited at other than annual periods, the number of accounts opened or reopened, the number closed during the year and the number of open accounts at the end of the year.

Such reports shall be verified by the oath of the president or cashier of said institution, and any wilful false swearing in regard to such reports or in regard to any reports made to the Auditor General pursuant to the provisions of this act, shall be deemed perjury and be subject to the prosecutions and punishments prescribed by law for that offense. If any such bank shall fail to furnish to the Auditor General any report or statement required by this act at the time so required, it shall forfeit the sum of one hundred dollars per day for every day such report or statement shall be so delayed or withheld, and the Auditor General may settle an account to recover such penalty in the manner now provided by law.—Act of 20th of May, 1889, Sec. 23, P. L. 246.

Auditor General and Court of Common Pleas to Appoint Examiners.
—Their Powers.—Expenses.—Their Compensation.—Duty of Auditor General and Attorney General in Case Corporation Violates its Charter, Etc.—Proceedings by Attorney General.—Powers of the Court.

Sec. 323. It shall be the duty of the Auditor General and of the court of common pleas of the county in which any savings institution incorporated under this act may be carrying on business, once in two years, each to appoint an examiner to visit and examine every savings institution incorporated under this act within the limits of the county, and such examiners shall have power to administer an oath to any person whose testimony may be required on such examination, and to compel the appearance and attendance of any such person by subpoena or attachment, issuing out of said court, and all books and papers which it may be deemed necessary to examine by such examiners shall be produced, and their production may be compelled in like manner; the expense of such examination shall be paid by the corporation examined; the rate of compensation to said examiners shall be fixed by the Auditor General. And the court making the appointment.

And whenever it shall appear on the report of any examination made by such visitors, either to the court or to the Auditor General, that any corporation has committed any violation of its charter or is conducting its business and affairs in an unsafe and unauthorized manner, the said Auditor General by an order under his hand and seal, shall direct the discontinuance of such illegal and unsafe or unauthorized practices, and whenever such corporation shall refuse or neglect to comply with its direction in the premises he shall communicate the fact to the Attorney General, who shall thereupon institute such proceedings as the nature of the case requires The proceedings instituted by the Attorney General may be by quo warranto, in the county where the institution is situated, for the removal of one or more of the trustees, or for the withdrawal of corporate powers, or consolidation and merger of the corporation with any other saving corporation that may be willing to accept the trust, or of such other or further relief or correction as the particular facts communicated to him shall seem to require. And the court before such proceeding shall be instituted shall have power to grant such orders and, in its discretion, from time to time to modify or revoke the same, and grant such relief and render such judgment as the facts or evidence in the case, and the situation of the parties and the interest involved seem to require. And the court, on being satisfied that it is necessary so to do, may appoint a receiver to take possession and to hold all the assets of such corporation until the further order of the court.—Act of 20th of May, 1889, Sec. 24, P. L. 246.

Duty of Trustees to Examine Books, Etc., at Least Once a Year.

Sec. 324. It shall be the duty of the trustees of every corporation incorporated under this act to make a thorough examination, at least once in every year, of the books, vouchers, assets and affairs generally, and the statements furnished to the Auditor General, and to see that accurate balances of the depositor's ledger have been made, and to see if any discrepancies exist between the amount due the depositor, as shown by such balances, and the amount due the depositor as shown by the general ledger.—Act of 20th of May, 1889, Sec. 25, P. L. 246.

Changing the Number of Trustees.

Sec. 325. It shall be lawful for the board of trustees of any such savings corporation, by a resolution of its board, a copy, of which shall also be filed to the Auditor General, to reduce the number of trustees named in the original charter of such corporation to a number not less than the minimum named in this act, such reduction to be affected gradually by the occurrence of vacancies by death, resignation or forfeiture, until the number is reduced to thirteen, or to such greater number as shall be designated in the aforesaid resolution; or the number of trustees may be increased to any number designated in the resolution for that purpose, where reasons therefor are shown to the satisfaction of the Auditor General, and his consent in writing obtained thereto.—Act of 20th of May, 1889, Sec. 26, P. L. 246.

Compensation to Trustees.

Sec. 326. It shall be lawful for the trustees of such corporation, acting as officers of the same, whose duties require and receive a regular and faithful attendance at the institution, to receive such compensation as in the opinion of a majority of the board of trustees shall be just and reasonable, but such majority shall be exclusive of any trustee to whom such compensation shall be voted; but it shall not be lawful to pay trustees as such for their attendance at the meetings of the board.—Act of 20th of May, 1889, Sec. 27, P. L. 246.

Trustees Must be Residents of the State.

Sec. 327. No person shall be elected a trustee of any savings bank who is not a resident of this State, and removal from the State by any trustee hereafter elected shall vacate his office.—Act of 20th of May, 1889, Sec. 28, P. L. 246.

Change of Name of Corporation.

Sec. 328. The names of any institutions incorporated under this act may be changed by complying with all the rules and regulations in force in the State in regard to changing the names of corporations. —Act of 20th of May, 1889, Sec. 29, P. L. 246.

How Solvent Saving Bank May Discontinue or Close Business.— Trustees to File in Auditor General's Office a Statement of Depositors not Claiming Sums Due Them.—Balances to be Paid to State Treasurer.—Dissolution of Corporation by the Court.

Sec. 329. Whenever the trustees of any solvent saving bank shall deem it necessary and expedient to close the business of such corporation, they may, by the affirmative vote of not less than two-thirds of the whole number of trustees, at a meeting to be called for that purpose, of which all the trustees shall have notice, declare by resolution its determination to close such business and pay the money to the depositors and creditors and surrender the corporate franchise. The vote upon such resolution shall be taken by ayes and noes, and the resolution and the votes thereon shall be recorded in the minutes of the board of trustees, and a copy of the record of such proceedings, certified by the president and secretary of the corporation, shall be filed with the Auditor General. The trustees shall therefore give notice to all the depositors and creditors of the adoption of such resolution by publication thereof in the newspaper or newspapers most likely to give the same publicity, and by printed or written notices, personally served upon or mailed to every depositor and creditor of such saving bank, at their last known residence, postage prepaid.

When the trustees of any such saving bank shall have paid the sums due respectively, to all the depositors and creditors whom they can discover, and who claim their deposits or the moneys due them, it shall be the duty of said trustees to make a transcript or statement from the books of said saving bank, of the names of all the depositors and creditors who do not claim, or have not yet received, the balances to their credit, or due them, and of the sums due them respectively, and to file such transcript in the Auditor General's Department, and to pay over and transfer all such unclaimed and unpaid deposits, credits and money to the Treasurer of the State. The trustees shall thereupon report their proceedings, duly certified to, before the court of common pleas of the county in which the corporation is situated, and upon such report, and the petition of the trustees, and upon notice to the Attorney General and the Auditor General, and such other notice as the court may deem necessary, the court shall adjudge the franchise surrendered and the existence of the corporation terminated.—Act of 20th of May, 1889, Sec. 30, P. L. 246.

Associations Incorporated Under Act to be Taxed as other Corporations Without Capital Stock.

Sec. 330. The associations incorporated in pursuance of this act shall be taxed in the same manner as other corporations without capital stock.—Act of 20th of May, 1889, Sec. 31, P. L. 246.*

*It appears that the Commissioner of Banking is to be substituted under the act in place of the Auditor General. Act of 11th of February, 1895, P. L. 4.

CHAPTER 11.

MISCELLANEOUS ACTS RELATING TO BANKS, TRUST COMPANIES, BUILDING AND LOAN ASSOCIATIONS, SURETY COMPANIES, SAVING FUND SOCIETIES, ETC.

ACT OF 22ND DAY OF APRIL, 1854, BEING A SUPPLEMENT TO THE ACT OF 1850, RELATING TO BANKS.

Total Liabilities of Banks.—Proviso.

Sec. 331. From and after the passage of this act the total liabilities of any bank in this Commonwealth, exclusive of the capital stock, shall not at any time exceed three times the amount of the capital stock paid in: Provided, That, when the deposits shall exceed one-fourth of the capital stock, such excess shall not be counted as a liability, in the meaning of the above prohibition, nor shall the debts due and to become due to any such bank, ever amount to more than four times the capital stock paid in, in loans to the Commonwealth excepted.—Act of 22nd of April 1854, Sec. 1, P. L. 467.

Change of Sections 17 and 18 of Act of 1850.

Sec. 332. That the seventeenth section of the act regulating banks, approved the 16th day of April, 1850, so far as the same is not hereby altered, and the eighteenth section of the same act, be and are hereby extended to all the banks chartered prior to 1850; Provided, That the provisions of this act shall be applicable only to such of the banks of this Commonwealth heretofore chartered, as may accept the same by written evidence of such acceptance to be deposited with the Auditor General.—Act of 22nd of April, 1854, Sec. 2, P. L. 467.

Duty of Auditor General.

Sec. 333. That it shall be the duty of the Auditor General to ascertain what banks of this Commonwealth have failed to comply with the provisions of the forty-seventh section of the act of 16th of April, 1850, entitled: "An act regulating banks, etc.," and, if any banks have so failed and have not paid the forfeit specified in said section, he shall demand the same and if necessary bring suit therefor in the name of the Commonwealth, and no objection of form shall defeat or prejudice such action, but the same shall be tried and determined on the merits.—Act of 22nd of April, 1854, Sec. 3, P. L. 467.

Treasurers of Savings Institutions Liable as Cashiers.

Sec. 334. That all general laws relative to cashiers of banks shall be deemed and held applicable to the cashiers of banks or treasurers of savings institutions.—Act of 22nd of April, 1854, Sec. 4, P. L. 467.

Act Extending Article Five of Section Ten of the Act of 1850 to all Banks.

Sec. 335. The provisions of article fifth, section ten, of an act regulating banks, approved the 16th day of April, one thousand eight hundred and fifty and the supplement thereto approved the seventh day of May, one thousand eight hundred and fifty-five be and the same are extended to all the banks of the Commonwealth.—Act of 18th of April, 1856, Sec. 1, P. L. 403.

Act of 21st day of April, 1858, Relating to Savings Institutions, Insurance and Trust Companies and Loan Association.—Such Institutions May Make Investments in Ground Rents.

Sec. 336. All insurance and trust companies, saving funds and building associations incorporated under, or by any law of this Commonwealth, are authorized to purchase, hold, sell and convey ground rents; and all conveyances of ground rents heretofore made by or to any such corporation, shall be good and effecutal, and have the same force and effect as if the same had been made subsequent to the passage of this act.—Act of 21st of April, 1858, P. L. 412.

Authorizing Vice-Presidents of Banks to Receive Salaries for Their Services.

Sec. 337. It shall be lawful for the duly elected vice-president of any bank within this Commonwealth, to receive such salary as may be fixed upon by the board of directors of said bank.—Act of 13th of April, 1859, Sec. 1, P. L. 613.

Mortgages May be Taken to Secure Payment of Notes and Renewals Thereof.

Sec. 338. It shall be lawful for mining and manufacturing companies organized under any special or general law of this Commonwealth, or for any other organized company or individual to execute and deliver and for all banks organized under any law under this Commonwealth or any other organized company, individual or individuals, to take and hold mortgages of real estate to secure payment of such notes, bills and other negotiable and other paper and renewals thereof belonging to or made by said companies as the said banks, company, individual or individuals shall agree to, and execute from time to time for discount or otherwise: Provided, That such mortgage shall operate as a lien from the date of the record of such instrument.—Act of 17th of February, 1873, Sec. 1, P. L. 35.

Liability of Stockholders Fixed.—Proviso.

Sec. 339. From and after the passage of this act, all stockholders in banks, banking companies, saving fund institutions, trust companies, and all other incorporated companies doing the business of banks or loaning and discounting moneys as such in this Commonwealth, shall be personally liable for all debts and deposits in their individual capacity to double the amount of the capital stock held and owned by each: Provided, That before such liability shall accrue, in case of banks already chartered, the stockholders shall, at a regular or adjourned meeting, declare by resolution or otherwise their intention to accept the provisions of this act, and notice of their action shall, within thirty days thereafter be filed in the office of the Auditor General and Secretary of the Commonwealth setting forth at length their proceeding declaring their intention to be bound by its provisions in the same manner and as fully as if the same had been part of the original act by which they were incorporated.—Act of 11th of May, 1874, Sec. 1, P. L. 135.

Repeal.

Sec. 340. All acts or parts of acts inconsistent with this act are hereby repealed.—Act of 11th of May, 1874, Sec. 1, P. L. 135.

Amendment of Criminal Code.—Unlawfully Obtaining Key or Combination to Bank, Vault or Safe, Etc.—Penalty.

Sec. 341. If any person shall by fraud, force, threats or menaces, or by seizing, gagging or trying, compel or attempt to compel another to surrender the key or other appliance, or to divulge the combination, secret or other means used to open any bank, vault, safe or other depository of money, securities or property, or if any persons shall administer or attempt to administer to another, any stupefying or overpowering drug, matter or thing for the purpose of enabling such offender to obtain such key or other appliance, with intent, in any of the cases aforesaid, to steal such money, securities or property, or any portion thereof, every such offender shall be guilty of a felony, and being thereof convicted shall be sentenced to pay a fine not exceeding ten thousand dollars and to undergo imprisonment at hard labor not exceeding twenty years.—Act of 8th of May, 1876, Sec. 1, P. L. 139.

Re-hypothecation of Stocks and Bonds, Prohibited.—Punishment for Violation of Act.

Sec. 342. It shall not be lawful for any person or persons, bank, savings fund, building association, or any corporation, to repledge or re-hypothecate any stocks, bonds or other securities, received by any of them for money lent and borrowed, during the continuance of the contract of hypothecation or pledging of such securities; and such re-pledging or re-hypothecation, without the consent of the party pledging the same, is hereby declared a misdemeanor, triable in the courts of quarter sessions, and on conviction thereof, any person or persons, or the officers of any corporation, violating the provisions of this act, shall be sentenced to a fine not less than five hundred nor more than five thousand dollars, and undergo imprisonment for a period not exceeding five years, or both or either, at the discretion of the court before which such person shall be prosecuted. —Act of 25th of May, 1878, Sec. 1, P. L. 155.

Embézzlement by Officers and Employes of Bank and Other Corporations.

Sec. 343. The one hundred and sixteenth section of the act, entitled "An act to consolidated, revise and amend the penal laws of this Commonwealth," approved the thirty-first day of March, Anno Domini one thousand eight hundred and sixty, be and the same is hereby amended, so that it shall read as follows, namely:

If any person, being an officer, director, superintendent, manager, receiver, employe, agent, attorney, broker, or member of any bank or other body corporate, or public company, municipal or quasi municipal corporation, shall fraudulently take, convert or apply to his own use, or the use of any other person, any of the money or property of such bank, body corporate or company, municipal or quasi municipal corporation or belonging to any person or persons, corporation or association, and deposited therein or in the possession thereof, he shall be guilty of a misdemeanor.—Act of 12th of June, 1878, Sec. 1, P. L. 196.

Keeping Fraudulent Accounts.

Sec. 344. The one hundred and seventeenth section of said act, be and the same is hereby amended, so that it shall read as follows, namely: If any person, being an officer, director, superintendent, manager, receiver, employe, agent, attorney, broker or member of any body corporate or public company, or municipal or quasi municipal corporation, shall as such receiver (receive) or possess himself of any money or other property of such corporate or public company, municipal or quasi municipal corporation, otherwise than in payment to him of a just debt or demand, and shall, with intent to defraud omit to make or cause or direct to be made, a full and true entry thereof in the books and accounts of such body corporate, public company, municipal or quasi municipal corporation, he shall be guilty of a misdemeanor.—Act of 12th of June, 1878, Sec. 2, P. L. 196.

Destroying or Mutilating Books of a Corporation.

Sec. 345. The one hundred and eighteenth section of said act, be and the same is hereby amended, so that it shall read as follows, namely: If any officer, director, superintendent, manager, receiver, employe, agent, attorney, broker, or member of any bank or other body corporate, or public company, municipal or quasi municipal corporation, shall, with the intent to defraud, destroy, alter, mutilate or falsify any of the books, papers, writings or securities belonging to the bank, body corporate or public company, municipal or quasi municipal corporation, of which he is a director, officer, superintendent, manager, receiver, employe, agent, attorney, broker or mem-

'ber, or shall make or concur in the making of any false entry or any material omission in any book of accounts or other document, he shall be guilty of a misdemeanor.—Act of 12th of June, 1878, Sec. 3, P. L. 196.

False Statement by Officers.—Members and Employes of Corporations.

Sec. 346. The one hundred and nineteenth section of said act, be and the same is hereby amended, so that it shall read as follows: If any officer, director, superintendent, manager, receiver, employe, agent, attorney, broker, or member of any bank or other body corporate or public company, municipal or quasi municipal corporation, shall make, circulate or publish, or concur in making, circulating or publishing any written or printed statement or account, which he shall know to be false in any particular with intent to deceive or defraud any member, shareholder or creditor of such body corporate or public company, municipal or quasi municipal corporation, or with intent to induce any person to become a shareholder or partner therein, or to interest or advance any money or property to such body corporate or public company, or to enter into any security for the benefit thereof, shall be guilty of a misdemeanor.—Act of 12th of June, 1878, Sec. 4, P. L. 196.

Punishment for the Foregoing Misdemeanors.

Sec. 347. Every person found guilty of a misdemeanor under any or either of the preceding sections of this title, wherein the nature and extent of the punishment is not specified shall be sentenced to pay a fine not exceeding one thousand dollars, and undergo an imprisonment by separate or solitary confinement at labor not exceeding six years.—Act of 12th of June, 1878, Sec. 5, P. L. 196.

When Prosecutions May be Commenced.

Sec. 348. Indictments for misdemeanors committed by any officer, director, receiver, superintendent, manager, broker, attorney, agent, employe, or member of any bank, body corporate or public company, municipal or quasi municipal corporation, may be commenced and prosecuted at any time within four years from the time the alleged offence shall have been committed.—Act of 12th of June, 1878, Sec. 6, P. L. 196.

Stock May be Divided Into Shares of Par Value of $50.00.

Sec. 349. All banks and saving institutions of the Commonwealth of Pennsylvania whose capital stock under acts of incorporation is now divided into shares of a greater par value than fifty dollars, may by vote of the majority of the stockholders or corporators, increase the number of shares of the capital stock so as to represent par values of any desired amount: Provided, That the capital stock shall not be increased and no share made of less par value than fifty dollars.—Act of 14th of June, 1879, Sec. 1, P. L. 94.

Relating to Evidence by Bank Books.—Verified Copies of Bank Book Entries Made Prima Facie Evidence.—Bankers Need not Attend as Witnesses.

Sec. 350. Whenever any evidence shall be required in any civil suit or proceeding in any court of this Commonwealth, from the book entries of any bank or banker doing business at the time of said requirement, it shall be competent upon ten days written notice to opposite party, to produce verified copies of such entries, which shall be received in all legal proceedings as prima facie evidence of such book entry or entries, and a bank officer or banker shall not be compelled to produce the original book or attend as a witness thereto, unless a party to the record shall file an affidavit that injustice will likely be done unless the original book is produced.—Act of June 22nd, 1883, Sec. 1, P. L. 154.

Affidavit to be Made by Bank Officer.

Sec. 351. To warrant such copy as provided for in the foregoing section, there must be an affidavit or the testimony of an officer of the bank stating that the book is one of the ordinary books of the banks used in the transaction of its business, that the entry is as was originally made at the time of its date, and in the usual course of its business, that there are no interlineations or erasures, that the book is in its custody and control and that the copy has been compared with the book and is a correct copy of the same, and such book shall be open to the inspection of any interested party.—Act of June 22nd, 1883, Sec. 2, P. L. 154.

When Act Does Not Apply.

Sec. 352. That the provisions of this act shall not apply to any suit to which the bank or bankers is a party.—Act of 22nd of June, 1883, Sec. 3, P. L. 154.

Repeal.

Sec. 353. All acts or parts of acts inconsistent with this act be and the same are hereby repealed.—Act of 22nd of June, 1883, Sec. 4, P. L. 154.

Officer of Insolvent Bank Receiving Money on Deposit Guilty of Embezzlement.—Penalty.

Sec. 354. Any banker, broker or officer of any trust or savings institution, National, State, or private bank, who shall take and receive money from a depositor with the knowledge that he, they or the bank is at the time insolvent, shall be guilty of embezzlement, and shall be punished by a fine in double the amount so received, and imprisoned from one to three years in the penitentiary.—Act of 9th of May, 1889, Sec. 1, P. L. 145.

Method of Renewing and Extending Charters of Certain Financial Institutions not Being Banks of Issue, and Rights Thereunder.—Proviso.

Sec. 355. Provident institutions, savings institutions and savings banks, banks of discount and savings banks and trust companies, not being banks of issue, chartered under the laws of the Commonwealth of Pennsylvania, may renew and extend their charters, corporate rights, and franchises for the period of twenty years, in manner following, namely: When the board of trustees or board of directors of any such institutions or savings banks, or banks of discount, or savings banks and trust companies, not being banks of issue, shall deem it expedient to have such charter, corporate rights and franchises renewed and extended, and shall so decide at a meeting called to consider the subject they shall give notice, by publication for three months in two newspapers published in the city or town where said institution or savings bank or bank, or bank of discount, or savings bank and trust company, not being banks of issue, is located, that at a specified time, the stockholders, where there are stockholders, and the directors, managers or trustees, where there are no stockholders, of such institutions or savings bank, or banks, or banks of discount, or saving banks and trust companies, not being banks of issue, will meet at the office or place of business of such institution or savings bank, or bank, or bank of discount, or savings bank or trust company, not being banks of issue, and vote for or against the proposition to renew and extend said charter corporate rights and franchises.

If a majority in interest of said stockholders, or directors, managers or trustees, where there are no stockholders, shall decide in favor of such renewal an extension, said action shall be certified to the Secretary of the Commonwealth, together with a statement of the condition of such institution upon a blank to be furnished by the Auditor General upon application made, said statement to be made by the cashier, secretary or president, under oath, attested by at least three of the board of directors, trustees or financial board of said institution, and a copy of its charter and all special acts of Assembly relating to said institution or bank, or bank of discount, savings bank and trust company, not being banks of issue, who shall refer the same to the Governor, Attorney General and Auditor General; upon a certificate being given by them or a majority of them that such renewal is not inconsistent with the public interests, and thereupon the said Secretary of the Commonwealth shall issue a certificate, under the seal of said Commonwealth that the charter, corporate rights and franchises of said provident institution, savings institutions, or savings banks, or banks, or banks of discount, or savings banks and trust companies, not being banks of issue, are duly renewed and extended for a period of twenty years: Provided, That said provident institution, savings institutions or savings banks, or banks, or banks of discount, or savings banks and trust companies, not being banks of issue, shall thereafter hold its charter subject to the provisions of the Constitution of the State: Provided also, That no provident institution, savings institution or savings bank, having no capital stock, renewing or extending its charter, corporate rights and franchises under the provisions of this act, shall thereafter be allowed the privileges of a bank of discount, nor be allowed to loan any money received on deposit, except upon first mortgage or lien upon real estate within this Commonwealth, upon the bonds or securities of the United States or of this State, or upon county, city, borough, township or school bonds of any county, city, borough, township or school district, or any other good and valid securities: And provided, That no bank re-chartered under the provisions of this act, shall charge a greater rate of discount than six per centum per annum.—Act of 10th of May, 1889, Sec. 1, P. L. 185.

ACT REGULATING DEPOSITORIES OF STATE MONEYS.

Payment of Interest on State Deposits.—Rate of Interest.

Sec. 356. On and after the first Monday of May, one thousand eight hundred and ninety-eight, the State Treasurer of Pennsylvania shall require and collect from each bank, banking institution, or trust company, in which funds of the State are deposited, interest on the amount of said deposit at the rate of two per centum per annum.— Act of 15th of June, 1897, Sec. 1, P. L. 157.

Banks Shall Give Bond Before Deposits are Made.—Contents of Bond.—Amount of Deposit.—Bonds Shall Include Special Obligation.

Sec. 357. The State Treasurer before making such deposits shall require each bank, banking institution or trust company to give a good and sufficient bond, containing a warrant of attorney to confess judgment in favor of the Commonwealth in double the amount of the contemplated deposit, with sureties to be approved by the Board of Revenue Commissioners of the Commonwealth of Pennsylvania, and no deposit shall at any time be greater than one-half of the amount of the bond furnished by said depository. And further, the said bond or bonds so given shall include a special obligation to settle with and pay to the State Treasurer, for the use of the Commonwealth, the amount of interest as it shall become due, semi-annually.—Act of 15th of June, 1897, Sec. 2, P. L. 157.

State Treasurer Shall Select Banks.—Approval of Revenue Commissioners.—Proviso.

Sec. 358. It shall be the duty of the State Treasurer to select the banks, banking institutions or trust companies in which State moneys shall be deposited, subject, however to the approval of the Board of Revenue Commissioners: Provided, however, That nothing in this act contained shall be held to prevent the State Treasurer from withdrawing any or all of said funds so deposited, for the purpose of paying the appropriations and obligations of the Commonwealth.—Act of 15th of June, 1897, Sec. 3, P. L. 157.

Duty of State Treasurer.—Selection of Depositories.—Responsibility of State Treasurer.—Not to be Held Liable for Failure of Banks, Etc.

Sec. 359. It shall be the duty of the State Treasurer to keep a correct and accurate account of all moneys received for the use of the Commonwealth, and pay out the same only on authority of law, and it shall be his further duty to select the depositories in which said funds may be deposited, subject to the approval of the Board of Revenue Commissioners as herein before provided; and he shall be personally responsible for a faithful performance of his duties under the law, and for a proper accounting of all moneys paid to him as State Treasurer; but he shall not be held personally liable for any moneys that may be lost by reason of the failure or insolvency of any bank, banking institution or trust companies selected as aforesaid.—Act of 15th of June, 1897, Sec. 4, P. L. 157.

Revenue Commissioners to Prepare Bonds.

Sec. 360. It shall be the duty of the said Board of Revenue Commissioners to cause to be prepared proper bonds to carry out the provisions of this act, and require the same to be executed by the State Treasurer and the banking institutions receiving State deposits, at or before the date when this act shall go into operation.—Act of 15th of June, 1897, Sec. 5, P. L. 157.

Five Active Banks to be Designated.—Duties of the Active Banks.

Sec. 361. The State Treasurer may designate one bank in Dauphin county, two banks in Philadelphia county and two banks in Allegheny county, to be known as active banks in which shall be deposited a sufficient amount of the daily receipts to transact the current business of the Commonwealth. These active banks shall be required to make all collections for the Commonwealth, without cost or compensation, and shall be required to pay interest at the rate of one and one-half per centum, per annum, on all daily balances.—Act of 15th of June, 1897, Sec. 6, P. L. 157.

AMENDMENT OF ACT OF 31ST OF MAY, 1893, RELATING TO LEGAL HOLIDAYS.

———

Days to be Observed as Holidays.—Every Saturday Designated as Half Holiday.—Such Holidays Shall be Treated as Sunday in Presentation of Bills, Drafts, Etc.—Provision as to Non-presentation for Payment on Saturday.—Proviso as to Business Transactions on Saturdays.—Proviso.—Execution of Writs, Etc., Shall not be Prevented on Holidays and Half Holidays.

Sec. 362. The following days and half days, namely: the first of January, commonly called New Year's day; the twelfth day of of February, known as Lincoln's birthday; the third Tuesday of February, election day; the twenty-second day of February, known as Washington's birthday; Good Friday; the thirtieth day of May, known as Memorial day; the Fourth of July, called Independence day; the first Monday of September, known as Labor day; the first Tuesday after the first Monday of November, election day; the twenty-fifth day of December, known as Christmas day; and every Saturday after twelve o'clock noon until twelve o'clock midnight, each of which Saturdays in hereby designated a half holiday, and any day appointed or recommended by the Governor of this State or of the President of the United States as a day of Thanksgiving or fasting and prayer, or other religious observance shall, for all purposes whatever as regards the presenting for payment or acceptance, and as regards the protesting and giving notice of the dishonor of bills of exchange, checks, drafts, and promissory notes, made after the passage of this act, be treated and considered as the first day of the week, commonly called Sunday, and as public holidays and half holidays; and all such bills, checks, drafts and notes otherwise presentable for acceptance or payment on any of the said days shall be deemed to be payable and be presentable for acceptance or payment on the secular or business day next succeeding such holiday or half holiday except checks, drafts, bills of exchange and promissory notes, payable at sight or on demand, which would otherwise be payable on any half holiday Saturday, shall be deemed to be payable at or before twelve o'clock noon of such half holiday: Provided, however, That for the purpose of protesting or otherwise holding liable any party to any bill of exchange, check, draft or promissory note, and which shall have not been paid before twelve o'clock noon of any Saturday designated a half holiday as aforesaid, a demand for acceptance or payment thereof shall not be made and notice of protest or dishonor thereof shall not be given until the next succeeding secular or business day: And provided further, That when any person, firm, corporation or company, shall, on any Saturday designated a half holiday, receive for collection any check, bill of exchange, draft or primisory note, such person, firm, corporation or company shall not be deemed guilty of any neglect or omission of duty, nor incur any liability in not presenting for payment or acceptance or collection such check, bill of exchange, draft or promissory note on that day: And provided further, That in construing this section every Saturday designated a half holiday shall, until twelve o'clock noon, be deemed a secular or business day; and the days and half days aforesaid, so designated as holidays and half holidays, shall be considered as public holidays and half holidays for all purposes whatsoever as regards the transaction of business: And provided further, That nothing herein contained shall be construed to prevent or invalidate the entry, issuance, service or execution of any writ, summons, confession of judgment, or other legal process whatever on any of the holidays or half holidays herein designated as holidays, nor to prevent any bank from keeping its doors open or transacting its business on any of the said Saturday afternoons if, by a vote of its directors, it shall elect to do so.—Act of 23rd of June, 1897, Sec. 1, P. L. 188.

Monday to be Observed When Holiday Occurs on Sunday.—Checks, Etc., Falling Due on Mondays Shall be Payable on the Next Business Day.

Sec. 363. Whenever the first day of January, the twelfth day of February, the twenty-second day of February, the thirtieth day of

May, the Fourth day of July, or the twenty-fifth day of December, shall any of them occur on Sunday, the following day, Monday shall be deemed and declared a public holiday. All bills of exchange, checks, drafts or promissory notes falling due on any of the Mondays so observed as holidays shall be due and payable on the next succeeding secular or business day, and all Mondays so observed as holidays, shall, for all purposes whatever as regards the presenting for payment or acceptance, and as regards the protesting and giving notice of the dishonor of bills of exchange, checks, drafts and promissory notes, made after the passage of this act, be treated and considered as if the first day of the week, commonly called Sunday.—Act of 23rd of June, 1897, Sec. 2, P. L. 188.

Checks, Etc., Becoming Due upon Sunday Shall be Payable on Next Business Day.

Sec. 364. All bills of exchange, checks, drafts and promisory notes made after the passage of this act, which by the terms thereof shall be payable on the first day of the week, commonly called Sunday, shall be deemed to be and shall be payable on the next succeeding secular or business day.—Act of 23rd of June, 1897, Sec. 3, P. L. 188.

Holidays Shall be Regarded as Business Days for Other Purposes.

Sec. 365. That all the days and half days herein designated as legal holidays shall be regarded as secular or business days for all other purposes than those mentioned in this act.—Act of 23rd of June, 1897, Sec. 4, P. L. 188.

AN ACT TO PROVIDE REVENUE BY TAXATION.

Banks Savings Institutions Shall Report Annually to Auditor General.—When Report Shall be Made.—Contents of said Report.—Auditor General shall Assess Shares of Stock.—Rate of Assessment upon each Dollar.—How Value shall be Ascertained.—Auditor General may Summon Officers of Bank, Etc., and Bring their Books for Examination, Etc., and may Require Further Evidence.—Auditor General shall Transmit Settlement to Banks, Etc., and Amount of Tax Due Commonwealth.—Bank Officer Shall Post Settlement.—Auditor General shall Hear Shareholder Valuation.—Banks shall Pay Tax Within Forty Days.—Banks and Savings Institutions Failing to Pay Tax, etc., shall be Subject to Penalty.—Amount of Penalty.—Officers who Fail to Post Settlement, etc., Subject to a Penalty.—Amount of Penalty.—Banks Collecting Four Mills on the Dollar on Actual Value of Stock, Etc., shall be Exempt.—And shall not make Report to Local Assessors or Commissioners.—Exceptions and Exemptions.

Sec. 366. That from and after the passage of this act every bank or savings institution having capital stock, incorporated by or under any law of this Commonwealth or under any law of the United States and located within this Commonwealth shall, on or before the twentieth day of June in each and every year, make to the Auditor General a report in writing, verified by the oath or affirmation of the president, cashier or treasurer, setting forth the full number of shares of the capital stock subscribed for or issued by such bank or savings institution, and the actual value thereof, which shall be ascertained as hereinbefore provided; whereupon it shall be the duty of the Auditor General to assess such shares for taxation at the same rate as that imposed upon other moneyed capital in the hands of individual citizens of the State, that is to say, the rate of four mills upon each dollar of the actual value thereof; the actual value of each share of stock to be ascertained and fixed by adding together the amount of capital stock paid in, the surplus and undivided profits, and dividing this amount by the number of shares. The Auditor General shall have the power, and it shall be his duty in case he shall not be satisfied with the correctness of the report as made by the officers of any bank or savings institution, to summon the officers of said bank or savings institution to appear before him, upon notice to do so, on a day to be fixed by him, and to bring with them the books of said bank or savings institution for his examination; and he shall have the right to have further evidence to satisfy himself as to the correctness of the report made to him on the question of the value of the shares of stock of such bank or savings institution according to the rule herein before stated. After the Auditor General shall have fixed the value of the shares of stock in any bank or savings institution by the method herein before provided, and settled an account according to law, he shall thereupon transmit to the president, cashier or treasurer of such bank or savings institution, copy of such settlement showing the valuation and assessment so made by him, and the amount of tax due the Commonwealth on all such shares. And it shall be the duty of the president, cashier or treasurer of any such bank or savings institution, immediately upon the receipt of said settlement, to post the same in a conspicuous place in such bank or savings institution so as to give notice to the share holders of such valuation; and it shall be the duty of the Auditor General to hear any share holder upon the subject of the valuation of such shares of stock at the Auditor General's office within the period of thirty days from the date of said settlement. It shall be the duty of every bank or savings institution within a period of forty days after the date of such settlement by the Auditor General, at its option, to pay the amount of said tax to the State Treasurer from its general fund, or collect the same from its shareholders and pay over the same to the State Treasurer: Provided, That if any such bank or savings institution shall fail or refuse to make such report, or to pay such tax at the time herein specified, or shall make any false statement in such report or shall fail or refuse by its officers to appear before the Auditor General upon notice as aforesaid, or shall fail or refuse to produce its books for examination when required to do so by the Auditor General, he shall, after having ascertained the actual value of each share of the capital stock of such bank or savings institution from the best information he can obtain, add thereto fifty per centum as a penalty, assess the tax as aforesaid, and proceed according to law, to collect the same from such bank or savings institution: Provided further, That if the president, cashier or treasurer of any such bank or savings institution shall neglect or refuse to post the copy of the settlement in a conspicuous place in such bank or savings institution immediately upon the receipt of the same, so as to give notice to the shareholders, such president, cashier or treasurer shall be adjudged to be in default, and as a penalty for such default such bank or savings instiution shall be responsible to the Commonwealth for the amount of tax assessed against the shareholders of such bank or savings institution: And provided further, That in case any bank or savings institution having capital stock, incorporated under the laws of this State or of the United States, shall collect, annually, from the shareholders thereof said tax of four mills on the dollar upon the actual value of all the shares of stock of said bank or savings institution according to the rule herein before stated that have been subscribed for or issued, and pay the same into the State Treasury on or before the first day of March in each year, the shares and so much of the capital and profits of such bank or savings institution as shall not be invested in real estate, shall be exempt from local taxation under the laws of this Commonwealth; and such bank or savings institution shall not be required to make any report to the local assessor or county commissioners of its personal property owned by it in its own right for the purposes of taxation, and shall not be required to pay any tax thereon. Except however that any bank or savings institution incorporated as aforesaid, in lieu of the method herein before set out for ascertaining the actual value of the shares of capital stock thereof, may elect to collect annually from the stockholders thereof a tax of ten mills on the dollar upon the par value of all shares of said bank that have been subscribed for or issued, and pay the same into the State Treasury on or before the first day of March in each year; and the shares of such bank or savings institution, and so much of the capital and profits of such bank or savings institution, as shall not be invested in real estate shall be exempted from local taxation under the laws of this Commonwealth.—Act of 15th of July, 1897, Sec. 1, P. L. 292.

AN ACT AMENDING THE EIGHTH SECTION OF THE BANKING LAW OF 13TH DAY OF MAY, 1876.

Section Eight of Act of 1876 as Amended.—What Real Estate May be Held.

Sec. 367. It shall be lawful for any association incorporated under this act to purchase, hold and convey real estate as follows:

First. Such as shall be necessary for its immediate accommodation in the transaction of its business.

Second. Such as shall be mortgaged to it in good faith as security for debts.

Third. Such as it shall purchase at sales under judgments, decrees or mortgages held by such corporation, or shall purchase to secure debts due to said corporation.

Such corporation shall not purchase or hold real estate in any other case or for any other purpose than as specified in this section, nor shall it in any case hold the possession of any real estate under mortgage, or the title and possession of any real estate purchased by it except such as may be necessary for its immediate accommodation of its business, for a longer perior than five years.—Act of 19th of April, 1901, Sec. 1, P. L. 79.

AN ACT PROVIDING THAT WHEN CORPORATION BECOMES SURETY FOR OFFICER OR CONTRACTOR TO ANY MUNICIPALITY ACTION MAY BE BROUGHT IN COUNTY WHERE MUNICIPALITY IS SITUATED.

Action or Suit Upon Bond May be Brought in County in Which Municipality is Situated.

Sec. 368. It shall be lawful for any borough, city or other municipality of this Commonwealth, to which is given the bond or other obligation of any officer thereof for the performance of his duties, or the bond or obligation of any contractor therewith for the performance of his contract, in which bond or obligation any corporation or surety company is the surety, to bring any suit, action or other legal proceeding upon said bond or obligation in the county in which the respective borough, city or other municipality is situate, with like effect as if the said corporation or surety company were a resident of the said county.—Act of 2nd of May, 1901, Sec. 1, P. L. 111.

Service of Summons or Process.—On Officers.—At Residence.—Upon Registered Agent.

Sec. 369. The summons or other process shall be served upon the said corporation or surety company defendent by reading the same in the hearing of any president, vice president, secretary, chief clerk, treasurer, or in the hearing of any other officer of said company, or of any director or agent thereof; or by giving any of the aforesaid officers or agents notice of the contents of said summons or other process, and giving him a true and attested copy thereof. If any of the aforesaid officers or agents cannot conveniently be found, then such service can be made by leaving a true and attested copy of the summons or other process at the dwelling house of such officer or agent, with an adult member of the family; and if said officer or agent resides in the family of another, then said attested copy may be left with an adult member of the family with which such officer or agent resides. Where the corporation or surety company defendant is a foreign corporation, authorized to do business in this State, the summons or other process may be served in the manner provided by law for the service of a summons upon any duly appointed and registered agent of the said foreign corporation or company, resident in this State.—Act of 2nd of May, 1901, Sec. 2, P. L. 111.

Within County Where Writ Issues.—Within Other Counties.—Mileage.

Sec. 370. The said summons or other process, herein before provided for, shall be served by the sheriff or his deputy within the county in which the writ issues; but when the corporation, surety company, or the officers or agents thereof, are non-residents, the said sheriff shall deputize to serve said summons or other process the sheriff of.any other county in which the corporation or surety company defendent is located, or the officers thereof reside; or in which the registered State agent is resident, in cases where a foreign corporation or surety company is defendant; but the mileage for service in the later cases shall be computed only from the county seat in which the said deputized sheriff resides.—Act of 2nd of May, 1901, Sec. 3, P. L. 111.

EXTRACTS FROM THE NEGOTIABLE INSTRUMENT LAW OF 1901 RELATING TO PRACTICE OF BANKS.

When Negotiable Instruments Drawn or Endorsed to Cashier, Etc.

Sec. 371. When an instrument is drawn or indorsed to a person as "cashier" or other fiscal officer of a bank or corporation, it is deemed prima facie, to be payable to the bank or corporation of which he is such officer, and may be negotiated by either the indorsement of the bank or corporation or the indorsement of the officer.— Act of 16th of May, 1901, Sec. 42, P. L. 194.

Presentment of Instrument Payable at a Bank.

Sec. 372. Where the instrument is payable at a bank, presentment for payment must be made during banking hours, unless the person to make payment has no funds there to meet it at any time during the day, in which case presentment at any hour before the bank is closed on that day is sufficient.—Act of 16th of May, 1901, Sec. 75, P. L. 194.

Right of Bank Where Instrument is Payable at Bank.

Sec. 373. Where the instrument is made payable at a bank, it is equivalent to an order to the bank to pay the same for the account of the principal debtor thereon.—Act of 16th of May, 1901, Sec. 87, P. L. 194.

Definition of a Check.

Sec. 374. A check is a bill of exchange drawn on a bank, payable on demand. Except as herein otherwise provided, the provisions of this act applicable to a bill of exchange, payable on demand, apply to a check.—Act of 16th of May, 1901, Sec. 185, P. L. 194.

Presentation of a Check.

Sec. 375. A check must be presented for payment within a reasonable time after its issue or the drawer will be discharged from liability to the extent of the loss caused by the delay.—Act of 16th of May, 1901, Sec. 186, P. L. 194.

Certification of Check Equivalent to Acceptance.

Sec. 376. Where a check is certified by the bank on which it is drawn, the certification is an equivalent to an acceptance.—Act of 16th of May, 1901, Sec. 187, P. L. 194.

Discharge of Drawer and Indorser When Check Accepted or Certified.

Sec. 377. Where the holder of a check procures it to be accepted or certified, the drawer and all indorsers are discharged from liability thereon.—Act of 16th of May, 1901, Sec. 188, P. L. 194.

A Check not an Assignment.

Sec. 378. A check of itself, does not operate as an assignment of any part of the funds to the credit of the drawer with the bank, and the bank is not liable to the holder unless and until it accepts or certifies the check.—Act of 16th of May, 1901, Sec. 189, P. L. 194.

AN ACT TO AUTHORIZE BANKS TO IMPROVE REAL ESTATE FOR THE TRANSACTION OF BUSINESS AND TO DERIVE RENT THEREFROM.

Authorizing Banks and Banking Companies to Improve Certain Real Estate.—Proviso.—Repeal.

Sec. 379. It shall be lawful for any bank or banking company of this Commonwealth to improve any real estate it may now or hereafter hold for the accommodation and transaction of its business, by erecting new buildings, or by renewing or replacing any building or buildings thereon with such new or additional structures of such new dimensions as its board of directors may from time to time deem expedient; and to use such portion thereof as may be suitable and convenient for the transaction of its business for that purpose; and to lease and let from time to time, such portions or apartments of such building or buildings as it may not require for its banking business, and to receive rents for the use of the same: Provided, however, That no such bank or banking company shall, for the purposes aforesaid, reduce its surplus fund below fifty per centum of what its amount may be when such improvement, buildings, et cetera, may be commenced.—Act of 21st of May, 1901, Sec. 1, P. L. 288.

Repeal.

Sec. 380. That all acts or parts of acts inconsistent with this act be and the same are hereby repealed.—Act of 21st of May, 1901, Sec. 2, P. L. 288.

SUPPLEMENT TO THE ACT OF 1874.

Merger and Consolidation of Certain Corporations.—Proviso.

Sec. 381. It shall be lawful for any corporation now or hereafter organized under, or accepting the provisions of, the act, entitled "An act to provide for the incorporation and regulation of certain corporations," approved April twenty-ninth, one thousand eight hundred and seventy-four, or of any of the supplements thereto, or of any other act of Assembly authorizing the formation of corporations, to buy and own the capital stock of, and to merge its corporate rights, powers and privileges with and into those of any other corporation, so that by virtue of this act such corporations may consolidate, and so that all the property, rights, franchises and privileges then by law vested in either of such corporations, so merged, shall be transferred to and vested in the corporation into which such merger shall be made: Provided, That nothing in this act shall be construed so as to permit railroad, canal, telegraph companies, which own, operate or in any way control parallel or competing roads, canals or lines, to merge or combine; And provided further, That any corporation formed for the purpose of carrying on any manufacturing business under the seventeenth or eighteenth clause of section two of an act, entitled "An act to provide for the incorporation and regulation of certain corporations," approved April twenty-nine, one thousand eight hundred and seventy-four, with the powers conferred by section thirty-eight, or section thirty-nine, of said act, may be merged and consolidated, under the provisions of this act, with any other corporation formed for any purpose provided for in either the seventeenth or eighteenth clause of section two of the act above cited; but nothing in this act contained shall extend or enlarge beyond its former territorial limits the exclusive franchise of any gas or water company.—Act of 29th of May, 1901, Sec. 1, P. L. 349.

Joint Agreement.—To be Sumbitted to Stockholders.—Meeting.—
Certificates.—To be Filed.

Sec. 382. Said merger or consolidation shall be made under the conditions, provisions and restrictions, and with the powers herein set forth, to wit: First, The directors of each corporation may enter into a joint agreement, under the corporate seal of each corporation, for the merger and consolidation of said corporations; prescribing the terms and conditions thereof, the mode of carrying the same into effect, the name of the new corporation, the number and names of the directors and other officers thereof, and who shall be the first directors and officers and their places of residence, the number of shares of capital stock, the amount or par value of each share and the manner of converting the capital stock of each of said corporations into the stock of a new corporation, and how and when new officers and directors shall be chosen, with such other details as they shall deem necessary to perfect the said consolidation and merger; but said agreement shall not be effective unless the same shall be approved by the stockholders of said corporations, in the manner hereinafter provided.

Said agreement shall be submitted to the stockholders of each of said corporations, at separate special meetings, of the time, place and object of which respective meetings due notice shall be given by publication, once a week for two successive weeks before said respective meetings, in at least one newspaper in the county or each of the counties in which the principal offices of said respective corporations shall be situate; and at said meetings the said agreement of the directors shall be considered, and a vote of the stockholders in person or by proxy shall be taken, by ballot, for the adoption or rejection of the same, each share of stock entitling the holder thereof to one vote; and if a majority in amount of the entire capital stock of each of said corporations shall vote in favor of said agreement, merger and consolidation, then that fact shall be certified by the secretary of each corporation, under the seal thereof, and said certificates, together with the said agreement or a copy thereof, shall be filed in the office of the Secretary of the Commonwealth, whereupon the said agreement shall be deemed and taken to be the act of consolidation of said corporation.—Act of 29th of May, 1901, Sec. 2, P. L. 349.

Merger.—Proviso.—Letters Patent.—Bonus.

Sec. 383. Upon the filing of said certificates and agreement, or copy of agreement, in the office of the Secretary of the Commonwealth, the said merger shall be deemed to have taken place, and the said corporations to be one corporation under the name adopted in and by the said agreement, possessing all the rights, privileges and franchises theretofore vested in each of them, and all the estate and property, real and personal, and rights of action of each of said corporations, shall be deemed and taken to be transferred to and vested in the said new corporation without any further act or deed: Provided, That all rights of creditors and all liens upon the property of each of said corporations shall continue unimpaired, and the respective constituent corporations may be deemed to be in existence to preserve the same; and all debts, duties and liabilities of each of said constituent corporations shall thenceforth attach to the said new corporation and may be enforced against it to the same extent and by the same process as if said debts, duties and liabilities had been contracted by it. But such merger and consolidation shall not be complete, and no such consolidated corporation shall do any business of any kind, until it shall have first obtained from the Governor of the Commonwealth new letters patent, and shall have paid to the State Treasurer a bonus of one-third of one per centum upon all its capital stock in excess of the amount of capital stock of the several corporations so consolidating upon which the bonus required by law had been therefore paid.—Act of 29th of May, 1901, Sec. 3, P. L. 349.

Evidence.

Sec. 384. A certified copy of said certificate and agreement, or copy of agreement, so to be filed in the office of the Secretary of the Commonwealth, shall be evidence of the lawful holding and action of such meetings, and of the merger and consolidation of said corporations.—Act of 29th of May, 1901, Sec. 4, P. L. 349.

Petition.—Appraisers.—Award.—Appraisement.—Stock Transfer.

Sec. 385. If any stockholder or stockholders of any corporation which shall become a party to an agreement of merger and consolidation hereunder, shall be dissatisfied with, or object to such consolidation, and shall have voted against the same at the stockholder's meeting, it shall and may be lawful for any such stockholder or stockholders, within thirty days after the adoption of said agreement of merger and consolidation by the stockholders as herein provided, and upon reasonable notice to said corporation, to apply by petition to any court of common pleas of the county in which the chief office of such corporation may be situate, or to a judge of said court in vacation, if no such court sits during said period, to appoint three disinterested persons to estimate and appraise the damages, if any, done to such stockholder or stockholders by said consolidation. Upon such petition, it shall be the duty of the said court, or judge, to make such appointment; and the award of the persons so appointed, or a majority of them, when confirmed by the said court, shall be final and conclusive; and the persons so appointed shall also appraise the share or shares of said stockholders in the said corporation at the full market value thereof, without regard to any appreciation or depreciation in consequence of the said consolidation, which appraisement, when confirmed by the said court, shall be final and conclusive; and the said corporation may, at its election, either pay to the said stockholder or stockholders the amount of damages so found and awarded, if any, or the value of the stock so ascertained; and upon the payment of the value of the stock of the aforesaid, the said stockholder or stockholders shall transfer the stock so held by them to the said corporation, to be disposed of by the directors thereof or to be retained for the benefit of the other stockholders; and in case the value of said stock as aforesaid, shall not be so paid within thirty days after the said award shall have been confirmed by the said court, the damages so found and confirmed shall be a judgment against said corporation, and be collected as other judgments in said court are by law recoverable.— Act of 29th of May, 1901, Sec. 5, P. L. 349.

AN ACT AMENDING THE FIRST SECTION OF AN ACT RELATING TO PRIVATE BANKERS, ETC., OF THE 16TH OF MAY, 1861.

Return to Auditor General.—Contents of Return.—To Pay One Per Centum.

Sec. 386. Every stock broker, bill broker, exchange broker, merchandise broker and private banker in this Commonwealth shall, on or before the first Monday of December next, and on or before the same day in each year thereafter, make a written return, under oath or affirmation, to the Auditor General of this Commonwealth, in which return he shall exhibit and set forth the full amount of his gross receipts from commissions, discounts, abatements, allowances and all other receipts arising from his business during the year ending with the thirtieth day of November preceding the date of such annual return, and shall forthwith pay into the State Treasury one per centum of the aggregate amount of such gross receipts contained in such return, for the use of the Commonwealth.—Act of 13th of June, 1901, Sec. 1, P. L. 559.

Repeal.

Sec. 387. All acts or parts of acts inconsistent with this act, passed previous to the adoption of this amendment, are hereby repealed.—Act of 13th of June, 1901, Sec. 2, P. L. 559.

AN ACT LIMITING AMOUNT OF LOANS TO OFFICERS AND DIRECTORS
OF BANKS, TRUST COMPANIES AND SAVINGS INSTITUTIONS.

Limit of Loans.

Sec. 388. No director of any banking institution, trust company
or savings institution, having capital stock, heretofore or hereafter incorporated in this Commonwealth, shall receive as a loan an
amount greater than ten per centum of the capital stock actually
paid in, and surplus; and the gross amount loaned to all officers and
directors of such corporations, and to the firms or houses in which
they may be interested directly or indirectly, shall not exceed at
any time the sum of twenty-five per centum of the capital stock paid
in and surplus.—Act of 14th of June, 1901, Sec. 1, P. L. 561.

Capital Stock Not to be Taken as Security or Purchased.

Sec. 389. No corporation under this act shall take as security for
any loan or discount, a lien on any part of its capital stock; but the
same surety, both in kind and amount, shall be required of persons,
shareholders and not shareholders; and no such corporation shall be
the holder or purchaser of any of its capital, unless such purchase
shall be necessary to prevent loss on a debt previously contracted in
good faith, on surety which at the time was deemed adequate for
the payment of such debt, within a lien upon such stock, or in case
of forfeiture of such stock for the non-payment of instalments due
thereon; and the stock so purchased shall, in no case, be held by the
corporation so purchasing for a longer period than six months, if the
same can be sold for what such stock cost the corporation.—Act
of 14th of June, 1901, Sec. 2, P. L. 561.

AN ACT AUTHORIZING BANKS TO LOAN MONEY ON BONDS AND MORT-
GAGES ON REAL ESTATE, AND NOTES, SECURITIES, ETC.

Loans on Bonds and Mortgages, Etc.

Sec. 390. Banks chartered under the provisions of the laws of the
Commonwealth of Pennsylvania be and they are hereby authorized
to loan money on the security of bonds and mortgages on unincumbered real estate situated in this State, not in excess of their time
deposits, and to invest their funds, not exceeding twenty-five per
centum of their capital stock, surplus and undivided profits, in the
purchase of such mortgages; and may also purchase, for investment,
any interest bearing bonds or other obligations of any corporation
or individual.—Act of 10th of July, 1901, Sec. 1, P. L. 639.

Repeal.

Sec. 391. All acts and part of acts inconsistent herewith are hereby
repealed.—Act of 10th of July, 1901, Sec. 2, P. L. 639.

STOCKHOLDERS, DIRECTORS AND CLERKS OF, MAY BECOME COMMISSIONED NOTARIES PUBLIC.

Stockholders, Directors and Clerks May be Notaries Public.—
Proviso.

Sec. 392. Hereafter any stockholder, director, or clerk, in any bank, banking institution or trust company may, at the same time, hold, exercise or enjoy the office of notary public: Providing, That no stockholder, director, or clerk, in any bank, banking institution, or trust company, shall do or perform any act or acts as notary public or perform any duty or duties of notary public, for such bank, banking institution, or trust company, in which he or she may be a stockholder, director or clerk; and any act or acts, duty or duties, performed by any notary public of any bank, banking institution, or trust company, in which he or she may be a stockholder, director, or clerk, is and are hereby declared invalid.—Act of 24th of March, 1903, Sec. 2, P. L. 50.

CHAPTER 12.

AN ACT CREATING A BANKING DEPARTMENT.

**Banking Department Established.—Institutions Under its Control.
—Foreign Corporations.**

Sec. 393. There is hereby established a separate and distinct department to be known as the Banking Department, the Commissioner of which said Department shall take care that the laws of this Commonwealth in relation to banks and banking companies, cooperative banking associations, trust, safe deposit, real estate, mortgage, title insurance, guarantee, surety and indemnity companies, and all other companies of a similar character, savings institutions, savings banks, provident institutions and every other corporation having power and receiving money on deposit, and to mutual savings funds, building and loan associations and bond and investment companies incorporated, or which may hereafter become incorporated, under the laws of this State, or incorporated under the laws of any foreign State, and authorized under the laws of this State to transact business herein, shall be faithfully executed; and also that the greatest safety to depositors therein and other interested persons shall be afforded; and the said Commissioner of Banking and said Department shall be charged with the supervision of all of said corporations for said purposes. And it shall not be lawful for any foreign corporation to receive any deposit or deposits or transact any banking business whatsoever, in this Commonwealth, until it shall have first filed in the office of the Commissioner of Banking a certified copy of the statement required by law to be filed in the office of the Secretary of the Commonwealth.—Act of 11th of February, 1895, Sec. 1, P. L. 4.

**Chief Officer.—How Appointed.—Term of Office.—Salary.—Clerks
and Their Salaries.—Deputy.—Salary.—Examiners, Number and
Appointment Of.—Compensation.—Oath and Bond of Commissioner and Deputy.—Shall Not be Interested in Any Corporation
Under Their Supervision.**

Sec. 394. The chief officer of the Banking Department shall be denominated the Commissioner of Banking. He shall be appointed by the Governor, by and with the advice and consent of the Senate, and shall hold his office for the term of four years and until his successor is duly qualified. He shall receive an annual salary of six thousand dollars, payable quarterly by a warrant drawn by the Auditor General on the State Treasurer. He shall have power to employ from time to time such clerks, not to exceed three in number, whose annual salary shall not exceed fourteen hundred dollars each, to discharge such duties as he shall assign them, whose

10

salaries shall be paid monthly by warrant drawn by the Auditor General upon the State Treasurer. He shall also appoint one deputy who shall perform the duties attached by law to the office of Commissioner of Banking during the absence or inability of the Commissioner, and whose salary shall be twenty-five hundred dollars per annum, payable in the same way and manner as that of the Commissioner, and who shall give to the Commonwealth a bond in the penalty of ten thousand dollars, with one or more sureties to be approved by the Governor, conditioned for the proper and faithful performance of all his duties. The Commissioner of Banking may also from time to time appoint examiners in such numbers as may be necessary for the conduct of the business of the Department, not to exceed ten in number, who shall receive such compensation as may be fixed by said Commissioner for each day actually employed in making examinations of corporations under the order of said Commissioner, not to exceed ten dollars per day, and also actual expense incurred in making such examination, which compensation and expenses shall be paid by a warrant drawn by the Auditor General upon the State Treasurer. Within fifteen days from the time of the notice of their appointment, the Commissioner and his deputy shall take and subscribe the oath of office prescribed by the Constitution and file the same in the office of the Secretary of the Commonwealth, and the Commissioner shall also give to the Commonwealth a bond in the penalty of twenty thousand dollars, with two or more sureties to be approved of by the Governor, conditioned for the faithful performance of his duties, and neither said Commissioner nor his deputy nor examiners shall be interested as officer, director, trustee, manager or stockholder in any corporation subject to the supervision of this Department.—Act of 11th of February, 1895, Sec. 2, P. L. 4.

Corporations Shall Be Subject to Supervision in All Departments.—
Examiner Must Have Written Authority to Inspect.

Sec. 395. Every corporation, in all its departments, business and affairs, together with all its property, assets and resources included within the supervision of the Commissioner of Banking or his Department, as set forth in the first section of this act, shall be subject to inspection and examination by the Commissioner of Banking or his deputy, or any qualified examiner of the said Department, when such examiner is authorized, in writing, under the official seal of said Commissioner or his deputy, to make such examination of any said corporation.—Act of 11th of February, 1895, Sec. 3, P. L. 4.

Duties of the Commissioner of Banking.—Examiner.—Assignment Of and Powers Of.—Oaths May be Administered by Commissioner.—Deputy and Examiner.—False Swearing.—Procedure in Case of Failure to Make Answer.—Compensation of Examiner, Etc.—Fees to be Paid by Corporations.—Procedure in Case of Refusal or Neglect to Pay.—Proviso.

Sec. 396. It shall be the duty of the Commissioner of Banking, as often as he shall deem proper, to examine, or cause to be examined, the books, papers and affairs of each and every corporation subject to supervision as aforesaid, and whenever he shall deem it necessary or proper he shall assign a qualified examiner or examiners to make such examination, and who shall have power to make a thorough examination into all the business and affairs of the corporation in all its departments, and of all its property, assets and resources wherever situated, and in so doing, to examine any of the officers or agents or employes thereof, or any person or officers or employes of any corporation, or any firm in possession of any asset thereof, under oath, or otherwise, and shall make or cause to be made, in the manner aforesaid, a full and detailed report of the condition of the corporation; and the said corporation shall not be subject to any other visitorial power than such as may be authorized by this act, except such as are vested in the several courts of law. Said Commissioner and his deputy and any qualified examiner so as aforesaid appointed are hereby empowered and authorized to administer an oath to any of the persons aforesaid, and willful false swearing in any inquiry thereunder shall be perjury, and subject, upon conviction thereof, to the same punishment as provided by existing laws for the punishment of perjury. Upon failure of any of the persons aforesaid to make answer to any inquiries as aforesaid, the Attorney General, upon the request of the Commissioner of Banking, shall make information thereof to the court of common pleas of the county of Dauphin, whereupon said court, after hearing, shall make such order as occasion requires. The compensation of examiners and expenses of examinations provided for by this act shall be paid by warrant drawn by the Auditor General on the State Treasurer, upon requisition made by the Commissioner of Banking, and in order to help pay such expenses all corporations subject to the supervision of the Banking Department, (except Building and Loan Associations doing business exclusively within this State), shall annually, upon the first Monday of May in each year, pay into the Treasury of the State the following amounts in addition to any taxes or fees imposed by existing laws upon such corporations, the sum of twenty-five dollars each, and in all cases of such corporations having capital stock, for each one hundred thousand dollars of capital stock, or fractional part thereof in excess of one hundred thousand dollars, the sum of five dollars shall be paid annually at the time aforesaid; and all such corporations shall pay annually at the time aforesaid, the sum of two cents for each one thousand dollars of assets which it may have. In cases of corporations subject to the supervision of the Banking Department, which have no capital stock, they shall each, in addition to any taxes or fees imposed by existing laws, annually upon the day and year aforesaid, pay into the Treasury of the State the sum of twenty-five dollars, and for each one hundred thousand dollars of assets, or fractional part thereof in excess of one hundred thousand dollars, annually pay into the Treasury of the State the sum of one dollar. And in cases of neglect or refusal of any corporation aforesaid to pay said sums into the State Treasury at the time aforesaid, the Auditor General shall settle an account against such corporation for the amounts due and payable under this act, and shall proceed to collect the same in the same way and manner and under the same penalties as are provided for the collecting of taxes and penalties under the existing laws: Provided, however, That nothing herein contained shall impose upon building and loan associations, doing business exclusively within this State, the payment of any sum or sums of money whatsoever.—Act of 11th of February, 1895, Sec. 4, P. L. 4.

Reports.—Contents of Report.—When Reports Shall be Made.—Publication of Summary of Report.—Proof of Publication.—Special Reports.—Failure to Make Report.—Penalty For.—Refusal to Pay Penalty or to Furnish Proof of Publication, Procedure in Case of.—Sums Collected Shall be Applied to Expenses of Department.

Sec. 397. Every corporation, subject to the supervision of the Banking Department, as herein before provided, shall make to the Commissioner of Banking, not less than two reports of its condition during each year, according to the form and in the manner prescribed by the said Commissioner, which report shall be verified by the oath or affirmation of the president, cashier or treasurer or other managing officer of such corporation, and attested as correct by the signature of at least three of the directors, trustees or other managers of such corporation. Each such report of condition shall exhibit, in detail and under appropriate heads, the resources and liabilities of the corporation at the close of business on any past day by the Commissioner specified, and shall be transmitted to the Commissioner within five days (which time in the discretion of the Commissioner of Banking may be extended) after the receipt of a request or requisition therefor from him, and an abstract summary thereof shall forthwith be published by such corporation in a newspaper published in the place where such corporation is located, at least three times, and if there is no newspaper published in such place, then in the newspaper published nearest thereto in the same county; and upon completion thereof proof of such publication shall be furnished to the said Commissioner by such corporation. The Commissioner of Banking shall also have power to call for special report from any corporation whenever, in his judgment, the same may be necessary to a full and complete knowledge of its condition. The reports of condition and publication thereof provided for and required in this section shall be in lieu of all reports and of all publication for similar purposes heretofore required by law to be made by such corporations. In case any such corporation shall fail to make and transmit any of the reports, or furnish such proof of publication required by this act, such corporation shall be subject, at the discretion of the Commissioner of Banking, to a penalty of twenty dollars for each day after the time mentioned above, or the extension thereof by the Commissioner of Banking, for making such report or said publication. Whenever any such corporation shall delay or refuse to pay the penalty herein imposed for a failure to make and transmit a report or furnish proof of publication, the Attorney General, upon request of the Commissioner of Banking, is hereby authorized to maintain an action in the name of the Commonwealth against the delinquent corporation for the recovery of such penalty, and all sums collected by such action shall be paid into the State Treasury and applied upon the expenses of the Banking Department.—Act of 11th of February, 1895, Sec. 5, P. L. 4.

Impaired or Reduced Capital Stock.—Procedure in Case Of.—Commissioner Shall Require Deficiency to be Made Good.—Failure to Make Good Any Reduction or Impairment of Capital.—Procedure in Case Court Shall Hear Allegations and Proofs.—When Court Shall Decree Dissolution.—When Court Shall Annul Act of Commissioner.

Sec. 398. Whenever it shall appear from any report of the condition of any corporation made as hereinbefore provided to the Commissioner of Banking, or the said Commissioner shall have reason to believe that the capital of any such corporation is reduced, by impairment or otherwise, below the amount required by law or the articles of incorporation, or below the amount certified to the proper authorities as paid in, it shall be the duty of the Commissioner and he shall have power to require such corporation under his hand and seal of office, to make good the deficiency so appearing; and to give effect to such requisition he shall have power to examine, or cause to be examined, any such corporations, books, papers and affairs to ascertain whether such reduction or impairment of capital has been made good in compliance with his requisition; and if any such corporation shall neglect or refuse, for sixty days after such requisition has been made, to make good the reduction or impairment of capital existing, it shall be the duty of the Commissioner to communicate the facts to the Attorney General, whose duty it shall then become to apply to the court of common pleas of the county of Dauphin, or in vacation, to any of the judges thereof, for an order requiring said corporation to show cause why their business should not be closed, and the court or judge, as the case may be, shall thereupon hear the allegations and proofs of the respective parties. If it appears to the satisfaction of the said court or judge that such corporation has neglected or refused to comply with such requisition, and that such capital stock is reduced and impaired, and that such corporation is insolvent, or that the interests of the public so require, the said court or judge shall decree a dissolution of such corporation and a distribution of its effects, or shall make such other orders, from time to time, in the matter as the interests of the parties and the public may require. But in case it shall appear to said court or judge that said corporation has complied with the provisions of this act, and that it is not insolvent, a decree shall be entered annulling the act of the Commissioner in the premises and authorizing such corporation to continue business.—Act of 11th of February, 1895, Sec. 6, P. L, 4.

Duties of Commissioner Where Corporation Violates its Charter.— Commissioner to Report Facts to Attorney General.—Procedure by Attorney General.—When Court Shall Decree Dissolution.

Sec. 399. Whenever it shall appear to the Commissioner of Banking, from any report of condition of any corporation not having any capital stock and doing business exclusively for the benefit of depositors, or from any examination made by him, or from the report of any examination made to him, of the condition of the affairs of such corporation that any such corporation has committed any violation of its charter or law, or its conducting its business and affairs in an unsafe and unauthorized manner, he shall, by an order under his hand and seal of office, direct the discontinuance of such illegal and unsafe or unauthorized practice and direct strict conformity with the requirements of the law, and with safety and security in its transactions; and whenever any such corporation shall refuse or neglect to comply with any such order, as aforesaid, or whenever it shall appear to the Commissioner that it is unsafe or inexpedient for any such corporation to continue to transact business, or that any trustee or officer of any such corporation has abused his trust, or been guilty of misconduct or malversation in his official position injurious to the corporation, or to its depositors, he shall communicate the facts to the Attorney General, who shall thereupon institute such proceedings as the nature of the case may require. The proceedings instituted by the Attorney General may be by quo warranto in the court of common pleas of the county of Dauphin for the removal of one or more of the trustees or managers and the substitution of others, or for the transfer of the corporate powers to other persons, or for the withdrawal of corporate powers, or the consolidation and merger of the corporation with any other corporation of similar character that may be willing to accept of the trust, or for such other and further relief or correction as the particular facts communicated to him shall seem to require, and the court before which such proceedings shall be instituted shall have power to grant such orders, and in its discretion from time to time, modify or revoke the same, and to grant such relief and render such judgment as the facts or evidence in the case and situation of the parties and the interest involved shall seem to require, or if it shall appear to the said court that the interests of the public so require, the said court shall decree a dissolution of such corporation and a distribution of its effects.—Act of 11th of February, 1895, Sec. 7, P. L. 4.

Refusal of Corporation to Submit Books, Etc.—Commissioner May Refer Violation of Law to Attorney General.

Sec. 400. In case any corporation shall refuse to submit its books, papers and affairs to the inspection of the said Commissioner or his deputy, or of any examiner designated as aforesaid, or the officers thereof shall refuse to submit to be examined upon oath touching the affairs of such corporation, or if such corporation shall be found to have violated any law of this State binding upon such corporation, the Commissioner may refer the same to the Attorney General whose duty it shall then become to institute for such causes similar proceedings against such corporation as are authorized by the preceding section.—Act of 11th of February, 1895, Sec. 8, P. L. 4.

Duties of Commissioner When Corporation is in Unsafe Condition. —Duties of Attorney General.—Receiver May be Appointed.— Court Shall Approve Bond of Receiver.—Temporary Receiver May be Appointed in Certain Cases.—May Withdraw Temporary Receiver.—Corporation May File Answer in Court of Common Pleas of Dauphin County.

Sec. 401. If from any examination of the papers, books and affairs of any corporation, with or without capital, the Commissioner of

Banking shall have reason at any time to conclude that such corporation is in an unsound and unsafe condition to do business, or that its business or manner of conducting the same is injurious and contrary to the interest of the public. the Commissioner of Banking shall forthwith communicate the facts to the Attorney General who shall forthwith make application to the court of common pleas of the county of Dauphin, or to a law judge thereof, for the appointment of a receiver to take charge of such corporation's property and wind up its business. Such receiver shall proceed and wind up the business and affairs of said corporation under and subject to the orders of the court of common pleas aforesaid. Said court shall also approve the amount and security of the bond to be given by said receiver for the faithful performance of his duties: Provided, however, That if the Commissioner of Banking shall at any time deem it necessary for the immediate protection of the depositors and other creditors of any such corporation, he may, after hearing before the Attorney General of the Commonwealth, (of which hearing the said corporation shall have notice), appoint some suitable person as temporary receiver who shall first give to the Commonwealth a good and sufficient bond with two sureties to be approved by said Commissioner, conditioned for faithful performance of duty, and shall forthwith take possession of said corporation's property and business and retain possession thereof pending like proceedings, as aforesaid, which shall be forthwith instituted in the court of common pleas of Dauphin county, at which time the compensation of said receiver shall be fixed by said court. And said Commissioner of Banking after having so appointed said temporary receiver, shall, (if he deems it safe and to the best for all interests concerned), have power at any time to withdraw said temporary receiver and cancel his appointment and surrender possession of said corporation and its property to said corporation without further proceedings or order. Whenever a corporation which shall deny that there is a good reason for the institution of either of the proceedings, as aforesaid, or that its business should be closed, or that it should be dissolved, it shall forthwith file its answer in said court of common pleas of the county of Dauphin, or make application to said court, or the law judge thereof, and ask for an order to enjoin further proceedings in the premises; whereupon the said court or law judge thereof, after hearing the allegations and proofs of the respective parties, shall make such order in the matter as the interest of the parties and that of the public may require.—Act of 11th of February, 1895, Sec. 9, P. L. 4.

Duties and Powers of Auditor General Transferred to Banking Department.—Same as of the Banking Department.

Sec. 402. All requirements of law providing for supervision and regulation heretofore incumbent upon corporations now included by virtue of this act under the supervision of the Banking Department to be done and performed to the Auditor General, save requirements imposed by law for the purpose of taxation, shall hereafter be done and performed to the Commissioner of Banking, subject to the modifications herein provided. And all powers, duties, rights and privileges heretofore incumbent upon and belonging to the Auditor

General by virtue of the laws of this State regulating the business and for the supervision of the conduct of such corporations are hereby transferred to and made incumbent upon the Commissioner of Banking.—Act of 11th of February, 1895, Sec. 10, P. L. 4.

Visitorial Power Limited to Banking Department and That Authorized by the Courts.

Sec. 403. No corporation subject to the supervision of the Banking Department shall be subject to any visitorial power other than such as are authorized by this act, or are invested by law in the courts of this Commonwealth.—Act of 11th of February, 1895, Sec. 11, P. L. 4.

Annual Reports to be Made to Governor.—Contents of Said Report. —Corporations Closed During Year.—Suggestions of Amendments, Etc.—Names and Compensation of Clerks, Etc.

Sec. 404. The Commissioner shall make an annual report to the Governor, setting forth:

First. A summary of the state and condition of every corporation from which reports have been received during the preceding year, with such other information in relation to said corporations as in his judgment may be useful.

Second. A statement of the corporations under the supervision of the Banking Department whose business has been closed during the year, with such information relating thereto as he may deem useful.

Third. Suggestions of amendments to the laws relating to corporations under the supervision of his department by which the laws may be improved and the security of creditors and depositors may be increased.

Fourth. The names and compensation of the clerks and other employes and assistants employed by him, and the whole amount of the expenses of the Banking Department during the year, and also of the revenue received by the State under this act.—Act of 11th of February, 1895, Sec. 12, P. L. 4.

Seal of Office.

Sec. 405. The seal devised by the Commissioner of Banking for his office, and approved by the Governor shall be the seal of office of the Commissioner of Banking, and may be renewed when necessary. A description of the seal with the impression thereof, and a certificate of approval of the Governor, shall be filed in the office of the Secretary of the Commonwealth.—Act of 11th of February, 1895, Sec. 13, P. L. 4.

All Books, Etc., to be in Custody of Commissioner.

Sec. 406. All books, papers, records and securities, whatever, in the office of the Superintendent of Banking, and also in the office of the Auditor General, relating to the business of the corporations subject to the control of the department, shall, on demand, be delivered and transferred to the Commissioner of the Banking Department, and be and remain in his charge and custody.—Act of 11th of February, 1895, Sec. 14, P. L. 4.

Rooms, Furniture and Stationery to be Assigned Him.

Sec. 407. There shall be assigned to the said Commissioner of Banking by the Commissioners of Public Buildings and Grounds a suitable room, or rooms, for conducting the business of said department, and the Commissioner shall, from time to time, with the approval of the Commissioners aforesaid, procure the necessary furniture, stationery and other proper conveniences for the transacting of the said business, the expense of which shall be paid on the certificate of the Commissioner of Banking and the warrant of the Auditor General.—Act of the 11th of February, 1895, Sec. 15, P. L. 4.

Reports Not to be Divulged Unless Expressly Authorized.—Violation of This Section to be a Misdemeanor.—Penalty.

Sec. 408. The Commissioner of Banking. nor the Deputy Commissioner of Banking, nor any employe of said Department, shall not, directly or indirectly, wilfully exhibit, publish, divulge or make known to any person, or persons, any record, report, statement, letter or other matter, fact or thing contained in said Banking Department, or ascertained from any of the same, or from any examination of any corporation subject to the provisions of this act, excepting only by such publication in such manner as is herein expressly authorized, and any breach thereof shall be a breach of duty on the part of the Commissioner of Banking, Deputy Commissioner of Banking, or any employe of said Department, and the person so offending shall be guilty of a misdemeanor, and upon conviction thereof, shall be sentenced to pay a fine of not exceeding one thousand dollars, and be dismissed from his employment in said Department.—Act of 11th of February, 1895, Sec. 16, P. L. 4.

Repeal.

Sec. 409. That an act of the General Assembly of this Commonwealth, entitled "An act creating a Banking Department," approved June eighth, Anno Domini one thousand eight hundred and ninety-one, be and the same is hereby repealed, and that all other laws, or parts of laws. inconsistent with the provisions of this act are also hereby repealed.—Act of the 11th of February, 1895, Sec. 17, P. L. 4.

Amendment of the Fourth Section of the Act Creating the Banking Department.—Duties of the Commissioners of Banking.—Examiner.—Assignment of and Powers of.—Oaths May be Administered by Commissioner, Deputy and Examiner.—False Swearing.—Procedure in Case of.—Treasurer to Make Answer. —Compensation of Examiners, Etc.—Fees to be Paid by Corporations.—Procedure in Case of Refusal or Neglect to Pay.— Proviso.

Sec. 410. It shall be the duty of the Commissioner of Banking, as often as he shall deem proper, to examine or cause to be examnied, the books, papers and affairs of each and every corporation subject to supervision as aforesaid, and whenever he shall deem it necessary or proper he shall assign a qualified examiner or examiners to make such examination, and who shall have power to make a thorough examination into all the business and affairs of the corporation in all its departments, and of all its property, assets and resources wherever situated, and in so doing, to examine any of the officers or agents or employes thereof, or any person or officers or employes of any corporation or any firm in possession of any assets thereof, under oath, or otherwise, and shall make or cause to be made, in the manner aforesaid, a full and detailed report of the condition of the corporation; and the said corporation shall not be subject to any other visitorial power than such as may be authorized by this act, except such as are vested in the several courts of law. Said commissioner and his deputy and any qualified examiner so as aforesaid appointed are hereby empowered and authorized to administer an oath to any of the persons aforesaid, and any willful false swearing in any inquiry thereunder shall be perjury, and subject, upon conviction thereof, to the same punishment as provided by existing laws for the punishment of perjury. Upon failure of any of the persons aforesaid to make answer to any of the inquiries aforesaid, the Attorney General upon the request of the Commissioner of Banking, shall make information thereof to the court of common pleas of Dauphin, whereupon said court, after hearing, shall make such order as occasion requires. The compensation of examiners and expenses of examinations provided for by this act shall be paid by warrant drawn by the Auditor General on the State Treasurer upon requisition made by the Commissioner of Banking, and in order to help pay such expenses all corporations subject to the supervision of the Banking Department (except building and loan associations doing business exclusively within this State), shall annually, upon the first Monday of May in each year, pay into the treasury of the State the following amounts in addition to any taxes or fees imposed by existing laws upon such corporations, the sum of twenty-five dollars each, and in all cases of such corporations having capital stock, for each one hundred thousand dollars of capital stock, or fractional part thereof in excess of one hundred thousand dollars, the sum of five dollars shall be paid annually at the time aforesaid; and all such corporations shall pay annually at the time aforesaid, the sum of two cents for each one thousand dollars of assets, and the sum of two cents for each one thousand dollars of trust funds, which it may have. In cases of corporations subject to the supervision of the Banking Department, which have no capital stock, they shall each in addition to any taxes or fees imposed by existing laws, annually upon the day and month aforesaid pay into the treasury of the State the sum of twenty-five dollars, and for each one hundred thousand dollars of assets, or fractional part thereof in excess of one hundred thousand dollars, annually pay into the treasury of the State the sum of one dollar. And in cases of neglect or refusal of any corporation aforesaid to pay said sums into the State Treasury at the time aforesaid, the Auditor General shall settle an account against such corportion for the amounts due and payable under this act, and shall proceed to collect the same in the same way and manner and under the same penalties as are provided for the collecting of taxes and penalties under the existing laws: Provided, however, That nothing herein contained shall impose upon any building and loan association, doing business exclusively within this State, the payment of any sum or sums of money whatsoever.— Act of 29th of May, 1901, Sec. 1, P. L. 345.

An Act Authorizing the Employment of an Additional Clerk of Banking Department.

Sec. 411. One clerk, to be appointed by the Commissioner of Banking, at a salary of fourteen hundred dollars per annum.—Act of 8th of April, 1903, P. L. 159.

An Act Providing for Additional Bank Examiners.

Sec. 412. The Commissioner of Banking is authorized to appoint five additional examiners, who shall receive such compensation as may be fixed by said Commissioner, for each day actually employed in making examinations of corporations under the order of said Commissioner, not to exceed ten dollars per day, and also actual expenses incurred in making such examinations, which compensation and expenses shall be paid by warrant drawn by the Auditor General upon the State Treasurer.—Act of 7th of March, 1905, P. L. 33.

CHAPTER 13.

JUDICIAL DECISIONS AS TO BANKS, TRUST COMPANIES, BUILDING ASSOCIATIONS, ETC.

President.

Sec. 413. A president of a bank as his name indicates presides at the meetings thereof. He has no authority to make contracts binding on the bank without the control of the board of directors.—Bank vs. Williams, 100 Pa. 123.

He has no authority to part with collateral security held by the bank.—Day vs. Day, 32 Pitts. L. J. 75.

The Board of Directors.

Sec. 414. The business of the board of directors of a bank is generally to transact its affairs and business. They must meet collectively at a meeting of the board. They cannot act individually or separately.

If they allow the affairs of the bank to be carried on by another institution it is gross negligence which renders the directors liable for losses deriving therefrom.—Bank vs. Gregg, 27 Pitts. L. J. 26, P. & L. Dig. Dec. 2065.

Knowledge imparted by a director to the bank at a regular meeting binds the bank.—Bank vs. Whitehead, 10 Watts 397.

Notice to a director is not notice to a corporation.—Bank vs. Heppes, 23 C. C. R. 447.

The procedure to enforce the liability of bank directors for neglect must be under the 16th section of the act of 1850, and the act of 12th of April, 1867.—Ahl. vs. Rhoades, 84 Pa. 319.

When the directors use ordinary care in directing the business of the bank they are not liable for the fraud of its other officers.—Swentzel vs. Bank, 147 Pa. 140.

Declaring unearned dividends or withdrawing their individual deposits from the bank with knowledge of its insolvency are such acts as amount to fraud for which the directors of a bank are personally liable.—Gunkels Appeal, 48 Pa. 13.

The directors of a bank, who, by its charter were to conduct its affairs, delegated to the president and cashier the power to borrow money for the bank. It was held that the bank was liable on a bill of exchange signed by the president only. It was held that the bank was bound if the bill was issued for the use of the bank.—Ridgway vs. Bank, 12 S. & R. 256.

The managing partner of a firm doing a banking business, who is also the cashier, has authority to make an agreement by which a promissory note shall be charged to a third party in pursuance of a previous agreement between the bank and the maker of the note.—Wise vs. Loeb, 15 Pa. Superior 601.

The Cashier.

Sec. 415. As the name indicates, the cashier has charge of the money of the bank. He attends to the receipts and cash payments of the bank. To a certain extent he is like a treasurer of an association.

The ordinary duties of a cashier are to keep the notes. funds, bills and other choses in action of the bank, to be used from time to time for the exigencies of the bank, to receive directly or through subordinate officers all moneys and notes of the bank; to surrender notes and securities upon payment, to draw checks; to withdraw funds of the bank on deposit and generally to transact as executive officer of the bank the ordinary routine of business.—Williams vs. Dorrier, 135 Pa. 445.

Cashier of a national bank has no right to exempt the maker of a note held by the bank from liability.—Allen vs. Bank, 127 Pa. 51.

The cashier of a savings bank is not eligible to the office of notary public under the act of 1840.—Ruperts case, 16 C. C. R. 333.

The act of March 31st, 1860, P. L. 399, prohibiting cashiers from engaging in other business does not apply to national banks.—Allen vs. Carter, 119 Pa. 192.

Where an assistant cashier of a bank, upon his own responsibility receives bonds on deposit for safe keeping and subsequently as cashier, fraudulently pledges them for a debt of the bank, the fraud of the cashier becomes a fraud of the bank. The bank cannot retain the fruits of the crime and at the same time repudiate the fraud of the agent.—Hughes vs. Bank, 110 Pa. 428.

Deposits.

Sec. 416. The relation between a bank and its customer is that of debtor and creditor; but still it is not the ordinary case of one party owing another money. A bank is an institution of a quasi public character, and when the bank, without legal excuse refuses to honor a check drawn upon it by a depositor something more than a mere breach of contract is involved. and it is liable to the depositors for substantial damages. The agreement of the bank is to repay the deposits to the person who makes the deposit, or upon checks drawn by him. The bank cannot set up an adverse title to defeat the claim of its own depositor.—Penna. Title and Trust Co. vs. Meyer, 201 Pa. 299.

A deposit made to be applied to the payment of a special claim vests the title to the deposit in the owner of the claim, and the bank cannot in an action by that claimant to recover the same, set off the depositor's indebtedness to it.—Saylor vs. Bushong, 100 Pa. 23.

The design of the act of May 9th, 1889, P. L. 145, is to protect all depositors from loss through the fraudulent receipt of their moneys by insolvent bankers. A banker will not be permitted to fraudulently procure the moneys of A, B and C, because he has been punished in procuring money from D.—Comm. vs. Rockafellow, 3 Pa. Superior 588.

Three essentials which must be proved before a jury can find a defendant banker guilty of receiving deposits when insolvent. 1. Actual insolvency at the time the money was received. 2. Knowledge of insolvency. 3. Receipt of money as a bank deposit.—Comm. vs. Smith, 4 Pa. Superior 1.

A trustee or guardian is not liable for loss resulting from the failure of a bank, where money is deposited temporarily pending investment; but if a guardian leaves his wards money for an undue time on deposit without effort to invest the same, he is liable for the loss resulting from the failure of the bank.—Estate of Evance C. Pa. Superior 142.

Although the amount of a check left with a bank for collection has been credited to a depositor as cash, it may be charged back to him in case it turns out to be worthless, unless the bank has been negligent, or has done something to mislead the depositor, thereby inducing him to act as to his injury on the faith of the goodness of the check.—Union Safe Deposit Bank vs. Strauch, 20 Pa. Superior 196.

Trust funds not ear-marked cannot be recovered, on the assignment of a bank in preference to the general creditors of the bank.—In re Solicitors Loan and Trust Cos. Est. 3 Pa. Superior 244.

Where money received by trust companies as trustee, is not kept distinct nor invested in any specific way, but is mingled with the general mass of money on deposit and used in the general banking business, and there is no means of tracing or ascertaining its identity the cestuique trust is not entitled to a preference over general creditors in a distribution of the assigned estate of the trust company.—Cobsons estate, 3 Pa. Superior 248; Carmany's Appeal, 166 Pa. 622; Corn Exchange Nat. Bank vs. Loan Co., 188 Pa. 330.

Where a bank holds funds of the maker when the note matures, it is bound to appropriate his deposit to the payment of the note in the relief of the sureties, and the failure to do so to the loss of the sureties renders the bank liable.—Newbold vs. Boon, 6 Pa. Superior 511; Bank vs. Seitz Bros., 150 Pa. 632.

The act of May 9th, 1889, providing for the punishment of bankers receiving deposits with knowledge that a bank is insolvent is not in violation of article one, section fifteen of the Constitution that the person of a debtor shall not be continued in prison after the delivery up of his estate for the benefit of his creditors.—Com. vs. Sponsler, 16 C. C. 116.

On the trial of an indictment for a violation of the act of May 9th, 1889, P. L. 145, entitled An act relating to the receiving of deposits by insolvent banks in order to secure conviction the Commonwealth must prove beyond reasonable doubt first, actual insolvency at the time the money is received, second, the defendant's knowledge of the insolvency, third, the receipts of the money as a bank deposit.—Commonwealth vs. Junkin, 170 Pa. 194.

Where a check is received after banking hours, there is no unreasonable delay in depositing the check for collection in the usual course of business on the day after it was received, and presenting it to the bank for payment on the next day thereafter.—Loux vs. Fox, 171 Pa. 68; Willis vs. Finley, 173 Pa. 28.

When the maker of a negotiable note payable at bank has at the date of maturity a deposit to his credit, the bank should charge the note against the deposit.—Bank vs. Foreman, 138 Pa. 474.

A bank receiving a check for collection should send it to an independent bank, not directly to the bank on which it is drawn.—Hazlett vs. Bank, 132 Pa. 118.

A check by a depositor on his account certified by the bank becomes an obligation of the bank to the payee or holder, and in the absence of fraud or similar exceptional circumstances, the amount is as much withdrawn from the depositor's account as if the money had been paid over the counter.—Trust Co. vs. White, 206 Pa. 611.

A check on a bank when all the parties are residents of the same city must be presented on the day upon which it bears date, or on the next day, and if not, the risk of the solvency of the drawee is upon the payee.—Bank vs. Weil, 141 Pa. 457.

BUILDING AND LOAN ASSOCIATIONS.

Sec. 417. In carrying out the plan on which building associations are organized and conducted, it is not intended that a stockholder who borrows of the association will discharge the debt he incurs by direct payments on account of it. He pays at stated periods the dues on his stock, the interest on the money borrowed, and when the premium bid for the loan has not been deducted, the installments on it. When by the receipt of dues, interest, premiums and fines for non-payment of dues, all of the stock of the association or of the series to which the borrower's stock belongs, becomes full paid or matured. The value of his stock equals the amount of his debt, and the transaction is then ended by the surrender of the stock by him and the cancellation of his obligation by the association. When a borrowing member of a building and loan association gives the association an obligation which provides for the payment of the principal debt in equal monthly installments until the whole is paid according to the act of Assembly and the terms and provisions of the Constitution and by-laws of said association the monthly installments cannot be appropriated to a direct payment on account of the loan with the effect of leaving dues on stock unpaid.—Freemansburg B. & L. Assn. vs. Watts, 199 Pa. 221.

A foreign building and loan association having its office in the state of its domicile, where under its articles of association and by-laws, its business must be conducted and at which office all payments must be made to it, and all contracts passed upon, does not, in making a loan to a citizen of Pennsylvania on a bond, through an agent in Pennsylvania, and taking as security for the debt a mortgage on Pennsylvania real estate, make a Pennsylvania contract governed by the usury laws of this State; nor is the association doing business in Pennsylvania within the meaning of the act of April 22, 1874, requiring the registration of foreign corporations. In such case there is no employment by the association of any part of its capital in Pennsylvania. The capital if employed in Pennsylvania is employed by a citizen thereof.—People's B. L. and S. Assn. vs. Berlin, 201 Pa. 1.

The powers and immunities granted to building and loan associations incorporated under the act of April 29, 1874, P. L. 73, Sec. 37 and the several supplements thereto, do not extend to corporations not chartered under that legislation and managed and controlled in accordance with its provisions. The premiums, fines, and interest on such premiums accruing to such corporations, which the statute declares shall not be deemed usurious are those which accrue "according to the provisions of this act," the legislation was intended to regulate the dealings between a domestic corporation and its members, and not between it and those who are not members.—Trust Company vs. Fulmer, 24 Superior 256.

Domestic building associations act ultra vires when they (1) Establish and maintain branch offices; (2) Make permanent investments in office buildings; (3) Make collateral loans without limiting such loans as contemplated by the act of 1879; (4) Increase the expenses of management and salaries disportionate to services; (5) Charge an admission or withdrawal fee which is used to pay salaries, etc.; (6) Discriminate in the rate of interest paid to classes of shareholders; (7) Adopt the double mortgage feature (two bonds) and (8) Issue policies of insurance.—Domestic Building Associations; Opinion of Commissioner of Banking, 1905; 30 Pa. C. C. R. 616.

Whenever a tax is settled or assessed against a building association either domestic or foreign, it shall be four mills upon the return as made or certified to by the Auditor General. In the report to be filed by foreign associations, such associations may include such data as the Banking Department may require, but their report must include the amount of stock held by residents of Pennsylvania entitled to receive cash dividends or interest.—State Taxation of Building Associations, 20 Pa. C. C. R. 545.

A resident of Pennsylvania became a member of a New York building and loan association and received a loan from it for which he gave a mortgage of real estate in Pennsylvania. Held that the contractor was to pay money in New York and that the contract was subject to New York law as to usurious interest.—Bennett vs. Building Assn., 177 Pa. 233.

Building associations are doing business exclusively within this State (proviso of the fourth section of act February 11, 1895), although subscribers to stock have removed from the State, but continue to pay their dues, or although subscribers after removal assign their stock to non-residents, or although non-residents subscribe for stock without solicitation. Where building associations make their investments upon real estate in other states they are not doing business exclusively within this State and are not within the exemption proviso in Section 4, act of 1895. The stock of a building association should be valued at the amount actually paid in for the purpose of charging the fees in the banking act of 1895. Request of Commissioner for opionion.—Opinion by McCormick, Attorney General, October 17, 1895, 17 C. C. R. 62.

Where a building association has become insolvent a member is liable for the amount actually received on his loan with interest less actual payments of principal and interest thereon but he is not entitled to credit for payments on the stock assigned as collateral.— Strohen vs. Franklin S. F. and L. Assn., 115 Pa. 273.

Where a member of a building association borrows money from the association and to secure the loan gives a mortagage on his real estate, and makes an assignment of his stock, in which he elects to appropriate the amount realized from the stock at its maturity in payment of the loan, an attachment creditor whose attachment is subsequent to the mortgage and assignment cannót compel the association to exhause the security furnished by the mortgage before resorting to the security afforded by the assignment.—Hemperly vs. Tyson, 170 Pa. 385.

A defaulting borrowing stockholder of a building and loan association, whose stock is pledged to the association as collateral, is not entitled to withdraw and receive the same share of the estimated profits, as an ordinary withdrawing stockholder would be entitled to receive. The words "such borrower" in the proviso in section 4 of the act of April 10, 1879, P. L. 16, applied to a borrower who has repaid his loan and has no application to a borrower who has not only not paid his loan, but is in arrears, both as to dues and fines for several years. The dues and fines are payable under the by-laws and whether entered in the books or not are due and payable by a defaulting member.—Folsom B. and L. Association vs. V. Gogel, 24 Superior 539.

In entering judgment against a borrowing stockholder in favor of an insolvent building association on a mortgage given to secure the payment of a loan damages should be assessed by charging the defendant with the sum or sums actually received on the mortgage an interest on the same crediting him with all actual payments of interest and premiums, the installments on stock and fines will remain with the stock.—Twin Cities National B. and L. Assn. vs. Leport, 17 Pa. C. C. R. 426.

CLEARING HOUSE ASSOCIATION.

Sec. 418. The articles of association amount to an agreement with each other by thirty-eight national banks in the city of Philadelphia to facilitate and simplify the settlement of daily balances between them for their mutual advantage. This agreement substitutes a settlement made at a fixed place and time each day by representatives of all the members of the association, in the place of a separate settlement by each bank with every other made over the counter. No other object is contemplated or provided for. The association does not provide for any united action for business purpose. It does not contemplate the employment of capital or credit in any enterprise. It proposes and provides for co-operation to expedite and simplify the transaction by each member of the association of its own proper business in one particular, viz: the settlement of daily balances with the other national banks doing business in the city. Incidentally, co-operation in this particular would tend to bring the banks belonging to the association into closer relations, enable them to become more familiar with the volume of business and the actual condition of each other and open the way to make them mutually helpful in times of financial stringency; but these results are incidental only. The Clearing House Association is nothing more nor less than an agreement among thirty-eight national banks to make their daily settlements at a fixed time and place each day. To carry this agreement into operation it became necessary to determine the place and hour at which the settlement should be made. A suitable

11

room was secured fitted up with desks and other necessary appliances at the expense of the associated banks, and a manager chosen to preside over it and direct the action of the clerks and runners when in session. This room is the clearing place or in the language of the constitution of the association, the clearing house. It is the place where the representatives of the several banks meet and where the balances are struck and settled daily between the banks composing the association. At the close of each meeting the amount due to and from each bank is definitely ascertained. The debtor banks then pay over to the manager the gross balance due from them to settle their accounts with all the members of the association, and he makes distribution of the sum so received among the creditor banks entitled to receive them. The clearing house is not therefore a business organization, a corporation, a partnership or any artificial person of any sort, but a place in which the thirty-eight members of the association settle with each other daily. * * * Among the economies in time and labor contemplated by the banks was a settlement of daily balances without the necessity for handling and counting the cash in every case. To provide for this the banks agreed that they would deposit in the hands of certain persons, to be selected by them and to be called the clearing house committee, a sum of money, or its equivalent in good securities, at a fixed ratio upon the capital stock to be used for the payment of balances against them. For these sums the committee were to issue receipts or certificates in convenient sums, and these receipts or certificates were to be used in lieu of the cash they represented which remained in the hands of the committee pledged for the payment, when payment became necessary of the certificates. The committee held the funds and securities deposited with them in trust for the special purpose of securing the payment as far as they would reach of the balances due from the bank making the deposit. The committee were made trustees or agents for all members of the association with authority to accept deposits in money or securities and to issue their own receipts therefor, the money or securities remaining in their hands in pledge for the redemption of receipts or certificates so issued by them. Upon a bank failing to redeem the committee could collect the securities and apply the proceeds to the payment of the holders of certificates. It was held that the banks by above arrangements had not violated the statutes of the United States and had not transended the limits which those statutes have drawn about the business of banking. The same method has been adopted by the banks in every great city of the United States.—Philler vs. Patterson, 168 Pa. 468.

The issuing of certificates by clearing house is not the issuing of currency. The clearing house is not a bank.—Crane vs. Nat. Bank, 173 Pa. 566.

MISCELLANEOUS DECISIONS.

Sec. 419. Judgment notes and mortgages held by private bankers are subject to the four mill tax imposed by the act of June 8, 1891.—Commonwealth vs. McKean County, 200 Pa. 383.

Section 5242 of the revised statutes of the United States does not prohibit the issue of an attachment execution against an insolvent national bank for property or money of the third person in the custody of the bank, but the statute will prevent one creditor of an insolvent bank obtaining a priority.—Commonwealth vs. Bank, 189, Pa. 606.

The act of June 30, 1885, Sec. 3, P. L. 193, exempting banks from local tax on payment of State tax does not exempt banks in such case from the payment of license tax under the act of May 23, 1874. Sec. 20, 4, P. L. 239, such license tax being incidental to the exercise of the police power. The license tax on banks authorized by the act of May 23, 1889, P. L. 277 being for general revenue purposes, banks are exempt from payment of it upon compliance with the exempting provisions of the act of 1885.—Oil City vs. Trust Co., 151 Pa. 454.

The act of 1893 permits a married woman to make notes and contracts for three purposes. First, where she engages in trade or business. Second, in the management of her separate estate. Third, for necessaries.—Bank vs. Short, 15 Pa. Superior 64.

INDEX.

CHAPTER 1.

CONSTITUTIONAL PROVISIONS RELATING TO CORPORATIONS.

CHAPTER 2.

LEGISLATION RELATING TO BANKS PRIOR TO THE BANKING LAW OF 1850.

CHAPTER 3.

BANKING ACT OF 1850.

CHAPTER 4.

LEGISLATION RELATING TO BANKS FROM BANKING LAW OF 1850 TO THE BANKING ACT OF 1876.

CHAPTER 5.

BANKING ACT OF 1876.

CHAPTER 6.

LEGISLATION AS TO BANKS SINCE THE ACT OF 1876.

CHAPTER 7.

CO-OPERATIVE BANKING ASSOCIATIONS.

CHAPTER 8.

TRUST COMPANIES.

CHAPTER 9.

BUILDING AND LOAN ASSOCIATIONS.

CHAPTER 10.

SAVINGS INSTITUTIONS AND SAVINGS BANKS.

CHAPTER 11.

MISCELLANEOUS ACTS RELATING TO BANKS, TRUST COMPANIES, BUILDING AND LOAN ASSOCIATIONS, SURETY COMPANIES, SAVING FUND SOCIETIES, ETC.

CHAPTER 12.

AN ACT CREATING A BANKING DEPARTMENT.

CHAPTER 13.

DECISIONS OF COURTS AS TO BANKING, ETC.

CPSIA information can be obtained
at www.ICGtesting.com
Printed in the USA
BVHW08s1024210918
528173BV00022B/1426/P